Seel

Work

Get and

Education

Dance –

History

Look

CBI

Initiative Eastern Europe

DOING BUSINESS IN POLAND

BRITISH TELECOM · FRERE CHOLMELEY
THE POLISH INVESTMENT COMPANY
TOUCHE ROSS & CO

KOGAN PAGE

Note: This book has been written on the basis of information and law current as at April 1991.

First published in 1991

Kogan Page Limited
120 Pentonville Road
London N1 9JN

British Library Cataloguing in Publication Data

A CIP record for this book is available from the British Library.

ISBN 0 7494 0473 6

Typeset by DP Photosetting, Aylesbury, Bucks
Printed in England by Clays Ltd, St Ives plc

Contents

The Contributors

BT (previously known as British Telecom) is a worldwide telecommunications company with major operational expertise, as well as offering consultancy, investment finance and project management support in the provision and operation of telecommunication services. BT has a long-established and continually developing relationship with Poland.

Frere Cholmeley is a leading European law firm specialising in international business transactions. Lawyers in its London, Paris and Berlin offices have extensive experience of advising on Polish affairs and the Berlin office has special experience of handling transactions with Eastern European enterprises.

The Polish Investment Company is based in Warsaw, Krakow and London and is at the forefront of developing a market economy in Poland. It has been actively involved in Poland's first share flotations and privatisations, as well as leading the first commercial restructuring of a state enterprise.

Touche Ross & Co and ***DRT Poland*** are part of DRT International, one of the world's largest accounting, auditing, tax and management consulting firms. They have significant experience of assisting Western clients entering the Polish market, and of advising Polish enterprises and government on matters related to privatisation and of dealing with Western enterprises, capital markets and funding agencies.

Foreword

There is, I believe, a particularly close relationship between Poland and the United Kingdom. This results from our history but is linked also to the closeness of the Polish and British people - in part due to those Poles who have so happily settled in the UK.

When the monumental changes took place in Poland in 1989, the British government was very helpful. The Know-How Fund was a typical British response - fast, flexible and effective. The technical assistance provided under that programme has been a major contributor behind Poland's drive to become a market economy.

Now, I am delighted to see the launch of the CBI Initiative Eastern Europe. Poland needs, and welcomes, foreign investment and an initiative to provide necessary information to businessmen in making their investment decisions is a critical and valuable contribution.

Poland is a very attractive country in which to invest - the potential for growth is enormous. Clearly, early investors will have the edge and I encourage CBI members to take full advantage of the investment opportunities now offered in Poland - the region's largest country, and a country committed to free enterprise and market principles.

Jan Krzysztof Bielecki
Prime Minister of Poland
May 1991

Preface

It was in Poland that the most sustained challenge to the Communists' monopoly of political power in Eastern Europe was made prior to the revolutions of 1989 and it is in Poland that the most radical programme to establish a free market is being carried through. None the less, the legacy of 45 years of central planning and totalitarianism means it will be a battle to get the country moving again, but it is a battle the Polish government is set on winning.

The distortions that communist central planning created are being eliminated through a daring programme to establish sound money, free prices and private ownership. This has had dramatic results. In response to a comprehensive package of economic reform in January 1990, the private sector is rapidly developing throughout the economy, accounting for as much as one third of total value added. Manifestly, Poland's traditional spirit of enterprise lives on.

The government has been equally radical in re-integrating Poland into the world trading system; foreign investment rules are increasingly liberal and transparent, and a trade regime as open as *anywhere* in Europe has been created. All this is taking place in the largest consumer market in Central Europe. Foreign companies will be further drawn to Poland by its wealth of natural resources, by its skilled and relatively cheap labour force and by its ambitious programme to privatise 80 per cent of its industry.

This book concentrates on providing pragmatic business advice drawing on the expertise of British Telecom, Frere Cholmeley, The Polish Investment Company and Touche Ross. The CBI thanks them for the substantial efforts they have made towards putting the material together.

There are heartening examples of British companies who are

succeeding in this new economic environment and this book looks at the experience of five of these: Trusthouse Forte, Courtaulds, Radiotrust, ECH and Maiden, who have been generous - and honest enough - to spell out the realities of operating in Poland.

In addition, Saatchi & Saatchi have given us the benefit of their knowledge of marketing in Poland. Important contributions have also been made by Mike Dembinski, Jonathan Star, Stephanie Flanders, Mike Cronshaw and MarCo Ltd.

Readers should remember that Poland is a fast-developing market and that this book has been written on the basis of information and law current in April 1991. Although there can be no guaranteed returns on any involvement, there are undoubtedly great opportunities. Unless British business decides to take a long-term view and unless British business establishes its presence now, the rewards will inevitably go to our more daring trading rivals. It is our hope that this book will give British companies a competitive advantage when exploring and developing business in this new and exciting market.

Alan J Lewis, CBE
Chairman, CBI Initiative Eastern Europe
April 1991

Part I

A Business Revolution?

1

The Country and its Potential

The Polish Investment Company

Today, Poland is a free country open to the world with a well-educated population, a wealth of natural resources and a strong base in primary economic activities. This chapter looks at the revolution Solidarity carried through in 1989 against the context of Polish history, and then goes on to discuss some of the more enduring aspects of Poland: its geography, its people, agriculture, natural resources, power, communications, industry and finally the UK's trading record with Poland.

THE STRUGGLE FOR INDEPENDENCE

From its origins in the tenth century a strong united Poland emerged in the fourteenth century and enjoyed two centuries of strength and prosperity under the Jagiellonian dynasty. In 1569 a Union of Poland and Lithuania was established, forming the largest single kingdom in Europe, extending from the Baltic coast in the north to the Black Sea coast in the south. At the end of the sixteenth century, however, the dynasty fell and was succeeded by an elective monarchy controlled by the Polish parliament. Over the next two centuries, the state weakened and in the last quarter of the eighteenth century, ceased to exist. Poland was partitioned between Austria, Prussia and Russia. Poles fought five times to regain independence, in 1805, 1830, 1848 and 1863. They gained it only in the aftermath of World War I in 1918.

Newly independent Poland was immediately threatened by war with communist Russia in 1919–20 (which ended with the rebuffal of Russia) and by Germany's claims to Upper Silesia and Gdańsk.

Independence ended with the Nazi German invasion of Poland on 1 September, 1939, precipitating World War II and the partition of

Poland between Germany and the USSR. During World War II Poland fought for independence both on the home front and in exile with its government based in London. It provided the fourth largest army among allied nations after the USSR, the US and the UK; one in eight of RAF pilots in the Battle of Britain was Polish.

The fate of Poland after 1945 was decided between the superpowers at Yalta and Potsdam, when it was placed in the Soviet-European sphere against the will of its people. The communists won the rigged election in 1947 and thus established their rule which lasted until June 1989.

Riots in 1956 ousted the Stalinist regime which was replaced by a moderate communist, Gomułka. His rule ended in riots in 1970 in Gdańsk and Szczecin. Again in 1976, riots threatened the regime and these culminated in the now famous countrywide strikes in July and August 1980 which led to the birth of Solidarity, an independent trade union with over 10 million members, led by Lech Wałęsa.

The riots and the emergence of a clandestine opposition led gradually to a degree of liberalisation which went further than anything in neighbouring communist countries. This liberalisation was not only political but also economic. A large number of privately owned service and small-scale manufacturing activities became established.

During this period, a growing and influential role was played by the Catholic Church, led by Cardinal Wyszyński.

In 1980 and 1981, the emergence of Solidarity with its very strong political emphasis, created a new and powerful threat to the existing order. This, coupled with external pressures from the USSR and the orthodox Polish military hierarchy, led in December 1981 to the imposition of martial law by the then Prime Minister, General Jaruzelski. Solidarity was crushed, its leaders imprisoned and all opposition activities went underground.

As a consequence of the political unrest in 1981 and 1982, industrial output decreased by 25 per cent, with severe shortages and rising inflation. The Jaruzelski government made half-hearted attempts at economic reform . This process largely failed, but it did initiate substantial dismantling of the central planning system.

The growing underground activity of Solidarity, the further collapse of the economy, and external pressures led to further weakening of the communist regime. The reform communist Rakowski government of autumn of 1988 was a final attempt to make the old system work. But internal pressures at that time were too strong and they led in February-April 1989 to the historic 'round table' discussions between the Communist Party and the opposition.

Agreement was reached and elections were held which resulted in Solidarity-backed candidates obtaining 161 seats in the Sejm (lower house) and 99 out of 100 seats in the Senate (upper house). However, only one-third of the seats in the Sejm were contested; the remaining non-elected two-thirds of the Sejm was held by the Communist Party and its allies. Completely free elections for the whole Sejm are scheduled for autumn 1991.

A compromise between communists and opposition led to General Jaruzelski being elected in July 1989 to the newly created post of President, and the installation of the first non-communist Prime Minister, Tadeusz Mazowiecki.

The Mazowiecki Government instituted the first radical economic and political changes in the countries of Central and Eastern Europe. That policy has been continued by the present Prime Minister Jan Krzysztof Bielecki, who was appointed in January 1991, following the victory of Lech Wałęsa in the presidential elections.

The key elements of economic reform are contained in the Balcerowicz Plan (named after the deputy Prime Minister and Minister of Finance).

The plan contains the following principal elements:

- a tight monetary and credit policy to fight inflation;
- a freeze on wages in the state-owned sector;
- free convertibility of the zloty into all major currencies;
- the elimination of price control;
- privatisation of the state sector;
- the opening of the economy to free flows of foreign capital.

GEOGRAPHY

The Republic of Poland (Rzeczpospolita Polska) is a large country in Central Europe located between Germany, the USSR and Czechoslovakia. Poland lies almost wholly on the North European Plain and is a land of gentle relief; rarely rising above 300m, except along the southern border with the Sudety and Carpathian mountain ranges.

Only approximately one fifth of the land is maintained as pasture and meadows. Approximately 27 per cent of the total area is covered by forests, particularly in the north.

The climate is characterised by cold winters and warm summers. Winters become increasingly severe inland from the Baltic coast, with January temperatures averaging -1°C (30°F) in the north and going as low as -5°C (23°F) in the south east. July temperatures range from 16.5°C (62°F) near the coast to 19°C (66°F) in the south.

Rainfall varies with altitude from less than 500mm in a year to as high as 1,270mm in the southern mountains. The longest rivers are the Vistula, crossing the country in the centre which is 1050 kilometres in length, and the Odra which flows along the Polish western border.

DEMOGRAPHY

About 97 per cent of the population claims Polish and Slavic origins. This ethnic homogeneity contrasts with the ethnic diversity prevailing before World War II when large minorities of Ukrainians, Byelorussians, Jews and Germans constituted more than 25 per cent of the Polish population.

That population fell from almost 36 million in 1939 to 23,600,000 in 1946 as a result of World War II and Nazi and Soviet atrocities, but has since increased to 38,000,000 in 1989. The largest city is Warsaw with an estimated population of 1.7 million (1988). Other large urban centres are Łódź, Kraków, Poznań, Wrocław, Szczecin, Katowice, Bydgoszcz, Lublin, Gdańsk, Gdynia, Częstochowa and Radom.

Most Poles (approximately 90 per cent) are Roman Catholic. There are small Eastern Orthodox and Protestant communities.

Education is free and compulsory between ages of 7 and 16 and optional after the age of 16. Higher education to a good standard is available in 12 universities, 18 polytechnics and 65 specialised institutes of higher learning. Thirty per cent of all students in Poland go on to higher education.

The starting age for employment in Poland is 18 and the retirement ages of men and women are 65 and 60 respectively. Between these ages there are roughly 22 million people, and the active labour force amounts to 18.5 million (10.5 million men and 8 million women).

About 60 per cent of the labour force (in March 1991) is

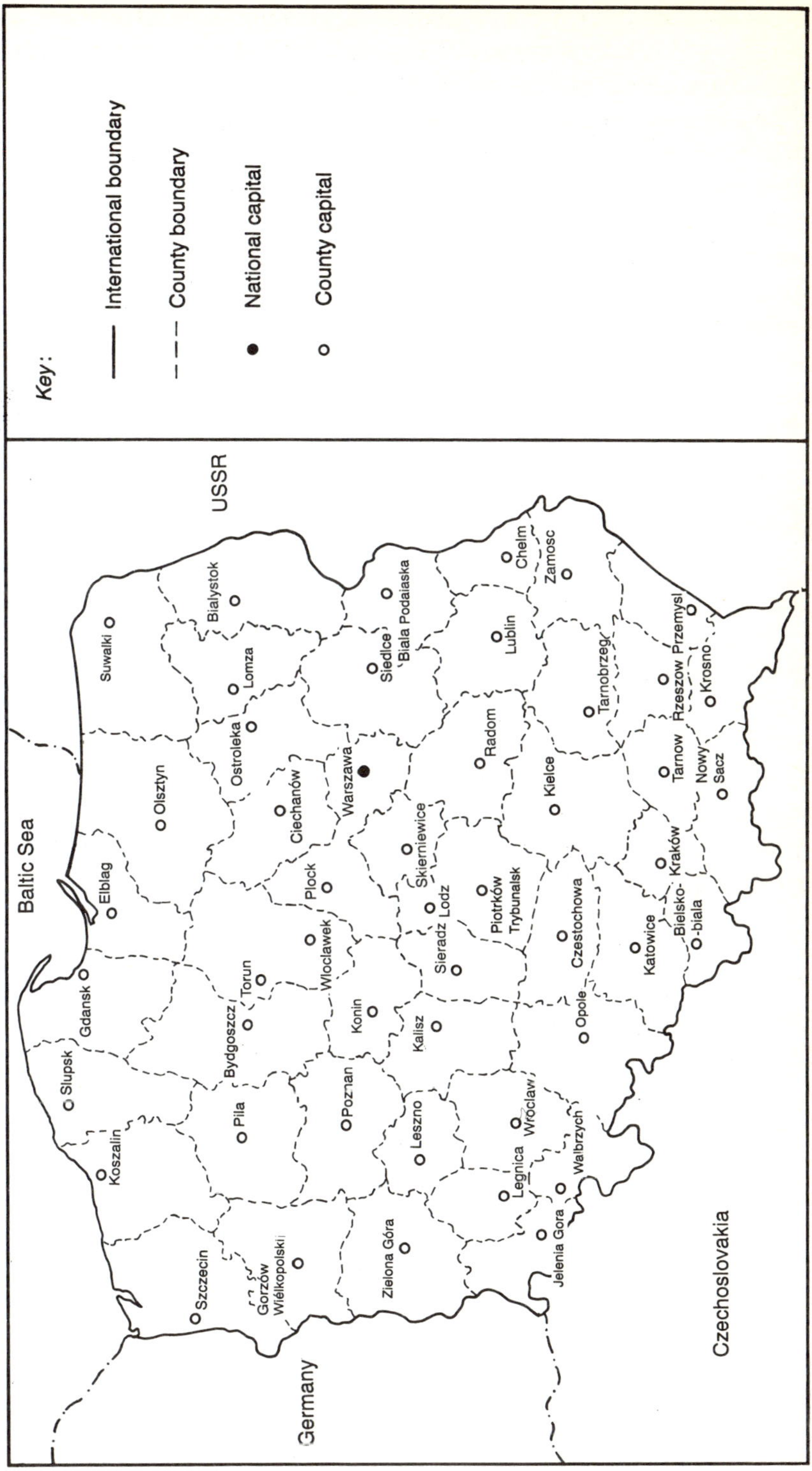

Map 1.1 *Poland and its neighbours*

employed in state-owned companies or cooperatives. The remaining 40 per cent is employed in the teaching profession, the civil service, the health sector and so on, as well as in the private sector. Of those employed in the private sector, half are small farmers while the rest are employed mainly in trade, service, manufacturing, and handicrafts.

During 1990 employment fell steadily with registered unemployment increasing from a negligible level at the beginning of the year to about 4 per cent of the labour force mid-year and to 6 per cent at the end of the year.

At present, there are favourable conditions for the supply of labour. More and more students are leaving further education colleges (potential blue-collar workers) and universities. By offering higher salaries than state-owned enterprises, foreign companies are being successful in attracting the best employees.

Culture and attitudes to work are varied in Poland, and potential investors looking for skilled workforces should consider carefully the geographical location of their planned investment. Higher quality output could be expected from workers in Warsaw, Silesia or Łódź, for instance, than from those in the east of the country.

AGRICULTURE

After 1945 the Communist government attempted to collectivise agriculture on the Soviet model but the process failed, and as from 1956 most of the farms returned to private ownership.

Table 1.1 *Analysis of land holdings*

Size (in hectares)		*% of farms*
Very small	0.5–2.0 ha	24%
Small	2.0–5.0 ha	27%
Medium	5.0–10.0 ha	28%
Large	over 10.0 ha	21%

Less than 20 per cent of all agricultural land was held by the government and over 80 per cent of the land was in private hands. Unlike many countries in Western Europe the Polish rural sector is of major importance to the social and economic make-up of the country. The rural population has remained approximately at the same level (15 million) since 1950 and now accounts for 40 per cent of the population. The average size of a farm is six hectares. A breakdown of land holdings is set out in Table 1.1.

Out of the total rural population, only 20 per cent make their income exclusively from farming; 40 per cent supplement their income from other activities and the rest are part-time farmers.

Polish agriculture is one of the world's largest producers of potatoes, vegetables and fruit and is a major producer of meat. In all such basic products Poland is self-sufficient and is gradually becoming a net exporter. Projections indicate that total domestic food demand will increase with population growth at an average annual rate of between 0.6–1.2 per cent over the period 1990-2000.

With the introduction of modern farming methods and technologies it is likely that the gap between supply and demand will rise, releasing more food and related products for export.

Table 1.2 *Comparative crop yields 1982–84, average kg/ha*

Crop	*Poland*	*W. Germany*	*UK*	*USA*
All grain	2,777	4,879	5,798	4,139
Meat	3,331	5,723	6,810	2,539
Rye	2,545	4,009	4,233	1,942
Corn	4,109	5,912	1,000	6,425
Potatoes	15,869	28,856	34,351	30,847
Sugar beet	32,711	37,514	43,222	45,179

Source: US Department of Agriculture in 'Poland: Reform, adjustment and growth' the World Bank, 17 August 1987.

RAW MATERIALS

The country is rich in natural resources of which coal (hard and brown coal), sulphur, copper and zinc have traditionally been exploited. In 1990 coal accounted for over 95 per cent of primary energy production and over 75 per cent of primary energy use. Hard coal is produced in 71 coal mines located predominantly in Upper Silesia. This makes Poland the sixth largest hard coal producer and exporter in the world, with 148 million tonnes of production in 1990

(1988 = 191 million tonnes). Despite falling demand and the start of the restructuring process, it is expected that hard coal production in the year 2000 will still achieve around 140 million tonnes. In 1990, open coal mines produced around 70 million tonnes of brown coal. This is used on the spot to fire mine-mouth or nearby power stations.

Oil production in Poland is currently negligible (around 1 per cent of oil consumption - the rest is imported primarily from the USSR). Natural gas production is larger and has far more potential. In the past Poland produced approximately 6.7 million cubic metres per annum. A recent study by AMOCO and the Polish Oil and Gas Company indicated the presence of commercially viable deposits of both natural gas and methane.

Another major natural resource is sulphur, with reserves estimated at 900 million tonnes and annual production at around 5.0 million tonnes. Production costs are low, at around 30–45US$/tonne (1985). At present, around 80 per cent of production is exported.

In 1981 refined copper production reached some 317,000 tonnes rising in 1985 to 378,000 tonnes. It is important here to note the relative cost position of Poland vis-a-vis other producers. The 1985 figures are set out in Table 1.3.

Table 1.3 *Comparison of copper production costs*

Country	*Gross cost (1985) (cents/lb)*
USA	71.9
Chile	51.0
Zambia	65.8
Poland	40.0

Another factor in Poland's copper industry is the production of silver as a by-product.

Copper is a major export commodity with an annual average value of around US$270 million. The total Polish reserve base of copper is estimated at 15 million tonnes, out of total world reserves of 525 million tonnes (USA = 41 million tonnes, Chile = 97 million tonnes, Zambia = 34 million tonnes).

Prior to 1982, virtually all basic materials were centrally allocated but over the next eight years the scope of central planning was reduced and by the end of 1990 central allocation was practically abolished.

Currently, difficulties are occurring in some supplies, although almost no materials are now being rationed. Foreign companies are free to import raw materials or to purchase them on the domestic market on the same basis as Polish companies.

POWER

Poland has a comprehensive energy distribution network. Power stations are state owned. Due to decreasing demand there is an abundant supply of electricity. Energy prices are administered by the government and, despite increases, are still relatively low. The price of hard coal was freed from administrative control in the second half of 1990.

Electricity production amounted to 1475MWH in 1989 and accounts for over 55 per cent of primary energy use. During the cold season 34 out of the 56 power generating plants also produce steam and hot water for district heating purposes.

Most electricity is produced in coal-fired thermal plants, with severely adverse environmental effects. This situation is being gradually rectified with the assistance of credits from the World Bank, the European Bank for Reconstruction and Development (EBRD), the EC and the US.

Energy production is highly inefficient: it requires around 700 grams of coal to produce 1MWH of electricity compared to around 250 grams in Western Europe. Consumption is equally inefficient: prices have been held well below world levels, and metering is often inadequate, giving little incentive to economise.

Poland's energy profile is dominated by coal (70 per cent of primary energy requirements) and oil (20 per cent). The nuclear programme, based on Soviet technology, has been halted by the Solidarity government. Oil prices have risen significantly with the switch to hard currency trading at world prices with the Soviet Union, the traditional source of non-coal supplies.

MANUFACTURING

Industrial enterprises were estimated (end 1990) to contribute some 60 per cent of Poland's gross domestic product (GDP), a significant advance on the 1960 level of 35 per cent. Close to 30 per cent of the labour force is engaged in manufacturing.

Generally, Poland has a well-developed manufacturing industry in almost all sectors (except sophisticated, high-tech areas), staffed by very able and highly skilled labour and engineers. According to the 1986 World Bank report on Poland, management is of a very high technical capability. What it lacks, however, is modern Western methods of management and knowledge of the market economy.

Forty years of a centrally planned command economy have nevertheless taken their toll. Industry is concentrated in large state enterprises (a total number of 8000 or so) with the vertically integrated management and production systems which were typical of central planning. These huge state 'imperia' are only now starting to put into effect the gradual restructuring and privatisation programmes brought about by the policies of the Mazowiecki and Bielecki governments.

In all areas of industrial activity, state enterprises are encountering difficulties in adapting to market forces. The government faces a difficult task in balancing the need to expose firms to competition and to allow bankruptcies where necessary, and the need to avoid the complete collapse of the state sector. It is worth noting that approximately 15 per cent of industrial output is already delivered by Polish private industry, which, though small compared to the state sector, has managed to increase its total output substantially in the last three years.

Between 1982 and 1988, the net output of industry as a whole grew at an annual rate of 4.6 per cent. This was significantly lower than the average rate of growth of net output in the private sector, which was about 11 per cent. Output in the state sector of industry fell over 20 per cent in 1990, while the private sector reported a 9 per cent increase (and even this is probably an understatement).

Poland's leading industries are metallurgy and heavy industry, concentrated in Upper Silesia. The chemical industry is well developed; fertilisers and petrochemicals are important products. Textile production is also well developed, particularly in Łódź, Bielsko-Biała and Białystok and is expanding with an emphasis on exports. Other major industries are light engineering, pharmaceuticals, leather and leather products, wood products and food processing.

The fuel and energy sectors as well as the metallurgical industry have experienced a significant contraction, due partly to a fall in demand. Food processing declined in the socialised sector, while expanding in the private sector.

The cities of Szczecin, Gdynia and Gdańsk have been the centres of development of shipbuilding. The engineering industry is based in Warsaw, Poznań, Wrocław, Radom, Elbląg, Mielec, Rzeszów and Gliwice.

Profitability has been highest in light industry, engineering and minerals. Foreign companies are finding food processing, light industry and the service sector (hotels, transport and consulting services) as the current most advantageous prospects for investment.

COMMUNICATIONS

Poland's rail network is huge - about the size of France's and the former West Germany's combined. It is also relatively efficient and is being modernised with financial assistance from the World Bank and other financial institutions.

The country's road system, by contrast, is seriously under-developed and in a poor state of repair. The provision of public road transport and petrol stations is low.

The major ports are Szczecin, Gdynia and Gdańsk.

More than 75 per cent of all freight moves by road, 20 per cent by rail and the rest by water.

In a region world famous for its poor telephone networks, Poland still manages to be outstanding. The problem is beginning to be

Table 1.4 *Breakdown by country of exports and imports to Poland*

Country	*Exports from Poland (%)*			*Imports to Poland (%)*		
	1988	*1989*	*1990*	*1988*	*1989*	*1990*
Germany	12.4	14.2	25.3	13.0	15.7	22.0
USSR	24.5	20.8	15.3	23.3	18.1	18.7
UK	5.0	6.5	7.0	4.2	4.5	5.5
Switzerland	2.6	2.6	4.6	4.5	5.3	5.9
Czechoslovakia	6.0	5.5	4.0	6.4	5.7	3.3
Austria	3.1	3.5	3.9	4.4	6.0	5.7
France	2.3	2.4	3.3	2.5	3.1	2.9
Netherlands	2.2	2.6	3.2	2.7	3.0	3.0
Italy	2.3	2.3	3.1	3.3	4.1	7.2

overcome by the availability of satellite communication. Plans to modernise the internal system are well advanced.

UK/POLISH TRADE

The share of UK companies in Polish imports and exports is small but has been rising for the last four years following the decline in significance of the USSR as the main Polish trading partner (see Table 1.4).

UK exports to Poland are largest in the fuels, engineering and chemical sectors. The sale of fuels has shown the most significant growth, while exports of agricultural products suffered their worst decline in 1990. UK imports from Poland are concentrated on the metallurgical, food and engineering sectors (see Table 1.5). This has been true of the last two years.

Although in 1990 exports from the UK have shown some signs of decline, it is expected that in 1991 both exports and imports will show significant growth.

Table 1.5 *Breakdown by sector of UK imports from and exports to Poland*

Sector	*Imports from Poland (US$)*		*Exports to Poland (US$)*	
	1989	1990	1989	1990
Metallurgical	274,097	371,189	124,753	45,606
Chemical	72,677	88,298	118,218	71,405
Mineral	18,377	20,014	11,170	10,165
Wood/Paper	62,657	57,753	2,541	2,308
Textiles	58,495	75,345	29,140	19,690
Food	85,811	155,822	55,711	49,511
Agricultural	5,996	13,276	33,558	14,171
Other	7,996	11,052	8,352	7,701
Total	**774,016**	**961,078**	**518,655**	**479,634**

2

Economic Transformation

The Polish Investment Company

BACKGROUND

Internal

Political transformation was an indispensible condition for transition from the communist command economy to a market-based economy. Economic reforms attempted by the communists - sometimes even in good faith - could not be radical, comprehensive and effective because that would have led to a transformation of the political system, which the communists were not in a position to accept. Economic transformation and the establishment of a market economy require political changes that recognise the value of diversity and individual initiative.

The political changes thus facilitated the introduction of an economic transformation programme, announced in the third quarter of 1989 and put into operation from the beginning of 1990.

BACKGROUND

External

At the beginning of 1991 Poland owed some US$39 billion in foreign debt to a combination of Western governments and banks. In 1989 debt servicing obligations absorbed as much as 54 per cent of Poland's export earnings.

The IMF and the World Bank, both of which Poland joined in 1986, have been at the forefront of negotiations between Poland and its creditors. In January 1990, following IMF approval of the Polish government's recovery programme, the Paris Club of creditor governments agreed to restructure US$9.4 billion of Polish debt over 14 years.

There is a feeling within Poland that the West should reward and encourage Poland's unqualified commitment to swift market-oriented reform with the cancellation of all, or a substantial part of its debts, and agreement to cancel the debt by 50 per cent was recently reached with a number of sovereign creditors. The US (which has a low level of debt due to it) has offered a 70 per cent reduction. These measures and further negotiations with the London Club which are now proceeding should allow Poland to become a fully performing debtor country without placing an unbearable strain on its foreign currency earnings and reserves. This will provide conditions which will reduce any external constraints on the increasing momentum of the transformation process within the country.

THE BALCEROWICZ PLAN

The new government of Tadeusz Mazowiecki faced a serious dilemma: whether to choose swift, radical and comprehensive change, or to adopt a gradualist approach. The government's programme, commonly referred to as the Balcerowicz plan (after the Deputy Prime Minister responsible for economic policy), adopted the first approach. The choice was based upon three main considerations. First, that all aspects of an economic system are fundamentally interdependent and, therefore, its transformation needs a comprehensive and co-ordinated effort. Secondly, that the introduction of a market economy does not lend itself to a gradualist approach; a critical mass of reforms must be introduced without delay. Thirdly, that in view of the weak response of those accustomed to operating under the command system to policy changes requiring autonomous and spontaneous reaction, only drastic economic policy instruments could be effective.

The launching of the transformation programme took place under unfavourable economic conditions. The Polish economy entered 1989 with stagnating output, a rapidly shrinking foreign trade surplus, disequilibrium in the domestic market, and rampant inflation. These conditions were aggravated by lax government fiscal and price policies and a mounting budget deficit (probably prompted by a pre-electoral increase in consumption subsidies), which resulted in hyperinflation exceeding 50 per cent a month at the end of 1989. Thus, the transformation programme had to be underpinned by economic stabilisation measures, without which structural reforms would remain ineffective and the response to change would be distorted.

The stabilisation programme

The stabilisation programme comprised five principal elements:

1. With only minor exceptions (the most important being energy and transport), almost 90 per cent of prices (including those for intermediate and investment products) were freed from control. The difference between freeing prices to be determined by the market and an increase in administered prices (even if the end result in terms of price level is the same) should be stressed. Unlike the situation in several Central and Eastern European countries, society at large became accustomed to prices being determined by the market and not by government fiat. Corrective inflation ensued in the first months of 1990 and was higher than expected. Price liberalisation was combined with a withdrawal of the majority of subsidies.

2. Fiscal policy became extremely restrictive. Budgetary outlays and revenues were balanced by a reduction of subsidies, elimination of most tax reliefs, and increases in taxes or quasi-taxes (such as social security contributions).

3. A restrictive monetary policy was introduced with the aims of achieving positive interest rates and limiting access to credit.

4. Income and (especially) wage policies provided for progressive and heavy taxation of wage increases exceeding the inflation rate.

5. The zloty has been drastically devalued but, at the same time, full internal convertibility was introduced with all people and economic agents having unrestricted access to convertible currencies, the latter being simultaneously obliged to sell their foreign exchange receipts to the banking system. The new rate of exchange, fixed at Z9500 = US$1, was intended to be maintained for at least 3 months, but has remained stable until the devaluation to Z11,100 = US$1 in May 1991.

The stablisation programme led to the establishment of a market equilibrium, albeit at a depressed demand level. It caused industrial recession and a decline in output of over 20 per cent, predominantly in consumer goods industries. Inflation was much higher than predicted (especially in January February 1989, and again at the end of the year) and farmers and workers began to voice their grievances openly. The adjustment of the government's policy in July 1990, aiming at economic stimulation through demand expansion and support for new enterpreneurial activity and certain increases in agricultural support, resulted primarily in augmenting inflationary pressures. On the other hand, export expansion, initially assisted by drastic devaluation and later by demand contraction, counteracted the industrial recession to a certain extent and led to the accumulation of a considerable trade surplus both in convertible currency and in the rouble settlement areas. The surplus was increased by an import decline caused by a drop in domestic demand and the industrial recession, although some increase in certain consumer goods imports due to the release of pent up demand was recorded.

Structural change

The existing stabilisation measures already contain some rudiments of fundamental transformation. Freeing prices (restoring their allocative function) and foreign exchange liberalisation were among them. However, the programme also involved other important elements of structural change.

First of all, central planning has been abandoned and Civil Code rules have been applied to business and financial transactions. Secondly, efforts have been made to create a more competitive environment. An anti-monopoly law was enacted and an anti-monopoly board established to assist in breaking monopolistic structures in industry, trade, and services, and in counteracting restrictive business practices. At the same time, revenue boards were empowered to control price setting and they temporarily suspended price increases by firms considered to exercise a monopoly position in the market. Import liberalisation was reflected in formal abolition of the state foreign trade monopoly, elimination of all import restrictions and quotas, and in the suspension or lowering of tariff rates. The average nominal tariff rate decreased from 12 per cent at the beginning of 1990 to less than 4 per cent in the first months of 1991. All this contributed to a stimulation of the competitive environment and helped to reduce monopolistic practices. However, extreme concentration of production stemming from the very nature of central planning and investment, and built-in monopolistic structures (strengthened under the old system by strong interaction of these structures with the government and party apparatus) makes change far from simple.

At the same time, moves towards privatisation of trade and industry have been undertaken. The law now provides for free entry to, or exit from, business activities with practically no formalities besides registration. New foreign investment laws facilitated the inflow of foreign capital with tax holidays and exemption from wage increase taxation. However, profit transfers abroad were limited. This constituted an important disincentive to foreign investors and is to be corrected in the bill currently under parliamentary consideration.

Independent banking structures have begun to emerge; banking and insurance monopolies have been rescinded, and the banking system is being decentralised. Private and foreign banks and insurance companies are beginning to be established. The stock exchange is now operating on a limited scale but capital markets remain to be developed and a proper infrastructure for business operations is still awaited.

Political and economic difficulties

The transformation process also raises several political and economic dilemmas. First, there is the democracy dilemma. Although it is obvious that successful economic change can be achieved only within a democratic political environment, in a country that lacks a recent democratic tradition it is a difficult experiment. This was highlighted during the last presidential elections, when political infighting disrupted the precarious social consensus (underwritten by the Solidarity movement) that had secured acceptance of the hardships resulting from the transformation and stabilisation programmes.

Any emerging social discontent will be extremely difficult to neutralise, especially in view of the impending parliamentary elections. However, although sporadic strike action has occurred as a result of specific grievances over pay in certain areas of the public sector, the general consensus appears to be holding.

Completion of the legislative programme, crucial in establishing a firm legal framework for the transformation process needs to be achieved. If elections lead to a lack of clear parliamentary majority, a series of weak governments could emerge that are unable to drive the reform process to a successful conclusion. The President has recently sent back to Parliament for reconsideration the bill containing an over-complex electoral system.

Second, there is an inflation/recession dilemma. Certain political and social groups, and some noted economists, press for demand expansion (mostly through wage increases) as a means of reviving production and increasing employment. However, as the experience of the second half of 1990 has amply shown, under conditions of unchanged industrial structures and in an imperfect competitive environment, demand increases translate into higher inflation rather than supply growth.

Third, there is a difficult choice between exchange rate stability and devaluation. An anti-inflationary policy stance militates against devaluation, but combined pressures for market protection and for export support are hard to ignore.

Fourth, growing protectionist pressures in the form of calls to erect tariff walls (or even introduce non-tariff barriers) will also need to be faced.

Although the political changes are far from complete, the will of the people and the government make the market economy more of a reality each day. Though the state sector still grapples with recession, a more flexible private sector is adjusting to the changing conditions, and is booming.

CONCLUSION

Since the start of the transformation programme, queues have disappeared and, in 1990, exports to hard currency markets increased by over 40 per cent. Imports of consumer goods have increased considerably. These are palpable changes which can be experienced by all Polish citizens.

Privatisation of state enterprises has proceeded with five public offerings by the end of the first quarter of 1991; over 140 management/worker buy-outs have been affected. This process is being further accelerated.

More than one third of the total Polish economy is now estimated to be in private hands; private enterprise dominates the service sector and is a large force in the wholesale and retail trades. Five hundred thousand new businesses of all kinds were registered in 1990. Such a sea change puts the market-oriented development of the Polish economy in advance of any of its central European neighbours.

Internationally, Polish tariffs have been cut or suspended and international trade and investment facilitated by convertibility of the zloty and increasingly liberal foreign investment laws. All signs indicate that in the course of 1991 and beyond, those changes will take permanent hold, firmly keeping the country on the road to full recovery and a market economy.

3

The Legal Framework

Frere Cholmeley

The events of the last decade and the ending of one-party rule have inevitably brought about major constitutional and legal changes in Poland.

This chapter outlines the structures of national and local government and of the legislature. In practice, there is still some uncertainty as to where effective power will ultimately reside, and elections in the autumn of 1991 may have a material effect on the balance of power.

PARLIAMENT AND THE GOVERNMENT

The National Assembly was created in 1989 after the 'Round-Table' talks between Solidarity and the government. It is comprised of two chambers, the Senate and the Sejm:

- The Senate is comprised of 100 Senators. As a result of the free voivodship constituency elections held in June 1989, 99 Senators were elected from Solidarity candidates. There is one independent Senator.
- The Sejm is the main legislative body comprised of 460 Deputies. Elections took place in June 1989 according to the electoral law established under the Round-Table deal, which applies only to the present Assembly. Thirty-five per cent of the 460 seats were available for open contest. The remainder were guaranteed to the communists and their allies. Solidarity secured all the 161 seats open to them.

The government consists of a President and a Council of Ministers. Lech Wałęsa was elected President at the end of 1990 for a term of six years. The Council of Ministers consists of appointees approved by the Sejm and led by the Prime Minister. The President proposes the Prime Minister subject to approval by the Sejm. His term of office is undefined. The current Prime Minister is Jan Bielecki, appointed in January 1991.

The date for the first entirely free elections has been set for the autumn of 1991. In the meantime a Constitutional Commission has been working on reform of the electoral law. Controversy has arisen over the voting system to be used and over the power of the Communist Party to submit candidates for seats in parliament. The issue is whether this should be in the hands of political parties or whether it should be given to social organisations or even groups of citizens.

THE LAW

The main sources of law are:

1. The Constitution;
2. Statutes and decrees;
3. The Codes:
   - The Civil Code;
   - The Commercial Code;
   - The Civil Procedure Code;
   - Miscellaneous other codes;
4. Regulations.

The role of the principles of social co-existence as a moral code having binding force in a socialist society has now been diminished.

The Constitution

As a result of the political changes the Constitution as the foundation of the legal system has required radical alteration. In particular, changes have been necessary to eradicate those provisions which were incompatible with an economy moving towards private enterprise. Revision of the Constitution is continuing and it is anticipated that in the future there will be an entirely new Constitution of The Republic of Poland.

Statutes and Decrees

The legislation passed by parliament is published in the *Journal of*

Laws (*Dziennik Ustaw*). In the move towards a market economy the pace of legislation has been rapid.

Decrees

Decrees are supplementary provisions either envisaged by legislation and introduced by delegated power or introduced to clarify existing legislation. They are divided into two categories, according to the body issuing them: Council of Ministers decrees are equivalent to legislation and are passed by the Council of Ministers or Cabinet in areas reserved to them. The decrees are published in the *Journal of Laws*. Ministerial decrees may be introduced by a single minister and represent delegated or implementing rules. Ministerial decrees are published in an official journal, the *Monitor Polski*.

Regulations

Legislation may delegate power for the creation of secondary regulations to an appropriate body.

The Codes

The most important of these for current purposes are the Commercial Code of 27 June 1934 and the Civil Code of 23 April 1964. The Commercial Code has been largely repealed. However, some of its provisions have been maintained in force, in particular those relating to the structure and organisation of corporate bodies.

Legislative process

Legislation is initiated in either the Senate or the Sejm. Sometimes both initiate conflicting legislation on the same subject at the same time. It is initiated either by a commission of the Senate or Sejm, or by the President or Council of Ministers.

1. The Senate can amend or reject any proposal by a two-thirds majority with at least 50 per cent of the total Deputies present;
2. The President has a power of veto which can be overridden by the Sejm, again by two-thirds majority with at least 50 per cent attendance.

At present an extensive programme of liberalising legislation is being put through the Assembly at very great speed to implement the wide-ranging programme of economic and political reforms that has been adopted. Where appropriate, Western models are used, either from Germany, France, the UK or elsewhere. Increasingly the need to tailor these models to Poland's own situation has become apparent. Forecasting the pace and direction of new legislation remains a major difficulty for a foreign investor in Poland, particularly as English language translations are often unreliable and take time to become available.

LOCAL GOVERNMENT

Poland is divided into 49 voivodeships and 2121 gminas or communes.

- Voivodeships are provincial administrative bodies each of which is headed by a Voivode who is nominated by the Prime Minister. They provide the co-ordination of local services and supervise the communes.
- Communes (*gminas*) are controlled by a Mayor and a Management and Consultative Council, all elected by the inhabitants.

Local government elections

The first fully democratic local elections in post-war Poland were held in the spring of 1990. The election turnout was estimated at 42 per cent. Over 41 per cent of seats went to representatives of citizens' committees, which constituted the local organisations of Solidarity.

4

Polish Business Culture

Touche Ross & Co

In this chapter, the types of business structure operating in Poland, their make-up and the way they are managed, will be discussed.

Any understanding of the current business culture in Poland requires an appreciation of the background against which business activity has been conducted over the past decades, and of the changes which the system and its structures are now undergoing.

State enterprises, used to monopolistic production arrangements, are suddenly competing against each other - and, with the removal of external tariffs, against foreign imports. Centrally planned distribution suddenly gave way to selling in the market. Prices were freed, subsidies removed and the shock to the system cannot be underestimated. The managers of enterprises were most often, but not always, 'nomenklatura' bureaucrats (there were also technocrats - engineers and economists), and the wheels of central planning were kept turning by networks of patronage and favours. They had very quickly to come to terms with a new set of business concepts - making profits, producing what the market wants, efficiency, accountability and taking risks.

These concepts, with the lack perhaps of accountability, had hitherto been the stock in trade of the practitioners of the black economy who operated the black market in currency, food, consumer goods and from whom anything was available, for dollars. The black marketeers have now been displaced by ever rising numbers of small traders, and over one million private businesses were set up in 1990. An enterprise culture appears to be taking root.

Although we are here mainly concerned with industry and commerce, it is always worth remembering that 40 per cent of the population (and, by extension, of voters) is rural and that 80 per cent of the land - 2.7 million, mainly small, farms - is privately farmed, having survived attempts at collectivisation.

BUSINESS STRUCTURES

Under the socialist system, the state enterprise was the principal vehicle through which the state organised economic activity. State enterprises are still responsible for the bulk of Poland's industrial production. State-owned enterprises, and cooperatives, which together comprise the 'socialised' sector of industry, accounted for about 91 per cent of industrial value added in 1989, while the figure for 1990 dropped to some 80 per cent.

The present political and economic reforms in Poland aim, as a first step, to broaden the forms of state economic activity, so that in future the state will conduct such activity not only through state enterprises under direct ministerial control and government ownership, but through joint stock and limited liability companies, with 100 per cent share ownership by the state. The law on the privatisation of state enterprises, passed by the Sejm in July 1990, then allows, as the second step - the privatisation programme - sale of shares to privately run legal entities, individuals, joint ventures, or non-residents. (Alternatively, state enterprises can also be 'liquidated', prior to being sold.)

State enterprises

State enterprises are already independent, self-governing and self-financing economic entities with their own legal status.

The management of state enterprises make independent decisions in all business matters and organise the enterprise's activity. However, they can only make fully independent decisions concerning the enterprise's activity to the extent authorised by the company statutes. (For public utilities and all enterprises involved in foreign trade, radio and television, electronics, transport, telecommunications, vehicle manufacture and the repair of railway carriages, the statutes must have been adopted by the founding body, which is a ministry, local authority or state bank.)

If such powers are present, the government and its administration can only overrule the management's decisions if specifically empowered to do so by parliament. Now that enterprises organise their own supplies of raw materials, this theoretical protection from state interference is becoming more important, but it is still difficult for a state enterprise to be truly independent. In order to secure real independence from the state, a new law on state enterprises is to be introduced in 1991.

In practice, the management of the majority of state enterprises and cooperatives are free to decide what they should manufacture and in what quantities. In most cases, they are free to determine prices at which their products are sold, although in some circumstances, enterprises which wish to increase prices significantly are required to inform the Treasury Office of their intention. Only in some cases are prices controlled centrally (for example, energy, coal, gas, housing and rents).

Again, generally, management is free to employ and to lay off workers as well as to determine wages. However, the salary increase tax (podatek od ponadnormatywnych wynagrodzeń, or 'popiwek'), which applies to state enterprises and cooperatives, effectively discourages them from increasing wages. (The tax does not apply to private companies, to joint ventures formed before 1991 and to newer joint ventures if there is majority private participation.)

State enterprises are subject to registration procedures in district courts. There is free access to the registers, although information deemed to constitute a state or economic secret may be withheld. From its registration, a state enterprise becomes a legal entity.

State enterprises are self-financing, and must generate sufficient income to cover their costs, their development expenses, and their payments to the state Treasury. (In return for the initial funding of the enterprise by the state, the enterprise has to pay the Treasury a dividend paid out of profits, calculated on the value of fixed assets owned by the firm.) All enterprises must keep accounts and prepare periodic reports in specified formats. The annual financial report and accounts are subject to audit by the tax authorities.

Management structure and decision making in state enterprises

The law on state enterprises defines their management as comprising a general workers' assembly, the workers' council, and the enterprise director.

The director manages the enterprise and represents it in its relations with other organisations. He is usually independent and responsible for his own decisions. However, in some cases, the workers' bodies (ie, a general workers' assembly or the workers' council) have decision-making powers. These will be discussed in more detail later. Trade unions are also now an effective force and will also influence management decisions.

Although the director is the authorised legal representative of the enterprise, if legally binding commitments are being made which have a value of more than Z50 million (over US$5000), the agreement of at least two persons is required. In such cases, this is usually the director and either his deputy or the chief accountant. Deputy directors may represent the enterprise only to the extent of their authorisation to do so, and legally binding commitments can be made by them only in the presence of another authorised person. Information as to who has been authorised to act on behalf of the enterprise is included in the register.

The director of an enterprise is usually selected by means of open competition. In enterprises other than public utilities, where the founding body is responsible for the appointment and dismissal of the director, he is elected by the workers' council, which also has the power to dismiss him. (The first director of a newly established enterprise would have been appointed by the 'founding body'.)

For state enterprises of a general character (ie not public utilities), the founding body determines only the name, the type of company and its location, as well as the goal of its activity.

The basic internal structure of a state enterprise is specified in its statutes. These are normally drafted and proposed by the enterprise director and determined by the general workers' assembly. The internal structure of a state enterprise, the scope of its activities and the distribution of administrative duties and responsibilities are normally determined by regulations which are made by the director of the enterprise after consulting the workers' council.

Worker participation Worker participation in the management of state enterprises is guaranteed by law. Workers' councils and general workers' assemblies have certain decision-making powers and also the right to be consulted on matters affecting the enterprise and to state their opinions.

Specifically, general workers' assemblies have the authority to do the following:

- to adopt, on the motion of the enterprise director, the statutes of the enterprise;
- to decide upon the distribution of profits for the workers;
- to review annually the activities of the enterprise and of its director;
- to adopt the long-term plans and objectives of the enterprise.

The most important powers of workers' councils are:

- to decide upon the appointment and dismissal of the director and other persons having administrative functions in the enterprise;
- to adopt the annual plans and reports on the management of the enterprise's operations;
- to adopt resolutions concerning decisions on the merging of the enterprise with other enterprises or its transformation into a company and the issuing of shares;
- to approve the liquidation of fixed assets. (Since November 1990, state enterprises now also have the right to dispose of land which they own.)

The rights of workers in the management of state enterprises are thus strong. Paradoxically, this does not necessarily give rise to strong worker power - under the previous communist governments, the theoretical legal rights were effectively stifled by cosy Party arrangements. Now Poland is once more subject to the rule of law and those rights are real, but the overriding reality of the economic situation gives workers' bodies (and management) little effective room for manoeuvre, and they are queuing up to be privatised, exchanging effective control for 20 per cent employee share ownership and one-third of the places on the supervisory board.

Cooperatives

Cooperatives are voluntary, self-governing associations with an unlimited number of members and variable funds consisting of the members' contributions. Members may be both individuals and legal entities, but at least 10 individuals are required in order to establish a cooperative.

The founders of a cooperative draw up its statutes, sign them and elect the cooperative's authorities. Although these statutes do not have to be in the form of a notarised deed, they must regulate all the issues essential for the operation of the cooperative, as set down by law, and must be registered by the relevant district court, at which point the cooperative acquires legal status. Relations between the members of the cooperative and its management are stipulated in detail by law. There are special rules which apply to agricultural, farming, production, services and housing construction cooperatives.

Cooperatives may establish joint ventures in whatever corporate form they wish, including partnerships and limited liability companies. Thus while foreign participation in a cooperative is not possible, a foreign company may establish a limited liability company as a joint venture with a Polish cooperative.

Management structure and decision making in cooperatives

The supervision of a cooperative's activities is carried out by the general meeting of its members, its board of administration and its management.

The general meeting, held at least once a year, decides on the following:

- the cooperative's business planning;
- acceptance of the accounts presented by the management;
- distribution of any surplus revenue;
- sales of property;
- establishing the maximum liability for which the cooperative may be responsible;
- the merger or sub-division of the cooperative;
- any amendments to the statutes.

The board of administration, composed of at least three people, exercises control and supervision over the cooperative's operations. *Inter alia* it approves business plans, examines the management's reports and the accounts, and decides on the purchase or mortgage of property. Board members are appointed by the general meeting.

The management administers the cooperative's operations day to day and represents it in its relations with other organisations. It decides all issues which are not subject to decision by other bodies (as defined by law or by the cooperative's statutes). The management is composed of at least three members of the cooperative, and they are appointed by the board of administration or at the general meeting. The statutes of the cooperative may provide for the management of day-to-day operations by one manager if the other members of the management agree.

In order to commit the cooperative, it requires at least two members of management acting together, or else one member of management and a person authorised by the management to act on their behalf.

All independent, self-financing cooperatives which employ over 50 people (apart from service cooperatives and cooperative farms) must introduce self-government by workers, workers' general assemblies and a workers' committee. General assemblies of workers (which in practice have little power) pass opinions on development plans and evaluate the cooperative's operations each year. Workers' committees pass opinions on candidates who have been put forward to be employed in the cooperative's management.

The Chief Cooperative Council is the central organisation of the cooperative movement and it acts as the movement's representative in Poland and abroad. It also lobbies the government on the movement's behalf and provides information and statistical support to cooperatives.

Cooperatives are independent in the financing of their operations and supplement their own resources with bank credits and other loans. Cooperatives guarantee their liabilities with all of their property. Government subsidies, although now to a more limited extent, are available for construction and housing cooperatives, cooperatives for the disabled and for cooperatives producing basic services and commodities.

Private companies

Although the regulations concerning the establishment of companies can be found in the Commercial Code dating from 1934, following the regulations introducing the Civil Code (the law of 23 April 1964) only the rules on general partnerships, and limited liability and joint stock companies, including the regulations concerning their formation and commercial registration, remain in force.

For over 40 years since World War II, with the exception of a few joint stock companies which were created chiefly to conduct business abroad (such as the WARTA Insurance Company, the Bank PKO and some other foreign trade organisations with either 100 per cent or majority state ownership), the form of a private company has hardly ever been used.

At present, the most common vehicles for non-state business activities are limited liability and joint stock companies (for more information on both forms see, in particular, Chapter 31).

Joint ventures

The President of the Foreign Investment Agency (FIA) fulfils the functions of the central government agency responsible for foreign investments. The establishment of a company requires a permit. Such permits are usually issued without any difficulties and the law specifies that the refusal to issue a permit may be applicable only in the case of a threat to the national economy, for reasons of environmental protection, or in the interests of national security. Permits are also required for the following:

- transfer of shares between partners in the company;
- admission of a new partner to the company;
- when the field of operations changes.

Set out below are some indicators of the state of joint ventures as of 31 December 1990:

- Registered capital Z5.168 billion;
- Registered capital US$544.1 million;
- Foreign registered capital US$373.8 million;
- Average registered capital of foreign partner(s) US$133,500;
- Number of joint ventures 2,799.

This number can be divided as set out in Table 4.1.

Table 4.1 *Country of origin of joint ventures*

Germany	35.0%
Sweden	9.0%
USA	7.6%
Austria	7.1%
Great Britain	5.0%
48 others	36.3%

The value of the registered capital of all joint ventures created under the joint venture legislation amounted to US$544.1 million of which US$373.8 million (ie 68.6 per cent) was accounted for by foreign partners. These have come from 53 countries, mainly in Western Europe and the USA. Slightly over 100 companies raised capital from more than two foreign countries.

Both the registered capital and the number of joint ventures increased in 1990. The number of joint ventures rose from 1,935 to 2,799 (by 45 per cent), while the value of registered capital increased by some 40 per cent.

Between January and December 1990 about 3,000 joint venture applications were received by the FIA. Over 90 per cent were approved. So far, the biggest registered capital was declared by KVAERNER Gdynia Shipyard. Some other well-known companies were: Coca Cola, Hyatt, Johnson & Johnson, Kodak, Marriott Corporation, Procter & Gamble, General Motors and Siemens.

Table 4.2 *Joint venture participation by foreign partners*

Percentage of all joint ventures	*Participation of foreign partner in the shares*
29%	91%–100%
26%	61%–90%
8%	51%–60%
37%	1%–50%

The data in respect of percentages of foreign partner participation in joint ventures is set out in Table 4.2. It is estimated that in 1990 about 20 per cent of all foreign firms operating in Poland were involved in the clothing industry, and foreign firms are also highly active in cosmetics, plastics, construction and food processing. Nearly 40 per cent of all foreign companies conduct operations in more than one sector.

5

Market Intelligence

Touche Ross & Co

Since the inception of the Balcerowicz plan, the Polish economy now functions in a radically changed way. A modern market economy requires that its participants have access to information - historical information about what has gone before, market derived information about the value of assets and businesses, and statistical information about the markets for specific products and services - permitting the analysis of trends and generally giving sufficient information for making valid business decisions.

Currently, there are still inherent difficulties in using most available information for valuing businesses or for profit forecasting: it is often not possible to base decisions on historic information because even when it is available it can be unreliable and, because it relates to performance in a command economy, it can be misleading; and the lack of a developed capital market makes it impossible to value businesses in relation to their market worth - as yet (there has been, since 16th April 1991 a fledgling stock exchange occupying, by a nice irony, the former central committee headquarters building of the Polish Communist Party).

The changing conditions within which the economy now operates have revealed, among other things, the ineffectiveness of both the information gathering process as well as of the techniques for processing and presenting it. This gives rise to the lack of much of the information base needed for the carrying on of a market economy.

The Polish information system is characterised by a lack of consistent programmes for information gathering at a national level, by a low degree of computerisation, and by limited cooperation between agencies operating in this field. There may also be constraints on access to information which has been gathered in the case of some data requiring the permission of the appropriate authorities.

Another problem arises from the lack of suitably qualified personnel, at all levels. Marketing was a field neglected in Poland for many years - not only is there a lack of training in marketing, but there is little experience within Polish business of using information on the market when taking strategic business decisions.

SOURCES OF INFORMATION

The Main Statistical Office (Głowny Urząd Statystyczny - GUS)

This is a government body and is the largest institution operating in Poland gathering and processing information. It has offices throughout the country. All enterprises operating in Poland were required to file reports of their activities with GUS. Data on foreign markets is also compiled by GUS, but this is generally not very detailed.

Much information is published and openly accessible, but more is available on request. The difficulty arises in ascertaining what is available, and it is often a case of simply having to go and make enquiries. As in dealings with government ministries, it can be helpful to use the assistance of locals, businessmen or consulting firms, who have done it before and know what questions to ask and of whom.

Institutes

There are also several research and development institutes operating in Poland. These concern themselves with research on specific economic issues and sectors. Data which is gathered by them will be specific to the issues and subjects relevant to their field of interest. However, these data are not necessarily published in the form of analyses which may be of use to the businessman.

Firms are also now appearing who offer information and statistical services to businesses, and who analyse data available in raw format from official sources and present it in a usable form.

Ministries

Individual ministries have within them departments of analysts whose function is to gather and process data relating to the specific responsibilities of the relevant ministry. Access to this data is generally limited as it is primarily collected and processed for the use of the ministries themselves.

Centres for Overseas Trade and Chambers of Commerce

These bodies, because of the nature of their work, gather data on markets for specific products, on volumes and types of exports and imports, and on international trade.

The press

Information on the functioning of the economy, individual enterprises, and commodity exchanges, as well as the announcement of new legislation and regulations is published in papers such as *Rzeczpospolita* (*The Republic* - the nearest Polish equivalent to a 'paper of record'), *Życie Gospodarcze* (*Economic Life*), *Gazeta Bankowa* (*Banking Newspaper*), and in monthly periodicals such as *Handel Zagraniczny* (*Foreign Trade*), *Firma* (*The Company*) and *Problemy* (*Issues*). The Ministry of Ownership Changes places announcements of companies which it intends to sell in *Rzeczpospolita*.

INFORMATION TECHNOLOGY

In terms of the ways in which information technology is used, it is generally thought that in comparison with western Europe, Poland is currently at the level of the early-1970s.

This low level of utilisation of information technology in government, industry and commerce contrasts sharply with the achievements of Polish academics in the theoretical study of computer science - the Polish Computer Society and the Polish Cybernetic Society, as well as Professors Turski, Blikle, and Winkowski are highly regarded internationally.

The most common type of computer in Poland is the microcomputer or PC, and minicomputers manufactured in the west are also readily available. Although some years ago, in cooperation with other Comecon countries, minicomputers similar to the (now obsolete) IBM System 32 and 34 were produced, Poland now has no mainframe computer manufacturer. There is also a lack of large-scale computer networking. The majority of existing networks are local area networks (LANs) based on Novell technology.

Because of a lack of legislation which might have regulated the software market, there are an enormous number of copies of pirated software programs in existence, with all the attendant dangers to computer security. However, firms are now appearing on the Polish market offering licensed programs from leading western firms, such as Microsoft.

6

Poland and its Trading Partners

Frere Cholmeley

This chapter outlines Poland's relations with: the old Comecon system; the USSR and Eastern Europe in the post-Comecon environment; the EC; the UK; the USA; and Germany.

Other territories with which Poland has significant and growing business connections include Sweden, originating historically with Baltic trade, and the leading economies of the Far East.

SOVIET AND EAST EUROPEAN RELATIONSHIPS

On 26 February 1991 the military function of the Warsaw Pact was wound up at a meeting of member countries in Budapest. It was expected that Comecon, the socialist trading organisation, would be formally brought to an end at the same time but this has been temporarily postponed. Nevertheless, the organisation is unlikely to have much longer to live.

These events represent the end of security and trade structures that have sustained the region, however inadequately, for the last 40 years. Nevertheless a knowledge of the old structures is still relevant while the structures themselves are being removed. Also, the trading relationships that they produced are still very much in operation.

Comecon

The organisation was founded in 1949 'to assist in the economic development of its then member states' and also to 'further deepen and perfect the cooperation and development of socialist economic integration'. It formed part of Stalin's process of consolidation of Soviet rule in the satellite states through closer political and economic ties. Member countries are Bulgaria, Cuba, Czechoslovakia,

Hungary, Poland, the Soviet Union, Vietnam and, until reunification last year, the German Democratic Republic.

The official function of Comecon is to:

1. encourage the interchange of goods and services between members;
2. to promote synchronisation/harmonisation of the member countries' individual five-year plans; and
3. to provide funds via the International Investment Bank (headquarters in Moscow) to finance industrial development.

A major pre-occupation of Comecon has been the attempt to co-ordinate economic production and planning between the member countries, the goal being a centrally planned transnational economy orchestrated from Moscow by the Secretariat. This started in 1971 when the 'Complex Plan' for economic integration was adopted. The scheme was expanded in 1976 to include such industries as fuel and power resources, raw materials, machinery building, agriculture and transport.

The Comecon system covered primarily:

- Foreign trade, handled through state monopolies (such as Poland's Foreign Trade Enterprises) each having a sectoral responsibility. These followed targets set out in five-year plans. Trade was by barter or through the convertible rouble. A mainstay was the USSR's supply of oil in exchange for manufactured goods.
- Cooperation in the development of new industrial projects. Poland and Hungary cooperate in a joint venture known as Haldex for the development of mining technology, for example. There are numerous joint industrial, trade and transport organisations between member countries (ie the Office for Maritime Freight, INSA and Interport, all co-ordinating maritime freight).

Huta Katowice, Poland's largest integrated steel plant, is an example of the way in which industrial development took place in the context of Comecon central planning. Originally intended for East Germany, the Soviet planners moved the site to Katowice in southern Poland in part to quell simmering Polish dissent against Soviet domination. The plant was built using a mixture of Soviet and Western technology and involved the construction of 800 kilometres of railway linking it with iron ore mines in the Ukraine. The finished product was then transported back to the Soviet Union using the same line. Until 1 January 1991 when hard currency replaced the transferable rouble as the means of payment, the true economics of the plant were obscured by Comecon rules attaching artificial prices to the raw materials supplied by the Soviet Union and to the finished product sent back by Poland.

The reasons for the decline of Comecon are of course inextricably bound up with the political changes of recent years. Political change was to a great extent prompted by the failure of central planning at the domestic and supranational levels to meet the economic needs of people in Eastern Europe.

The linchpin of multilateral trade within the Comecon countries was and remains the USSR. The faltering economies of Eastern Europe were and to a great extent still are propped up by the provision of cheap natural resources (ie oil sold at 10 per cent of world prices) by the USSR in exchange for low quality manufactured goods. In recent years the USSR has become increasingly reluctant to continue this trade because its economy can no longer afford it and also because, with Poland and its Eastern European neighbours now committed to democracy and the free market, the political benefits from supporting the Comecon nations have now fallen away.

NEW EASTERN EUROPEAN RELATIONSHIPS

Poland and the Soviet Union

With the opening up of Poland from 1988 there were calls in some circles for a more bullish approach to relations with the USSR. This involved:

- calls for official recognition and support for the aspirations of the Soviet Republics;
- a swift winding up of the Warsaw Pact; and
- the departure of 50,000 Russian troops located in the country.

Poland's policy has been very cautious towards the USSR, particularly in the light of recent events in the Baltic Republics. The rationale for this policy given by the Foreign Minister, Skubiszewski, is a realistic one, namely that 'Poland is not a major power'.

Poland's economic interests lie in good relations with the USSR.

Some 30 per cent of its foreign trade is still with the Soviet states. In particular:

1. The survival of many of the country's steel and engineering companies since their exposure to the free market has been due to the availability of low-cost energy and raw material supplies from the Soviet Union, although the switch to hard currency accounting in intra-Comecon trade on 1 January 1991 is expected to reduce the scope for such deals.
2. For the moment, Poland is dependent upon the USSR for its oil, although import facilities at the Baltic ports are being improved to correct this.
3. An element of dependence also arises from the relative technical obsolescence of a good deal of Poland's manufactured produce; the main markets in which it will sell are Soviet and East European ones.

For these reasons it would be premature to assume that trade links with the Soviets are now forgotten and irrelevant.

Poland, Hungary and Czechoslovakia

Poland's natural partners, for the present at least, should be Hungary and Czechoslovakia. All three countries have a common post-war experience, extensive trading links and similar economic problems. In fact there are signs of the development of new political and economic links between these countries to replace those imposed upon them by the Warsaw Pact and Comecon:

- There have been a number of trilateral meetings between the Presidents of the three countries, the latest in Visegrad on 15–16 February 1991. Aside from smoothing over personal rivalries between Lech Wałęsa of Poland and Vaclav Havel of Czechoslovakia, potential areas of greater cooperation were discussed.

- There have also been a number of bilateral agreements reached between the three countries concerning military training and approaches and attitudes to Nato and the EC.

Poland is now interested in joining a multilateral organisation known as 'the Pentagonale' whose present members are Italy, Austria, Yugoslavia, Hungary and Czechoslovakia. This is an Italian sponsored organisation which grew out of a cooperation agreement signed in Budapest in November 1989. Its goals are, first, 'to contribute to regional growth and stability in the current period of change in Central and Eastern Europe' through cooperation in specific areas of common interest. These include transport, telecommunications, the environment, support to small- and medium-sized enterprises, culture and tourism; and, second, to 'complement the construction of the EC' and to provide a medium-term structure for Central European economic cooperation as a preliminary to full integration into the EC.

These developments should not disguise the existence of rivalries between the Eastern European states. This is partly the legacy of a Soviet policy of divide and rule. There are also clear divergencies of interest in such areas as competition for Western investment and membership of the EC. For the present, the greatest obstacle to formal economic and political arrangements between the three countries is the USSR. The aim is therefore to find methods of cooperation which will not be perceived by the USSR leadership as contrary to USSR interests.

POLAND'S LINKS WITH THE WEST

The EC

Until very recently the bulk of Polish foreign trade took place within Comecon. Exports to the West were material but of much less significance. The position now is the reverse. Access to Community markets and funding (in the form of loans, aid or otherwise) is vital to the future of the Polish economy.

There are two aspects to the issue of access to Community markets:

1. Polish industry needs to be able to generate hard currency by exporting to Community countries; and

2. Foreign investors must not be dissuaded from investing in Polish industry for fear that goods manufactured there might be excluded from Community markets.

The regulatory framework for entering the market is the Community's 'Common Commercial Policy'. This consists of trade agreements reached between the Community and non-member states and trade restrictions created by Community legislation. Until recently the Policy represented a significant barrier to free trade between East and West, imposing tight limits on the quantity of goods that could be imported and excluding goods on the basis of the Community's anti-dumping provisions. The position changed in 1988 because Comecon finally recognised the Community as a legal organisation, paving the way for the negotiation of less restrictive bilateral agreements between the Community and each of the Comecon countries. The absence of formal recognition until this time had the unfortunate side effect of the proliferation of separate commercial policies by each of the Community's member states with individual Eastern European countries, thus adding a second complicating tier of restrictions to East–West trade.

The Community signed a trade and cooperation agreement with Poland on 19 September 1989. It provided as follows:

1. progressive abolition of quantitative import restrictions applicable to imports into the European Community;
2. EC and Poland accorded each other 'most favoured nation' status; and
3. promotion of cooperation between the contracting parties in areas other than trade in goods (ie industry, mining, agriculture, research and development, energy, environment, transport and tourism).

The conclusion of bilateral trade agreements between the Community and each of the Eastern bloc countries is gradually re-instating the 'Common Commercial Policy' as the sole framework for restrictions on East–West trade.

The natural conclusion of Poland's policy to obtain unrestricted access to the Community's market is membership. Interest in obtaining membership has been expressed by the Polish authorities. The Community is not as yet prepared to commit itself to a fixed timetable for Poland or any of its other former Comecon partners to join. A prerequisite is that they first adjust their economic and social structures to the same standard as member countries. Until then the Community is negotiating 'association agreements' with the Eastern European countries. These will create a situation halfway between the current position and full membership. They will cover the following areas: free movement of people, services and capital; close economic cooperation in a variety of specialist fields; and close cultural cooperation.

The Community also has a variety of aid programmes targeted at

Poland and Eastern Europe generally. Details of these are given in Appendix 3.

The United Kingdom

The UK's links with Poland are strong, particularly as the result of relationships forged between the two countries during World War II. One in eight of the Battle of Britain pilots, for example, were Polish. The War also resulted in an exodus of Polish refugees to the UK forming the basis of the present Anglo-Polish community of some 150,000 people.

The UK's consistent policy on East-West relations and the assistance that it has provided to Poland in various international fora (for example the 'four plus two' negotiations concerning German reunification which settled Germany's eastern border with Poland) have formed the basis of solid diplomatic relations between the two countries. Since the appointment of the Solidarity-led government in 1989, bilateral governmental relations have flourished.

There are a number of UK government agencies, administered by the Department of Trade and Industry, with responsibility for promoting trade between the UK and Poland. These include the British Overseas Trade Board, The East European Trade Council and the Export Credit Guarantee Department.

On 8 December 1987 Poland and the UK signed an 'Agreement for the Promotion and Reciprocal Protection of Investments' which came into force on 14 April 1988. The Agreement set out to 'create favourable conditions for greater investment by investors' of both countries and to this end makes provision for compensation in the event of financial loss or in the event of nationalisation or other expropriation of a foreign investor's property.

The UK and Poland are also signatories to a double tax convention dated 16 December 1976.

The United States

Between 1945 and 1970 the United States imposed stringent restrictions on exports to the Eastern bloc, including Poland, as part of its overall policy of denying economic benefit to its cold war adversaries. In 1969 the position eased with the passing of the Export Administration Act which established the structure presently in use for the licensing of trade with Eastern Europe. The Department of Commerce, which is responsible for controlling exports, issues a commodity control list establishing details of all commodities which will require a licence prior to export. A number of goods fall into a general authorisation category for which no licence will be required.

Since the opening of Poland to the West in 1988–89, the United States has been swift to establish government agencies whose function is to assist American business in the country. These include the Eastern European Business Information Centre, the Overseas Private Investment Corporation and the Polish-American Enterprise Fund. There are also a number of agencies with funds to assist US-Polish enterprise including the US Trade and Development Programme.

In March 1990 Poland and the US signed a business and economic agreement with the purpose of improving the framework for bilateral trade.

Germany

The newly united Germany is already a major trading partner with Poland. According to statistics released by *The Warsaw Voice* (the local English language newspaper), in July 1989 German investors were involved in 367 inward investments into the Polish economy, by far the highest number from any one country, the next highest being Sweden with 84 investments. Most analysts are agreed that German investors will be the most active in the Polish economy over the next decade and that Germany will replace the Soviet Union as Poland's most important trading partner. The two countries are presently negotiating the terms of a 'General Cooperation Treaty' covering economic, political and cultural issues. There is already in place a double taxation treaty.

The relationship between the two countries is not without its tensions, though:

- Historically, the repositioning of Poland's western border some 60 miles into former German territory at the end of World War II and other issues continue to cause tension. The boundary was only formally accepted by the German government last year with the signing of a border treaty on 14 November 1990.

- There is a concern that the powerful German economy will come to exercise too much influence over Polish economic and industrial affairs. For this reason the Polish authorities wish to establish a diverse base of foreign investment in the country.

Part II

The Business Infrastructure

7

Foreign Investment

Frere Cholmeley

There are three ways in which a foreigner can invest in Poland:

1. Acquisition of real property; this option is dealt with in Chapter 13.
2. Acquisition of an interest in an existing Polish venture. Opportunities in this area will arise as the result of the programme of privatisation of state-owned enterprises that is to take place over the next five years. A stock exchange is also being established in Warsaw so that it will be possible for foreign and domestic investors to trade in Polish quoted stocks.
3. Investment in newly formed businesses.

In each case, a Polish partner may or may not be involved.

HISTORY OF FOREIGN INVESTMENT LEGISLATION

There have been a number of attempts to encourage foreign investment in Poland by means of legislation establishing structures for this purpose:

- In 1976 the Gierek administration issued the 'Regulation of the Council of Ministers on Permits to Foreign Individuals to Run Certain Types of Economic Activities'. This was largely abortive, attracting only nine foreign investors over the period 1976–82, and was repealed in 1982.
- In 1982 a wider attempt was made with the 'Law on Principles of Running Small Scale Industry Businesses by Foreign Persons'. This was aimed at small manufacturing businesses with a maximum workforce of 200.

- In 1986 The 'Law on Companies with Foreign Capital Participation' was passed which enabled foreigners to invest in the public sector as well. It lead to the establishment of a number of substantial joint ventures between foreign and Polish partners.

All this legislation operated in a communist and centrally planned economy. The role assigned to the foreign investor was marginal. Since the democratic elections of June 1989, foreign investment has been seen as fundamental to the establishment of a market-oriented economy. The passing of a new, more liberal, foreign investment law was regarded as a matter of priority by the new government. The result was the 'Law on Economic Activity with the Participation of Foreign Parties' (the Foreign Investment Law - 'FIL') passed on 23 December 1988, and amended on 28 December 1989.

The new legislation and the old

The 1982 'Law on Principles of Running Small Scale Industry Businesses by Foreign Persons' remains in force but was updated by the FIL to bring it into line with the new procedures. Companies that were set up under the 1982 law have the option either of continuing to trade under that law as amended or of registering under the FIL.

The 1986 'Law on Companies with Foreign Capital Participation' was repealed by the FIL. Companies established under the 1986 law were automatically brought within the system of regulation established by the FIL.

Thus there are now two structures for foreign investment, the first being the 1982 law and the second being the FIL. The FIL provides the more liberal framework for setting up in business in Poland and will normally be the investment route followed.

THE FOREIGN INVESTMENT LAW

Summary of principal features

The FIL establishes a more favourable climate for investment than its predecessors by giving the investor a greater degree of freedom:

- In deciding the nature of its investment and the legal structure through which the investment may take place.
- In the amount of control that it may exert over the investment entity.

- In the movement of funds into and out of that entity.
- Legal structure: the investment entity may be a joint stock or limited liability company.
- Management and control: the only restriction on equity participation is that the investor must acquire more than 20 per cent of the equity with a value in excess of US$50,000. Otherwise control may be to the extent of 100 per cent ownership and Polish involvement is not required (although such involvement may reduce the need for other licences, eg on real property acquisitions). Overseas personnel are free to hold management positions.
- Area of investment: while certain areas of business activity have been prioritised by the Polish government as being areas where foreign investment is to be particularly encouraged, there is little restriction on the choice of activity.
- Bureaucracy: some red tape is involved. The investor is required to obtain a permit from a government agency, the Foreign Investment Agency, but by comparison with the requirements of earlier legislation the procedure has been streamlined.
- Taxation: companies doing business under the FIL have the benefit of a number of tax breaks (discussed later).
- Compensation guarantee against nationalisation: this is not dealt with directly under the FIL, but a number of trade and cooperation agreements that Poland has signed with its principal trading partners (including the United Kingdom) provide for compensation in the event of expropriation of a foreign investor's investment assets.

The material that follows consists of a more detailed analysis of the FIL, how it works and the procedures that will need to be observed in order to set up a business in Poland.

The foreign investor

For the FIL to apply there has to be a degree of involvement by a foreign entity. Foreign entities are defined in Article 3.2 as being:

1. individuals domiciled outside of Poland (whether Polish or not);
2. companies with a foreign shareholder owning more than 20 per

cent of the shares (the definition of 'foreign' in the corporate context being registration outside Poland and, in the case of private individuals, domicile outside Poland).

Business entity

Article 2 of the FIL provides that the 'conduct of economic activity with the participation of foreign parties' may be carried on 'either in the form of a limited liability or a joint-stock company'.

It is possible to carry on business in Poland simply by means of the establishment of a branch office; such an investment would fall outside the terms of the FIL's regulatory structure and the incentives that go with it.

Contributions to equity

Contributions by Polish and foreign investors may be made in money and/or in kind. Contributions by a Polish party may, additionally, be made in the form of the transfer of rights to state-owned real property.

- The value of any contribution in kind may be subject to verification by independent experts should the Foreign Investment Agency require it. A right to occupy land is valued by capitalising the market rental value. If the valuation by the Agency is lower than that originally claimed the cost of verification will be borne by the investor making the contribution.

- The monetary contribution of a foreign investor must be made in zloty acquired from the sale of foreign currency at a Polish foreign exchange bank.

- A contribution in kind of a foreign investor may be either transferred from abroad or acquired in Poland in exchange for zloty (again acquired from the sale of foreign currency at a Polish foreign exchange bank). Customs duty is not payable.

- The Minister of Finance may, in some circumstances, approve foreign contributions made in another manner, such as debt-equity swaps whereby the foreign party assumes debt obligations of the Polish state in exchange for credits to its account at a Polish foreign exchange bank.

Management of the company

Article 9 of the FIL provides that 'Parties ... may, without restriction, arrange their relationships and the internal affairs of the company in its founding act [ie its Memorandum and Articles] unless provisions of the Commercial Code or this Law state otherwise'. The foreign investor has, accordingly, been given a free hand to establish and/or negotiate the terms upon which the company is to be managed. This is a considerably more liberal position than that adopted by earlier legislation.

The FIL permits investors, with consent, to appoint foreigners to key management positions in companies set up under it. Article 31.2 provides that 'a company can employ persons not having Polish citizenship or a permanent residence card with the consent of the local State Administrative Authority'. A permit is not required, however, where the foreign investor seconds one of its employees to the Polish company.

Other issues

Other relevant issues include:

- employment/labour;
- land ownership;
- tax (corporate and personal);
- distribution of profits;
- exchange control and repatriation of investments and profits;
- foreign trade.

Each of these topics is covered in separate chapters.

Obtaining authorisation

Commencement of business in Poland by a foreign investor within the terms of the FIL, whether by way of a joint venture or a wholly-owned company, requires a permit. The issuing authority is the Foreign Investment Agency, the central authority responsible for foreign investment policy.

Certain information must be supplied with the permit application. This includes:

- the name(s) of the party or parties to the investment;
- the subject and parameters of the business activity of the company;
- the anticipated duration of the investment;

- the estimated setting-up costs and the capital of the company;
- the ratio of capital contributions to be made by the parties to the company and the nature of their contribution (whether cash or in kind);
- the registered office;
- an indication of the proposed location of the company's production facilities;
- the draft constitutional documents of the company (which should be initialled by all the prospective parties);
- information on the identity and financial standing of the proposed shareholders in the company. Photocopy extracts of passports will be sufficient to establish the identity of individuals. Evidence of financial standing that will be acceptable include letters of financial standing from bankers and audited accounts.

The degree of complexity and detail required in relation to the feasibility study will depend upon the monetary value of the venture. Where the initial capital outlay is in excess of US$500,000, or where the Polish public sector is participating to the extent of US$100,000 or more in a venture, a full plan will be required. In all other cases a short study will suffice.

A number of practical points should be remembered:

1. The application and supporting documents should be submitted in Polish.
2. The trade mission to the Polish Embassy in London has available a specimen application form which may be a useful guideline in relation to such matters as style and layout.
3. The application may be filed by the Polish or foreign investor. If only one of a number of the prospective investors makes the application, the application should be accompanied by evidence of appropriate authorisation from the other parties.

Priority investment areas

Investors proposing to set up business in 'priority areas of investment' (as designated by the Polish authorities) will be viewed with particular favour. 'Priority areas' include:

- Businesses which will be particularly active in the provision of products and services for export.

- Businesses which will lead to the introduction of new technology and management systems.
- Businesses which facilitate the transfer of know-how and management skills.
- Businesses which are intended to lead to the improvement of the environment.

Grant of authorisation

Authorisation is granted on the basis and on the terms of the information set out in the application. Accordingly, the authorisation will specify:

- the names of the joint venture partners;
- the name of the company and its registered office;
- the geographical location of its production sites;
- the type of activities to be carried on by the joint venture company and the anticipated duration of the joint venture;
- the ratio of capital contributions;
- the period of time for which authorisation is granted.

Authorisation is granted on the basis of the information submitted in the application. Any significant change to it without prior approval can result in withdrawal of authorisation.

Conditional authorisation

The Agency may impose conditions on the grant of authorisation. It may, for example, make authorisation conditional upon the involvement of a Polish partner or upon a different ratio of capital contribution.

Post-authorisation requirements

Once authorisation is granted, the joint venture company must be registered in the Polish Commercial Register. An application for registration must include the written authorisation. Companies must then provide proof of registration to the Agency and, within two weeks of registration, a copy of the final constitutional documents of the joint venture company (its Memorandum and Articles of Association).

Refusal of authorisation

The Foreign Investment Agency's decision must be given within two months of the date of receipt of the application. This provision has been inserted to allay well-founded concerns about Polish bureaucratic delay.

An application can be refused only on certain specified grounds. Those are that it is likely to affect adversely: the Polish economy; the environment; public safety; national defence or state secrets.

Appeal

It is possible to appeal against decisions of the Foreign Investment Agency. Appeals must be made within 14 days from the notification of the refusal of the permit application.

FUTURE DEVELOPMENTS

A new foreign investment law was due to be passed in the first half of 1991. The current draft of the new law indicates that the structure and procedure for foreign investment are to be amended in the following areas.

Permits

Foreign investors will only need to obtain permits from the Foreign Investment Agency in two instances:

1. If the activity of the investment is in a 'sensitive' area of the economy (eg air, sea or rail transport, telecommunications services, turnover in real estate, defence industry).
2. If the Polish partner, in the case of a joint venture, is a state-owned or municipal enterprise which is contributing, as part of the founding capital of the company, an enterprise such as a plant or branch.

These proposals represent a massive reduction in the regulatory role of the Foreign Investment Agency. In the great majority of cases, a permit will no longer be required. It is thought, however, that the Agency will still have an overall supervisory function, particularly to ensure that whole sectors of the economy are not monopolised by foreign investors.

Tax concessions

The present FIL grants companies set up under it a blanket exemption from corporation tax for the first three years of trade. It is proposed that this exemption be amended so that companies will only be exempt if:

- the capital contribution of the foreign investor is in excess of US$3 million;
- the venture is active in 'preferred areas' which are as yet undefined; and
- the investment occurs prior to the end of 1993.

If a company satisfies these requirements then it will be exempt from tax for up to the first six years of its trade. This proposed amendment obviously represents a considerable reduction in the scope of tax exemption.

Profit

The proposed reduction in the scope of tax exemption will be compensated for by a relaxation of the restrictions on repatriation of profit made by foreign investors. Foreign investors will be able to repatriate all their profits, including proceeds from the sale of shares in the investment entity. Employees of a joint venture will be able to transfer abroad the equivalent of their salaries in foreign exchange.

The law will no longer define the minimum level of foreign investment. Currently, this is 20 per cent of the start-up capital of the company (being not less than US$50,000). At the same time, it is proposed that the minimum required capital for the establishment of limited liability and joint-stock companies will be increased to Z10 million and Z250 million respectively (US$1052 and US$26,315 at current exchange rates).

8

The Convertibility of the Zloty

The Polish Investment Company

BACKGROUND

Prior to the economic reforms initiated in 1989, the zloty was not convertible. Its rate was set by the National Bank of Poland and based on a basket of Western currencies. Officially, foreign currencies could be purchased only through the (state-owned) banks for authorised transfers (eg, in payment for imports). Throughout the post-war period there was an active black market where the zloty experienced considerable volatility and traded, at times, at less than 10 per cent of its official value.

In 1989 the government authorised the establishment of private sector money exchange bureaux, known as 'kantory'. Until the end of that year Poland had a 'dual' exchange rate system: authorised transactions were effected through the banks at the official exchange rate, while individuals could buy or sell zlotys in exchange for convertible currencies at the 'market' rates quoted in the kantory. The kantor rates proved highly volatile, reflecting the very unclear political and economic situation of Poland during this period.

Significant price differences were occasionally evident between kantory in different geographical locations, creating arbitrage opportunities for some well-organised groups with access to good telephone communications.

The new economic programme launched in January 1990 envisages the eventual full convertibility of the zloty. As from the beginning of that year the zloty became 'internally convertible' at the new official exchange rate of US$1 = Z9500. The rate is market-driven, but remained relatively stable, hovering between Z9344 and Z9764 (June 1990), until the 16 per cent devaluation in May.

Dollar shops ('Pewex') now accept the zloty as well as foreign currencies, and all prices are displayed only in zlotys. Taxi drivers now prefer to be paid in zlotys, and the black market has virtually disappeared.

CURRENT REGULATIONS

There are still restrictions, however, on the export of currencies and the foreign exchange legislation does not permit Poles to hold assets overseas. Foreign visitors are not allowed to bring zlotys into, or take them out of the country.

Internal transactions

All commercial transactions between Polish enterprises (including Polish-registered joint ventures) must be invoiced and settled in zlotys; enterprises are no longer permitted to maintain foreign currency accounts in Polish banks. It is not uncommon, however, for contracts to be expressed as the zloty equivalent of a fixed amount of dollars, particularly where capital goods are involved or delivery is scheduled some time into the future. Foreign companies, on the other hand, may hold foreign currency accounts at Polish banks.

External transactions

Foreign exchange regulations relating to foreign trade have been significantly relaxed. Funds may be remitted freely in payment for goods and services. This can be effected through any of the licensed banks on presentation of appropriate documentation. No import licences are generally required. Loans in foreign currencies may only be taken through authorised banks.

Exchange facilities

At the beginning of 1990, only a few banks were licensed for foreign exchange transactions: Bank Handlowy, Bank Pekao SA, the Export Development Bank, and the Food Economy Bank. During the course of the year the National Bank of Poland issued licences to each of the nine state-owned commercial banks as well as to the government-owned National Economy Bank and State Savings Bank (Bank PKO). In addition, licences were granted to two private sector banks, the Bank Inicjatyw Gospodarczych and Kredyt Bank, and to the joint venture bank, the American Bank in Poland.

Remittance of profits

Remittances of dividends and capital resulting from investments in Poland are governed by the Foreign Investment Law (FIL). Under present legislation remittance of dividends is restricted to the surplus of export earnings over imports generated by the enterprise, plus 15 per cent of net profits derived from sales in the domestic market. Any additional transfer of profits requires the approval of the Minister of Finance. Proceeds from the sale of an investment to a foreign party in foreign currency may be transferred abroad; where the proceeds are received in zlotys, they may be transferred abroad 10 years after the date of registration of the company.

As discussed in Chapter 7, the Ministry of Finance is proposing to make significant changes to the FIL in the early part of 1991. Under the draft proposals dividends and capital will be freely remittable, although certain favourable tax provisions for foreign investors will be withdrawn.

THE FUTURE

In May 1991, principally in response to pressure from exporters experiencing internal inflation, the zloty was devalued to 11,100 zlotys = US$1. Its value will henceforth be measured against a basket of currencies rather than tied directly to the dollar.

The International Monetary Fund organised a Stabilisation Fund of US$1000 million to be available in support of the Polish currency, as exchange controls were lifted. However, Poland generated a strong balance of payments surplus in 1990 and the support was not required; the Stabilisation Fund remained unutilised.

The government succeeded in bringing down the rate of inflation from the exceptionally high levels of 1989 and the first quarter of 1990. However, retail prices continue to rise at a rate of over 5 per cent per month, thus creating increasing difficulties for the export sector and putting industry under pressure from imports. In these circumstances a realignment of the exchange rate was almost inevitable. However, having made a moderate adjustment, there is no retreat from the policy of achieving full convertibility of the zloty, to which the government appears to be wholly committed.

9

Prices

The Polish Investment Company

HISTORY

There was very little movement in prices in post-war Poland before the 1980s. The absence of inflation was, however, somewhat illusory, in that many articles were either not available or rationed or obtainable only after prolonged queuing or 'under the counter'. The official exchange rate was maintained unchanged, although the growing divergence with the black market rate pointed to the diminishing real purchasing power of the Polish zloty. The rate of interest was maintained low. It served mainly as an accounting instrument for state enterprises, rather than as a mechanism for balancing the supply and demand for credit or as a tool of macroeconomic policy.

From 1981 until 1987 annual inflation hovered between 15 per cent and 20 per cent per annum (see Table 9.1), with the exception of 1982 when it reached 100 per cent. The rising pace of inflation was caused by a series of price reforms which were introduced in reaction to social pressures, as a means of making the economy more market responsive.

Table 9.1 *Retail price indices 1981–1990 (previous year = 100)*

	1981	*82*	*83*	*84*	*85*	*86*	*87*	*88*	*89*	*1990*
Consumer goods	118.4	209.4	121.9	114.5	114.3	117.7	123.5	160.0	364.3	684.7
Food	114.6	262.8	113.1	116.9	115.7	114.6	118.2	148.3	437.7	674.7
Capital goods	118.6	236.1	114.2	110.9	112.3	116.7	128.8	171.6	287.1	990.8

Source: Central Statistical Office.

Table 9.2 *Average monthly earnings 1980–90 (excluding share of profits) (Z '000s)*

1980	*81*	*82*	*83*	*84*	*85*	*86*	*87*	*88*	*89*	*1990*
6.0	7.7	11.6	14.5	16.8	20.0	24.1	29.2	53.1	206.8	962.0

Source: Central Statistical Office.

A major attempt at reform took place in 1988. The immediate and most obvious consequence was that inflation rose significantly. It became apparent that no solution was possible within the existing state-controlled system. Pressures for the introduction of a free market system and the creation of a competitive environment became overpowering.

Between 1980 and end-1988 average prices had increased about tenfold, though there were significant variations between different items (see Table 9.3). The strength of the dollar on the black market rose steadily. During this period the black market value of the US dollar greatly exceeded the level that would have been justified by its purchasing power in Western Europe. Prices in Poland were generally far lower than in world markets, and this was particularly true in the case of energy prices.

Table 9.3 *Purchasing power of US dollar (31 December)*

Item	*1980*	*1988*	*1989*	*1990*
Petrol (litres)	6	15	4	2.4
Ham (kg)	0.6	1.2	0.4	0.15
Bread (loaves)	7	40	10	3
Bricks (number)	60	37	26	15
Cement (kg)	110	120	60	30
Taxi fare (km)	16	18	3	2
Domestic electricity (kwh)	100	300	450	20

Source: Polish Investment Company.

THE ROLE OF THE DOLLAR

The US dollar had an extraordinary role in the Polish economy at that time. It was the 'official' currency used in the so-called 'Pewex' shops ('internal export enterprises'), where a wide range of articles, not normally available elsewhere in the country could be purchased only with 'hard' currency. The 'Pewex' price of Polish vodka was maintained for a long time at US$1 for a half-litre bottle. As vodka could also be purchased in local shops, there was a close link between the black market dollar rate and the zloty price of vodka. Second, the state issued dollar-denominated bonds which could be used for domestic trade. Most significantly, dollar-denominated bank accounts became the most popular form of personal saving. By December 1989 foreign currency deposits accounted for 84 per cent of all funds held in bank accounts by individuals.

The pace of inflation started to rise in the early months of 1989. By then the political situation had deteriorated significantly and the economy had moved into crisis. On 1 August 1989 the communist government made a final attempt to reform the economy and liberalised the price of food products. Inflationary pressures were released, prices rocketed, and the Solidarity trade union won its battle for full indexation of pay.

By the middle of 1989 a network of foreign exchange shops ('kantory') were in operation. The dollar/zloty exchange rate was highly volatile. Panic buying at the end of August pushed the rate up to US$1 = Z18,000 (Z500 at end-1988), though the rate later settled down to Z12,000. With the establishment of the Mazowiecki government, notice of the Balcerowicz plan and news of the proposed Stabilisation Fund under the auspices of an IMF programme, the zloty's value rose and the official rate at the end of the year was Z6500. The same rate was obtainable at the kantory.

Meanwhile, prices were rising at around 30 per cent per month from August to December 1989. During the whole of the year they had risen by 650 per cent.

CONTROLLING INFLATION

The Balcerowicz plan came into effect on 1 January 1990. Its main priority was the control of inflation, which was viewed as an essential precondition to further economic reforms. The main mechanisms to achieve this were: free internal convertibility of the zloty; liberalisation of foreign trade in order to create a competitive environment; control of government expenditure; a firm exchange rate; and positive real interest rates.

Interest rates throughout the economy are determined in relation to the National Bank of Poland's Refinancing Credit (RC) rate. For the month of January 1990 this was set at 45 per cent per *month*. As inflation dropped, reaching a low of 1.8 per cent per month in August 1990 (see Table 9.4), so the RC rate was reduced;

in July it was quoted on an annual basis (34 per cent per annum). However it started to rise again in October (43 per cent) and reached 72 per cent in February 1991.

Table 9.4 *Monthly inflation rates during 1990 (percentage increase over previous month)*

Jan	Feb	Mar	Apr	May	Jun	Jul	Aug	Sep	Oct	Nov	Dec
78.6	23.9	4.7	8.1	5.0	3.4	3.6	1.8	4.6	5.7	4.9	5.9

Source: Central Statistical Office.

With the dollar/zloty exchange rate remaining fixed at Z9500 throughout this period, the purchasing power of the dollar dropped significantly (see Table 9.3).

Table 9.5 *Retail consumer goods price indices 1989–91 (previous month = 100)*

	Jan	Feb	Mar	Apr	May	Jun	Jul	Aug	Sep	Oct	Nov	Dec
1989	111.0	107.9	108.1	109.8	107.2	106.1	109.5	139.5	134.4	154.8	122.4	117.7
1990	179.6	123.8	104.3	107.5	104.6	103.4	103.6	102.8	104.6	105.7	104.9	105.9
1991	112.7	106.7										

Source: Central Statistical Office.

In the first three months of 1989 prices continued to rise at around 5 per cent per month. Pressure has been growing on the government from exporters to adjust the exchange rate; the rise in domestic costs is squeezing their profit margins and seriously threatening export markets. Many enterprises fear for their survival unless there is a significant devaluation of the zloty. At the same time, the markets are being increasingly swamped with imported goods. The balance of trade swung into deficit in the last two months of the year after recording surpluses every month from January until October 1990. This has resulted in the 16 per cent devaluation undertaken in May 1991.

UNION DISCONTENT

Pressures are also growing from the unions. A major plank of the government's policy in controlling salaries and wages has been the so-called 'popiwek', a penal rate tax applied on pay increases over a designated norm in state enterprises (the tax does not apply to the private sector, where it is presumed that shareholders will ensure that pay increases are not excessive). Strike threats have been made in several significant economic sectors: transport, coal mining, shipbuilding etc. Farmers have also been outspoken and have threatened to boycott the markets unless prices of farm produce are significantly raised. They claim that rising costs of energy, machinery and fertilizers are jeopardising their economic existence.

Despite the pressure the government's resolve to combat inflation is evident. One reason for this is to be able to reduce interest rates. At current levels, new investment has virtually halted.

By the end of 1990 95 per cent of prices were liberalised. The government announced that during 1991 rents for municipal housing and posts and telecommunications prices will be freed. It is envisaged that prices of only six categories of goods and services will remain subject to state control. These are:

1. heating and hot water for private accommodation;
2. gas and electricity for private dwellings and agriculture;
3. listed medicines, serums and vaccines;
4. services of social health institutions;
5. personal services provided for social health institutions (eg blood donations);
6. pure and rectified ethyl alcohol and domestically manufactured spirits.

Table 9.6 *Average monthly earnings during 1990 and 1991 (Z'000s)*

	Jan	*Feb*	*Mar*	*Apr*	*May*	*Jun*	*Jul*	*Aug*	*Sep*	*Oct*	*Nov*	*Dec*
1990	618	652	720	738	802	847	969	1026	1116	1269	1431	1521
1991	1451	1436										

Source: Central Statistical Office.

Pay had generally kept pace with inflation until the end of 1989. Living standards fell in the first half of 1990 (see Table 9.6), but in the second half of the year the rate of pay increases again exceeded inflation.

Table 9.7 *Current (March 1991) indicative prices (Z '000s)*

Rental of accommodation (50 m^2, Warsaw)	2000 per month
Purchase of flat	5000 per m^2
Salary – Chief Accountant	4000–8000 per month (+ca 65% by way of taxes and social security)
Electricity	4 per Kw/hrs
Hotel	700 (4)–2000 (Marriott)
Car hire	500–1000 per day
Domestic flights	350 (Warsaw-Krakow)
Rail (1st class)	70 (Warsaw-Krakow)
Restaurant meal	25–150
Average pay	1500 per month

Source: Polish Investment Company.

10

Banking and Financial Services

The Polish Investment Company

BANKING

The Polish banking system is in the process of a major restructuring, which was initiated in 1988. Prior to that date the banking industry consisted of a limited number of specialised institutions: the Narodowy Bank Polski (NBP); Bank Handlowy w Warszawie (BH); Powszechna Kasa Oszczędnościowa - Bank Panstwowy (PKO); Bank Pekao SA; and around 1600 small cooperative banks serving mainly the agricultural sector under the overall supervision of the Bank Gospodarki Żywnościowej (BGZ).

Bank functions under the old system

The Narodowy Bank Polski had two main functions. It acted as Poland's central bank, in so far as it was the custodian of the country's foreign exchange reserves, and it alone was authorised to issue notes and coins. Secondly, it serviced the banking needs of local authorities and state enterprises in the industrial and commercial sectors through its nationwide network of around 400 branches. It handled operating accounts for these entities, as well as providing long-term finance for major projects.

The Bank Handlowy w Warszawie was exclusively responsible for handling Poland's foreign trade. It operated and continues to operate through a network of seven branches in Poland with overseas offices in London and Luxembourg. BH provides a comprehensive range of foreign trade products, including letters of credit and pre-export finance. However, it has few customers of its own; generally, it acts on instructions of the customer's main bank, which was normally the NBP. BH was also the vehicle through which most of Poland's foreign borrowings were effected, both in the form of commercial loans and export credits.

PKO was and remains essentially a savings bank. It has a network of 355 branches throughout the country and its services can be accessed through a further 13,530 agencies, mainly at post offices. It serves only the personal sector, and has been the main form of saving available to the Polish citizen. It provides a variety of accounts for specific purposes (eg, savings accounts for the acquisition of a flat or car) and a limited number of ancilliary services, such as standing orders in favour of specified beneficiaries. It also provides cheque book facilities to its customers on a limited scale; it should be noted, however, that cheques are rarely accepted as a means of payment.

Bank Pekao SA was established with the chief aim of facilitating the remittance of funds by Poles overseas to their home country. It has a network of 73 branches in Poland and offices in Paris and Tel Aviv. It specialises in maintaining foreign currency (mainly US dollar) accounts for private individuals and servicing enterprises engaged in 'internal export'. Maintaining a foreign currency account has been traditionally the main form of personal saving in Poland: holding financial assets overseas is not legal. Until very recently securities have not been available in Poland and investment in property is feasible only for wealthier individuals. Following the substantial devaluation of the zloty during 1989 (from US$1 = Z530 on 1 January to Z9500 on 31 December), the balance sheet of Pekao ballooned significantly, and it is now second only to BH (whose balance sheet is also largely dollar denominated) in asset terms.

Poland's agricultural sector is serviced by a network of around 1600 small cooperative banks, which are supervised by the BGZ.

Reform of the banking system

In 1988 the government undertook a restructuring of the banking industry, starting with the reorganisation of the NBP. Nine new regionally-based state-owned banks were incorporated and the majority of NBP's branches, together with their assets, liabilities and personnel, were transferred to these new banks. Although initially organised on a regional basis, the banks are free to extend their activities throughout the country, and some have embarked on a rapid programme of branch expansion. The banks are listed in Table 10.1.

Table 10.1 *The nine banks arising from the 1988 reforms*

Bank	*Headquarters*
State Credit Bank	Warsaw
Deposit and Credit Bank	Lublin
Industrial and Commercial Bank	Kraków
Silesian Bank	Katowice
Bank of the West	Wrocław
State Economy Bank	Łódź
Bank of Wielkopolska	Poznań
Pomeranian Credit Bank	Szczecin
Bank of Gdańsk	Gdańsk

A new Banking Law was passed on 31 January 1989. This allowed the establishment of privately owned banks, and made provision for foreign banks to establish representative offices and joint ventures. By end-1990 a total of over 100 new banks had been licensed by the NBP, although fewer than half were operational by that date. The Export Development Bank was the first of the 'new' banks founded in 1987. Originally owned by the government and a number of state enterprises, it has developed close links with the International Finance Corporation, and is currently being privatised. The first joint venture bank, the American Bank in Poland, commenced operations towards the end of 1990. Among foreign banks which have obtained licences are Creditanstalt-Bankverein of Austria, NMB Bank of the Netherlands and American Express of the United States. Foreign banks with representative offices in Poland include Citibank (US), Deutsche Bank and Dresdner Bank (Germany), Société Générale and Crédit Industriel et Commercial de Paris (France), Banca Commerciale Italiana (Italy), and Barclays Bank (UK).

Current developments

The reform of the banking system has created a much more competitive environment. Most of the state commercial banks have ambitious plans to extend their branch networks, particularly outside their own regions. There is considerable competition between them to acquire the very limited number of available buildings which are suitable as bank premises. The commercial

Table 10.2 *Consolidated balance sheet of the banking system in 1990 (Z billions)*

Items	*XII 1989*	*Months of 1990* I	II	III	IV	V	VI	VII	VIII	IX	X	XI	XII
A. Domestic currency	26,350.1	37,279.7	45,346.7	55,148.6	63,098.7	70,430.8	80,095.1	91,445.6	102,867.7	110,468.5	117,827.2	126,362.8	132,514.3
1. Cash circulation (without cash in banks' vaults)	9,879.8	11,105.8	14,751.2	18,914.8	22,093.4	22,527.9	25,996.7	28,344.0	30,966.4	33,315.6	35,450.3	38,343.5	39,228.5
— Issue of cash	12,778.7	13,985.0	17,676.7	22,161.1	25,913.2	26,423.2	29,423.0	32,330.4	36,135.5	38,812.3	41,564.4	44,691.0	48,078.7
— Cash in banks' vaults	2,898.9	2,879.2	2,925.5	3,246.3	3,819.8	3,895.2	3,426.3	3,986.4	5,169.2	5,496.8	6,114.1	6,347.5	8,850.2
2. Individuals' savings deposits	8,628.9	10,975.0	13,583.2	16,514.2	18,315.8	20,294.1	22,678.3	25,236.2	27,577.7	29,870.9	32,659.9	35,712.4	41,293.0
— Demand	1,392.4	1,755.7	2,101.3	2,807.7	3,373.3	4,177.8	5,007.9	6,044.3	7,028.1	7,715.9	8,723.6	9,868.3	10,754.9
In that saving - settlement accounts	711.8	785.8	996.3	1,261.9	1,510.7	1,710.7	1,971.0	2,277.7	2,618.7	2,687.2	2,857.9	2,954.4	3,052.5
— Savings deposits	7,236.6	9,219.3	11,481.9	13,706.5	14,942.4	16,112.4	17,670.4	19,191.9	20,549.6	22,155.0	23,936.3	25,844.1	30,538.1
In that interest and bonuses accounts	2,158.7	2,947.1	3,956.7	5,048.1	5,245.8	5,587.4	5,836.3	6,013.7	6,104.4	6,478.2	6,513.2	6,694.0	8,031.7
3. Enterprises' funds	7,841.4	15,199.0	17,012.3	19,719.6	22,689.5	27,608.8	31,420.1	37,865.4	44,323.6	47,282.0	49,717.0	52,306.9	51,992.8
B. Foreign exchange accounts	68,609.1	60,012.2	57,706.1	57,081.0	56,660.4	56,614.6	56,133.1	57,198.0	58,266.9	58,775.5	59,252.5	59,316.7	59,239.2
— Individuals' accounts	45,926.1	45,904.7	46,509.7	47,232.1	48,058.3	49,000.3	49,444.6	50,976.2	52,388.5	53,192.6	54,044.1	54,599.6	55,100.9
— Enterprises' accounts	22,683.0	14,105.4	11,194.3	9,846.8	8,600.0	7,612.2	6,688.3	6,221.6	5,878.2	5,582.7	5,208.2	4,717.0	4,138.3
C. Dollar-denominated Bank Pekao SA coupons	880.6	749.5	698.4	649.3	608.7	532.0	448.1	410.3	373.8	378.9	346.8	326.2	258.9
Foreign reserves (gross)	23,780.4	23,257.9	24,529.0	26,944.9	27,916.7	33,742.1	36,636.8	40,936.5	45,195.3	50,843.0	52,025.8	51,441.5	46,741.9
In US$ mn	2,503.2	2,448.2	2,582.0	2,836.3	2,938.6	3,551.8	3,856.5	4,309.1	4,757.4	5,351.9	5,476.4	5,414.9	4,920.2
Domestic assets	72,059.4	74,783.5	79,222.2	85,934.1	92,451.1	93,835.4	100,039.6	108,117.4	116,313.1	118,779.9	125,400.7	134,564.1	145,270.5
1. Credit for businesses and individuals	33,476.5	33,006.3	40,774.4	48,076.4	61,588.9	67,639.3	74,543.2	85,671.8	93,836.3	99,876.0	108,235.5	114,628.3	118,591.0
1.1. Credits for socialised sector	31,489.4	31,791.0	39,450.4	46,087.9	58,787.1	63,633.9	69,170.3	78,383.7	84,414.8	87,600.9	92,669.3	97,662.7	100,314.6
1.2. Credits for private sector and individuals	1,987.1	1,215.4	1,323.9	1,988.5	2,801.7	4,005.4	5,372.9	7,288.1	9,421.5	12,275.1	15,566.2	16,965.6	18,276.3
2. Credit for budget (net)	6,495.9	6,403.4	2,587.9	2,694.7	-2,669.1	-8,602.9	-11,062.6	-14,933.6	-16,670.7	-18,079.9	-17,848.5	-17,648.8	-8,185.3
3. Balance of other items	32,087.1	35,373.7	35,859.9	35,163.0	33,531.2	34.798.9	36,559.0	37,379.3	39,147.6	36,983.7	35,013.7	37,584.6	34,864.8

Notes Data in December 1990 are preliminary ones and may be altered,
Data for previous months are derived from monthly balance sheets of the banking system.

Source: National Bank of Poland: *Monthly Information Bulletin*, January 1991.

banks are heavily asset-orientated and have hitherto relied on a Refinancing Credit from the NBP. This facility is gradually being withdrawn, and consequently the banks are seeking to strengthen their deposit bases. Their eagerness to attract personal deposits is evidenced first by increasingly competitive interest rate quotations (only minimum deposit rates are stipulated by the NBP) and secondly by longer opening hours.

BANK OPERATIONS

Payment and cash transfer

Virtually all financial transactions involving the personal sector are performed with cash. While most people have accounts with the PKO, these are mainly deposit accounts and frequently tied to some form of saving scheme. Salaries and wages are invariably paid in cash, a procedure which for larger enterprises is usually staggered over three days at the end of each month.

The commercial banks operate a funds transfer system between their branches, utilising regional settlement centres of the NBP. Most banks are now looking to a rapid introduction of computer technology, but most operations are still being performed manually. As a result, transactions take a long time to process. Money transfers between branches can take up to four weeks. Most inconvenient for the customer is the long wait normally associated with any visit to a bank branch.

Loans

Credit for the personal and private corporate sectors is extremely restricted. PKO provides personal loans for very specific purposes. Credit extended by the commercial banks has been largely limited to the state sector where decisions on credit allocation were made in the context of the government's economic policy.

Very high interest rates since the beginning of 1990 deterred bank borrowing, but have created a rapid growth of intra-company debt. In an effort to unwind this problem, the authorities have encouraged the use of the bill of exchange. Some banks have started to market bill discount facilities to their corporate clients. However, the development of this business has been slower than anticipated due to the reluctance of companies to add their names to bills of exchange in view of the consequences of non-payment on due dates.

Foreign exchange

Most of the state commercial banks and some of the private banks have licences to carry out transactions in foreign currencies, including foreign trade products such as letters of credit. While the BH still maintains a dominant position in this field, competition will increase as the newly licensed banks develop their own expertise and correspondent banking networks.

Foreign exchange transactions for the personal sector are normally carried out in the Kantory. These are licensed money shops offering two-way markets in several convertible currencies, mainly US dollars and German marks. Some kantory also make markets in Eastern European currencies and/or gold and silver.

Interest-bearing deposits

Controlling the accelerating rate of inflation (640 per cent in 1989) was the first objective of the 'Balcerowicz plan', and this was to have been achieved mainly by monetary policy. Interest rates throughout the economy are determined effectively by the NBP's Refinancing Credit (RC) rate - the rate at which the central bank provides refinancing facilities for the state banks' medium-term loans. This was set at 36 per cent per *month* in January 1990. As inflationary pressures eased during the first half of 1990 the RC rate was systematically lowered to 4 per cent per *month* in June 1990 and 34 per cent per *annum* in July 1990. It remained steady during the third quarter, but has been rising again since then, reaching 55 per cent per annum at the end of the year and 72 per cent per annum in March 1991.

Interest rates on personal deposits differ according to maturity and follow the trend of the RC rate. Twenty-four month deposits in December 1990 were paying 44 per cent per annum. It should be noted, however, that rates on fixed-term deposits were also adjusted monthly. Private individuals may hold deposits also in foreign currencies. Despite the significant difference in interest rates (US dollar deposits paid around 10 per cent per annum) and the fact that the exchange rate remained stable during the year, there has been little evidence of switching into zlotys, and the volume of foreign currency deposits held by individuals rose by 20 per cent during 1990. However, as a proportion of total bank deposits held by individuals, foreign currency holdings fell from 84 per cent to 57 per cent. Foreign currency holdings of enterprises fell to an insignificant

Table 10.3 *Interest rates 1989–90*

Items	Unit	XII 1989	Months of 1990: I	II	III	IV	V	VI	VII	VIII	IX	X	XI	XII
Refinancing credit interest rate[2]	%	140.0	36.0	20.0	10.0	8.0	5.5	4.0	34.0	34.0	34.0	43.0	55.0	55.0
Rediscount credit interest rate[1,6]	%	26.0	49.0	24.0	16.0	13.0	9.0	7.0	28.0	28.0	28.0	36.0	48.0	48.0
Interest rate on accounts with NBP[3]														
a) On current accounts:														
— Of banks	%	0.0	12.0	6.0	3.0	3.0	2.0	0.65	5.5	5.5	5.5	7.0	9.0	9.0
— Others	%	0.0	12.0	6.0	3.0	3.0	2.0	1.3	11.0	11.0	11.0	14.0	18.0	18.0
b) On fixed date accounts:														
6 months	%	33.0	20.0	11.0	5.0	5.0	4.0	2.2	19.0	19.0	19.0	24.0	30.0	30.0
12 months	%	44.0	26.0	14.0	7.0	7.0	5.0	2.8	24.0	24.0	24.0	30.0	39.0	39.0
24 months	%	56.0	33.0	18.0	9.0	9.0	6.0	3.2	27.0	27.0	27.0	34.0	44.0	44.0
Interest rates of credit in deposit and credit banks														
a) On credits with lowest risk rates[4]	%	143–195	38–55	19–25	8–13	7.5–9.5	5.5–7	4–5	34–36	34–36	34–36	35–47	42–59	54–68
b) Bills of exchange discount rate[7]	%	116–130	51–69	25–30	16.5–19	13–16	9–12	7–9	30–32	29–32	29–30	37–38	38–51	38–51
Interest on deposits and savings in deposit and credit banks[5]														
a) Demand	%	21–24	7–10	5–7	3–4	3.0	2–3	1.3–1.8	11–15	11–15	11–12	12–18	15–23	18–23
b) Short-term (under 1 year)	%	100–130	10–33	7–17	4–9	3.5–8	2.75–6.5	2–4.5	24–32	24–32	24–34	27–44.5	25–58.5	25–62
c) One year and longer	%	160–180	30–46	15–24	7–12.5	7–11	4.5–8	3.5–5.75	25–42	33–42	25–42	34–52.8	44–71	56–72
Official US$ exchange rate	zlotys	6,500	9,500	9,500	9,500	9,500	9,500	9,500	9,500	9,500	9,500	9,500	9,500	9,500
Average free market US$ exchange rate	zlotys	7,454	9,344	9,460	9,624	9,750	9,764	9,624	9,513	9,502	9,490	9,489	9,589	9,690

Note: Interest rates in December 1989 and since July 1990 are calculated on annual basis (excluding (1) for December 1989 when the rate was calculated on quarterly basis) and in the period from January to June 1990 interest rates were calculated on monthly basis (2, 3, 4, 5) or quarterly basis (6, 7). Presented interest rates come from the end of particular months.

Source: National Bank of Poland: *Monthly Information Bulletin*, January 1991.

level at the end of 1990 as a result of restrictions imposed by new foreign exchange regulations.

INSURANCE

The insurance industry is currently also being restructured. The industry is dominated by three state enterprises: Państwowy Zakład Ubezpieczeń (PZU) which deals with insurance for the agricultural and cooperative sectors and the insurance of motor vehicles; WARTA which handles insurance and re-insurance of commercial risks including shipping and export credits; and Zakład Ubezpieczeń Społecznych (ZUS) which acts as a social security fund.

Recent changes in legislation have permitted the creation of new insurance companies, of which the most significant is WESTA, established in 1988, which offers personal and property insurance. Over the past few months a number of broking firms have also been established.

The government is keen to encourage the entry of foreign insurance companies into the market and the regulatory changes now being undertaken will undoubtedly facilitate such investments. These could be linked to the government's plans for privatising the existing institutions, notably WARTA and PZU. Several major insurance companies from Europe and the USA are actively pursuing investment opportunities.

The Export Credit Insurance Corporation SA was established in January 1991 by the State Treasury together with a number of banks and trading companies. The State Treasury intends to sell its shareholding in due course to private investors. The main objective of the company is to promote Polish exports by providing suitable insurance cover to exporters. Its organisation, structure and activities will be based on the French COFACE and German HERMES export credit agencies.

THE STOCK EXCHANGE

Shares have been sold in Poland since 1989 when shares in newly privatised enterprises were first offered to the public by the government. Since the initial offering most of these enterprises have acted as brokers in their own shares on a matched bargain basis.

A properly regulated securities market is in the process of

creation. The securities law is in course of passing through the legislative process.

The official Stock Exchange was opened on 16 April 1991, in the old Communist Party headquarters building in central Warsaw. With more shares becoming available and a full securities law coming into effect the Exchange is expected to develop rapidly.

Trading currently takes place once a week, on Tuesdays, in shares of the five enterprises privatised in December 1990 with the support of the UK's Know-How Fund. Dealing is on a matched bargain basis with limits on the daily fluctuation of prices. Daily trading is expected to commence in June 1991.

11

The Economics of Privatisation

Touche Ross & Co

When one stands back and considers what it is that the Poles are trying to do, the very scale of what is happening is breathtaking. Approximately 80 per cent of the economy, 8000 enterprises (6000 state owned and 2000 municipally owned) which had hitherto operated within a command, socialised economy, were first of all exposed to the cold winds of competition and the laws of supply and demand, and are now being transformed into entities with recognisable corporate structures - and being put into private ownership. All this is happening within a ruined economy, in a country crippled by external debt, with negligible private savings, an inefficient banking system, and a new-born capital market. And although the word is the same, analogies to the UK privatisations are misleading. This has simply never been done before - there are no maps or signposts.

The first phase of the Balcerowicz plan brought hyperinflation under control and established a free pricing structure. The consequent slashing of the standard of living demonstrated, if demonstration were necessary, the true material poverty to which society had been brought after 45 years of communist economics and the distorted trading patterns within the Comecon bloc.

The legislation on the Privatisation of State Owned Enterprises and for setting up the Office of the Minister of Ownership Changes was passed in July 1990 and came into force on 1 August 1990. As a result of the latter, the Office of the Plenipotentiary for Ownership Changes was converted into the Ministry of Ownership Changes. The task now facing the new Ministry is to create ownership where there has been no ownership in place. The goal is to create an ownership structure similar to that of the Western economies within five years.

As a result of the depression, the pre-war Polish economy had a high proportion of nationalised and monopoly industry which would indicate no great tradition of free market economics, but there was also a large and active private sector, and of course private property rights. This points towards the most sensitive aspect of the whole privatisation programme - what to do about restitution of property to former owners. The problems of physical restitution appear intractable: even if one can establish someone's right to a particular piece of land, or to a share of a factory, how can 45 years of change and development, and any rights accruing to two post-war generations, be undone? The Ministry of Ownership Changes is putting together a framework for limited restitution, and one of the key criteria for transformation is that the property ownership position of an enterprise is clear.

VALUATION

Whether state enterprises achieve private company status (ie 51 per cent of the capital must be in private ownership) through the law on privatisation or the law on joint ventures, there is a requirement for the valuation of the enterprise to be privatised. Accounting and consulting firms are authorised to carry out such valuations, and lists of firms so authorised are published by the government bodies supervising the transformation process: the Ministry of Ownership Changes, the Foreign Investment Agency, and also those ministries who were the founding bodies of specific state enterprises responsible to them. The costs of carrying out the valuations are borne by the relevant enterprise, although in cases where there is special justification the costs can be borne by the Ministry of Ownership Changes.

The purpose of carrying out valuations is to determine the worth of the enterprise, that is the price which an investor should pay when buying the total assets of the enterprise from the state exchequer. Up to now, valuations have been carried out for no other reasons.

METHODS

In accordance with the recommendations of the Ministry of Ownership Changes, the valuation of an enterprise has to be carried out utilising at least two valuation methods. The Ministry recommends the following valuation methods:

- on the basis of discounted future cash flows;
- on a replacement cost basis;
- according to net book value of assets;
- at liquidation or break-up value;
- on the basis of price/earnings ratios.

The preferred method of valuation is discounted cash flow. Its application demands a very keen analysis of the future income streams which it is possible for the enterprise to achieve, as well as an assessment of the risks attaching to the attainment of that income. There are several factors hindering accurate forecasting of the future financial results of the enterprises activities:

- The radical changes in the economic environment often rule out extrapolation from historic figures.
- There are changes in the legal rules covering accounting, taxation and related issues.
- The high, and difficult to forecast, rate of inflation often forces the necessity of forecasting on the assumption of stable prices.
- There are changes in pricing and costing structures.
- There is often an unclear legal position as to the true ownership of particular assets making up the total property of the enterprise.
- Enterprise managements often do not have strategic plans and operating budgets.
- There is no developed capital market.

The above factors demand of the valuer a very good understanding of the Polish economic background, on the macro as well as the micro levels. The establishment in April 1991 of the Warsaw Stock Exchange, as well as the ever-increasing number of buy-sell transactions will give rise, in the near future, to some simplification in the procedures for the valuation of enterprises. In order to speed up the privatisation process, there are also plans for the introduction, by sector, of sets of simplified procedures for the valuation of small and medium-sized businesses.

PROGRESS IN 1990

The Ministry of Ownership Changes has established contacts with over 200 large enterprises. Five of them were transformed into joint-stock companies on 1 October 1990, and after preparation for privatisation by consultants, public offerings of their shares were made in November 1990. They were the following:

- Exbud - a construction company;
- Śląsk Cable Factory;
- Tonsil - an electronics company;
- Krośnieńskie Glass Factory; and
- Prochnik - a clothing manufacturer.

The number of shares offered was 4.33 million, worth some US$31 million. Each of the 5 companies was over subscribed and some 130,000 orders from private investors were taken. Priority in this pilot privatisation tranche was given to small investors who bought one or two packets of shares - small investors were finally allocated 80 per cent of the total shares issued.

Although the exercise was seen as a great success, and the long-term goal of the Ministry of Ownership Changes is to attract as many small investors as possible, it was also recognised that the process was very time consuming and expensive, and could not be applied to the whole privatisation programme.

Offerings for public subscription will continue, but the Ministry will also make direct trade sales and private placings. It is hoped to attract long-term, large scale investment. With this end in view, both domestic and foreign investors will be allowed to purchase significant portions of shares. It is felt that institutional investors will bring with them managerial oversight structures, thus contributing to the successful operation of those companies.

By the end of 1990, 58 state-owned enterprises had been transformed into joint-stock companies and now await privatisation. Local government authorities have also begun to privatise the enterprises which are under their control - typically through liquidations. Some 50 enterprises were privatised in this way in 1990.

1991 AND BEYOND

Following on from the first privatisations, the Ministry has prepared the next tranche of companies for privatisation. These include, among others, the following:

- ZPO Wólczanka - textiles and shirt manufacture;
- Swarzędzkie Fabryki Mebli - furniture;
- Otmęt Krapkowice - shoes;
- ZPT Brzeg - margarine and edible oils;
- ZPO Bytom - suits; and
- Huta Irena - glassware.

Enterprises which are earmarked for trade sales or private placements include:

- Świnoujście - ship repair yard;
- Huta Oława - metal processing;
- Zipo - computer software;
- Krakbud and Techma Kraków - contracting; and
- Milfor - food containers.

On 16 April 1991 the Warsaw stock exchange opened for business and trading took place in the shares of the five companies privatised in 1990. Legislation on the public sale of stock and mutual funds is in place and a State Securities Commission is being established.

There are plans for 40–50 companies to be privatised in 1991. It is recognised that offerings for public subscription, trade sales and private placements will not proceed quickly enough to effect the rapid ownership transformation that is overwhelmingly held to be essential for the Polish endeavour to succeed.

There are plans under examination for effecting 'mass privatisation'. The corner-stone of these plans involves the issue of privatisation vouchers to each citizen. These can be used to purchase shares in financial institutions (Privatisation Funds) which will themselves own shares in privatised enterprises. Under current thinking, the mass privatisation of 20 to 50 companies at a time would, for each company, give a Privatisation Fund 30 per cent, with 20 per cent each going to the state pension fund (ZUS) and the company's workers, and the Treasury retaining 30 per cent until the company is sold (while giving a proxy to the Privatisation Fund, thus providing it with managerial control). Each Privatisation Fund will then manage the companies in which it has a stake, restructuring and selling them as appropriate.

If this plan is adopted, every Pole will become a shareholder. Some will sell their shares, others buy more - it is after all a free market economy and no one can be forced to invest, but for an instant a country which until 1989 was communist will have achieved 'wider share ownership' beyond the wildest dreams of Western free market economists.

12

The Privatisation Process

Frere Cholmeley

NEW LEGISLATION

The framework for privatisation in Poland is primarily contained in two laws of 13 July 1990 - the State Enterprise Privatisation Law (SEPL) and the Ministry for Ownership Changes Law (MOCL). The legislation permits the commercialising and privatising of 'State' enterprises formed under the State Enterprises Law of 25 September 1981 at the instigation of various founding or instituting authorities. These are: the minister responsible for the relevant sector (eg Industry); or the president of a Voivodeship (province) or a commune.

The goal is to privatise 50 per cent of state assets in three years and to achieve a level of private ownership comparable to that found in a Western European economy in five years, although to date only five large-scale privatisations have been completed.

This chapter explains the functions of the Ministry for Ownership Changes, as established by the MOCL, the procedures to be followed under SEPL and the different methods of privatisation it allows, the framework for certain privatisations outside SEPL and finally the functions of the Anti-Monopoly Office.

MINISTRY FOR OWNERSHIP CHANGES

The functions of the Ministry of Ownership Changes (MOC) created under the MOCL include:

- implementation of the transfer of ownership from the state into private hands;
- preparation of annual policy guidelines for the privatisation of state enterprises and capital cooperation with foreigners (the

latter in conjunction with the Minister for International Economic Cooperation);

- analysis of the progress of privatisation;
- cooperation with trade unions, associations and local government to incorporate private companies;
- training of personnel and collection and distribution of information in relation to privatisation and capital markets.

The MOCL specifies that the Ministry for Ownership Changes should cooperate with the Minister of Finance and the President of the National Bank of Poland to establish a new Polish stock market. The Ministry for Ownership Changes' terms of reference and powers are limited by its statute and by orders of the Council of Ministers. It is intended to establish regional offices of the Ministry for Ownership Changes in the first half of 1991 to speed the privatisation process at a local level.

The MOCL provides for the establishment of the Ownership Transformation Board to advise the Council of Ministers on all matters relating to privatisation.

PRIVATISATION OF STATE ENTERPRISES

SEPL provides for the following privatisation procedures: transformation and the subsequent offer of shares to third parties; and liquidation followed by the offer of assets (which could include the whole business) directly to third parties either to purchase or on a lease.

The method chosen will depend on the type of enterprise involved. For large enterprises (the 500 largest enterprises in Poland by sales value), the shares of which are intended to form the basis of the future Polish securities market, a traditional form of privatisation by either public or limited offer is considered appropriate. The five pilot privatisations already completed under SEPL used this method. The enterprise is valued independently, prospectuses are issued, followed by subscription and finally allotment and issue of shares. Some large enterprises in the fats/oils and furniture sectors are to be privatised in this way during the early part of 1991.

Mass privatisation is planned for medium-sized or small enterprises, where the whole or substantial parts of an enterprise could be sold to a single buyer. There are about 2500 industrial enterprises and about 3000 construction, transport and other types of enterprise in this group; the numbers are increasing due to the break-up of larger enterprises under the anti-monopoly legislation. The method used may depend on the individual sector (eg, much of the food processing industry is to be privatised in 1991) and on the way the business is managed.

State enterprises of national economic importance will be listed by the Council of Ministers and their privatisation will be subject to its consent.

Transformation of a state enterprise into a corporation

Conversion into a corporation is the first step in the privatisation by transformation process for all enterprises, irrespective of size. It has two aims: to create a legal status compatible with the Foreign Investment Law; and to provide a clear management structure.

The company structures used are those described in a later chapter, with all shares being held by the State Treasury, pending an offer to third parties. About 60 new joint-stock companies have already been formed as a result of this process.

The initiative for transformation may come:

- from the enterprise itself (most usual);
- from the Prime Minister at the request of the Ministry for Ownership Changes or one of its prospective regional offices;
- from the enterprise's instituting authority.

A request should contain:

- an economic assessment of the transformed enterprise;
- a draft Charter; and
- the proposed extent of preferential share purchases by the employees.

Consent may be given subject to certain conditions or refused on the grounds of public interest or the financial situation of the enterprise. When the request has come from the Prime Minister, the Ministry for Ownership Changes commissions a valuation and prepares the Charter on behalf of the State Treasury; where the request is from the enterprise or the instituting authority the MOC could arrange for its own valuation and will have the final say on the Charter.

The newly created company assumes all the rights and liabilities of the transformed state enterprise and, subject to certain exceptions in SEPL, takes on most of the employees of the transformed enterprise. Its opening balance sheet is the closing balance of the state enterprise and its capital is the sum of the enterprise's basic assets and funds. The Charter specifies how the capital is to be divided into reserves and issued share capital. On conclusion of the Charter, the management applies for registration of the new company and the state enterprise is removed simultaneously from the state enterprises' register.

While more than 50 per cent of the company's shares are State Treasury held:

- one third of the new company's supervisory council must be elected by its employees, or their representatives, unless a majority of the employee-elected members has agreed otherwise;
- the other supervisory council members may be elected under the normal provisions of the Commercial Code.

Offering shares

Shares in a transformed company must be offered to investors within two years of incorporation, unless the Council of Ministers agrees to a longer period. For the purposes of the offer, the Ministry for Ownership Changes may:

1. Order an economic and financial study of the company before the share offer to value its assets and to establish whether it first requires re-organisation, particularly where there has been some time lapse between incorporation and the offer.
2. Order an analysis of the legal status of the company's assets and conflicting claims on these.
3. To make a company more attractive to potential investors, assume (with the consent of the Minister of Finance) some or all of the company's debts.

There are three general methods for offering shares: auction; publicly announced offers; and as a result of negotiations initiated by public invitation or as specified by the Council of Ministers at the Ministry of Ownership Changes' request. Any other form of transfer is unlawful. A separate decree has been issued specifying the acceptable methods of payment for shares which include cash, cheque and bank transfer.

As Polish people do not generally have sufficient capital to buy shares outright, SEPL suggests different ways of ensuring that they become shareholders:

- free of charge transfers;
- free distribution of capital vouchers;
- purchase by employees on preferential terms;
- allocation of shares to pension funds and financial intermediaries.

These methods are currently being considered in more detail and guidelines prepared in cooperation with foreign experts to facilitate the operation of the mass privatisation planned for the second half of 1991. The use of mutual investment funds, in particular for voucher schemes, is anticipated as a vehicle for mass popular shareholdings.

It is intended that all Polish citizens should receive some privatisation vouchers to serve as payment for:

- shares;
- interests in financial institutions (mutual investment funds) selling such shares;
- the whole or parts of an enterprise's business or assets.

Employees may acquire up to 20 per cent of a company's share capital on preferential terms (ie half the price set for Polish citizens on the first day of sale) subject to certain financial limits based on 12 months' average pay and number of employees. The entitlement remains open for a year and the offer must be made not later than two months after the first general share offer. Under certain circumstances farmers may acquire shares in companies with which they have long-term contracts on the same basis as employees.

Foreigners, including Polish companies which are 50 per cent plus foreign-owned, require a permit from the Foreign Investment Agency to acquire more than 10 per cent of a company's ordinary shares or any of its preference shares. This restriction may soon be removed. State enterprises need a permit from the Minister of Finance to acquire shares.

Privatisation by asset liquidation

With the consent of the Ministry for Ownership Changes a state-owned enterprise may be liquidated by the relevant founding authority, the decision being made on its own initiative or at the request of the enterprise's workers' council. Many consent applications have already been received. SEPL envisages three forms of disposal of the assets of an enterprise: sale; contribution to a corporation; and lease.

Where enterprises are to be split up for technological or regional reasons under the terms of the anti-monopoly legislation, the forms may be used jointly. SEPL permits liquidation only where an enterprise is in good financial condition so the founding authority should obtain a detailed draft of the liquidation procedures including:

- an economic analysis requiring MOC approval;
- information and proposals submitted by the enterprise; and
- (possibly) offers from potential investors.

Where the enterprise is in a poor organisational or financial state, it will be liquidated under the terms of the State Enterprises Law 1981, as amended by the Insolvency Law 1990. The three liquidation procedures are examined in turn.

Sale of assets

The whole or part of the assets may be acquired using the same methods as for an offer of shares (described earlier) by private domestic and foreign investors, without the need for a permit.

Contribution of assets

Assets may be contributed to an existing company or one incorporated for the purposes of receiving those assets, in exchange for shares. In the latter case the company could be established under the Foreign Investment Law as a joint venture between a foreign party and the State Treasury. The shares acquired by the Treasury in exchange would then be sold by public offer to private individuals. In such cases the employees do not have a right to acquire shares on preferential terms (see above).

Leasing of assets

SEPL sets out special conditions which must be fulfilled if this method is to be used:

1. The amount of registered share capital may not be lower than 20 per cent of the combined value of the liquidated enterprise's basic assets and its enterprise operations funds.
2. The lessee must be a company.
3. The majority of its members must be employees of the liquidated enterprise.
4. The shareholders must be natural persons unless the Ministry for Ownership Changes specifies otherwise.
5. The request for liquidation and lease must be adopted by the workers' council after consulting a general meeting of the employees.

A leasing fee must be paid. The contract is entered into by the enterprise's founding authority and the new company. It may give the lessee an option to purchase. The Minister of Finance will specify how fees are to be determined. Where only some of the assets have been leased the remainder may be sold or contributed to another company.

The lease form of liquidation is thought to be appropriate for small service-oriented firms - for example, retailing, transport or design firms. It is not thought appropriate for the privatisation of medium-sized or large industrial enterprises, especially those which have advanced technology and access to foreign markets through foreign investment.

PRIVATISATION UNDER OTHER LAWS

As SEPL covers state enterprises within the meaning of the State Enterprises Law 1981, the privatisation of particular enterprises which fall outside the scope of that law will require separate laws or amendments to SEPL. For example, banks are being privatised under the Banking Law, the Polish national airline LOT is being privatised on the basis of a separate law converting it into a 100 per cent State Treasury-owned joint-stock company and the telecommunications system is also in the course of separate privatisation. The strategic nature of the industries involved means that separate procedures and controls are being devised for each of them. Foreign investors should allow for the possibility that the rules will be substantially changed after the procedure has already begun, as with telecommunications where foreign investor restrictions were introduced.

In addition, as mentioned earlier, insolvent state enterprises may be liquidated on the basis of the Insolvency Law 1990 and any remaining assets may then be privatised by way of sale or contribution.

ANTI-MONOPOLY OFFICE ('AMO')

The AMO and its various regional agencies are involved in the privatisation process in two separate ways. Firstly, a state-owned enterprise which wants to be transformed under SEPL is obliged to notify the AMO of its intention, enclosing:

1. a draft company Charter;
2. a Ministry for Ownership Changes questionnaire containing information on the enterprise;
3. a detailed report on the applicant's percentage market share;
4. a list of competitors;
5. information enabling the AMO to consider the possibility of dividing the enterprise before privatisation; and
6. a declaration by the manager that persons holding managerial posts in the enterprise are not members of competitor companies.

Transformation may take place if the AMO fails to prohibit it within two months of notification. If the enterprise has a dominant position (30 per cent or more market share), the AMO may negotiate with the state authority to agree a split of the enterprise under the Anti-Monopoly Law 1990 before privatisation. For example, multi-plant enterprises may be divided into smaller units, which can then be privatised separately.

Secondly, an enterprise may apply to the AMO to be divided into its component parts or the AMO may on its own initiative approach an enterprise's founding authority to negotiate or even impose a division. The components may subsequently be privatised under SEPL.

CONCLUSION

Although a number of transformation privatisations are currently being undertaken, they are, for the most part, traditional customised privatisations of large enterprises. Until the regional offices of the Ministry for Ownership Changes have been established, the voucher system is in place, the industry-by-industry approach to privatisation has been streamlined and the stock market and connected infrastructure is in place, mass privatisation along this route on a national scale will be difficult to implement. Once acquired, it will be difficult to transfer the shares in such companies. The potential foreign investor may, in the meantime, find more opportunities to purchase assets or whole businesses via the privatisation by liquidation route directly from the Voivodeships or communes.

13

Property

Frere Cholmeley

Investors considering entering the Polish property market will find that it is in a state of evolution. As the socialist system is eroded a Western property market is beginning to emerge and with it a need for professionals such as estate agents and surveyors.

This chapter considers first the legal framework including the forms of holding available and special rules applicable to foreigners; secondly, the opportunities for investment in today's market; and thirdly, the potential risks.

THE LEGAL FRAMEWORK

Concepts

The transformation from a socialist to a market economy necessarily results in fundamental changes to the concepts of property use and ownership.

Property was formerly classified as social property, personal property or individual property. Each of these types of property enjoyed different levels of protection under the law with social property enjoying the maximum protection.

As a result of recent political events and economic reform the situation has now changed. Property can consist of state property or privately owned property, but both enjoy comparable treatment.

Forms of holding

A key area for the foreign investor is of course the acquisition of land and buildings, both as investments in their own right and as part of an investment in a different sector. Areas of interest include office and factory space, housing for employees and property development and construction.

The forms of holding which may be obtained and the types of property available are summarised in the following sections.

'Ownership'

The nearest equivalent to our own freehold is referred to as 'ownership'. The land is owned for an unlimited period of time and, within the general framework of the law, in particular relating to matters such as planning and the environment, there is freedom of use.

In general there is no restriction on the parties to the transaction or the type of land that can be purchased, subject to the fact that a foreigner requires a permit from the Minister of the Interior in most cases.

'Perpetual usufruct'

This is a type of lease which can only be granted by the state and has been utilised to enable the state to grant rights without relinquishing ownership. The term 'perpetual' is misleading as it is for a minimum of 40 and a maximum of 99 years, although there are rights of renewal. Legal formalities must be followed.

A distinction is made between land and buildings. On expiry of the term the tenant is entitled to compensation for buildings acquired or constructed on the land. A yearly fee is paid throughout the term. A foreigner may acquire this form of holding subject to obtaining the necessary permit from the Minister of the Interior.

In Warsaw the highest form of holding is the perpetual usufruct due to an anomaly caused by an unrepealed decree establishing state ownership of all real property in the City.

Other property rights

It is possible for a foreigner to acquire a lease or tenancy without the need for a permit.

Permission for foreigners

Foreigner

A foreigner is defined as:

- an individual who does not have Polish citizenship;
- a corporate body which is based abroad;
- a corporate body based in Poland but controlled by an individual without Polish citizenship, or by a company based

abroad. (Control is determined by direct or indirect ownership of at least 50 per cent of the company's share capital.)

Application

The application is made in writing to the Social and Administration Department of the Ministry of Internal Affairs (see Appendix 4). The following information is needed:

1. The location and area of the land with the borders indicated on a plan.
2. Details of the company seeking to purchase the land.
3. The purpose of the purchase/assignment and evidence that this is consistent with the land development plans.
4. A copy of the Land Register.
5. An official evaluation of the property in order to confirm the purchase price.
6. A statement from the seller confirming ownership of the land and a willingness to sell once permission has been granted.

The Minister must respond to the application within two months. The reply is likely to stipulate conditions for the grant of any permit such as any relevant permit being obtained from the Foreign Investment Agency or evidence concerning the company's status. In the past two years approximately 550 consents have been issued.

A fee calculated as a percentage of the purchase price is payable.

The Land Register

A large number of properties are registered although there are certain historical discrepancies. The Land Register contains details of the land, the proprietor, mortgages and other matters as with the English Land Registries.

In addition to the Land Register there are also ownership registers which are kept by local authorities for administrative purposes.

TODAY'S MARKET

Opportunities for investment

Office space

There are primarily three types of office space. First, the deluxe category where serviced space is available. These offices are located in buildings in Warsaw such as the Intraco II Tower, the Marriott Hotel and the Palace of Culture and Science. The middle range is located in existing office buildings and the lower bracket consists of non-dedicated office space which is usually in private ownership.

There is currently a massive demand for office space.

Retail property

There are few shopping centres, supermarkets, restaurants or fast food outlets and opportunities must therefore exist in these areas.

Residential property

There is a major shortage of housing and a tremendous need for modernisation. This is a difficult area as it is necessary to resolve the role of the state in the provision of housing in view of the financial difficulties for most Polish citizens in investing in the property market.

Country properties

Foreign investors may be tempted to acquire an historic palace or manor house. There are a number of these available for renovation at bargain prices. Information concerning property available may be obtained from the Ministry of Culture or local government offices. If a foreigner wishes to purchase an historic building, in addition to the consent of the Minister of the Interior it may be necessary to obtain the consents of the provincial monument conservator, the local authority and the Ministry of Culture. Conditions may be attached obliging the purchaser to renovate the property in a sympathetic manner. One problem that can arise is a difficulty over ownership as owners whose land was expropriated by the communists are now reclaiming their estates.

Hotel and leisure industry

There is a severe shortage of hotel accommodation; the greatest need is for two to three star hotels. Western-style leisure facilities are almost non-existent.

Industrial development

There is obvious scope for development although the position is somewhat hampered by the lack of infrastructure. Serviced greenfield sites can command a substantial premium.

Property development and construction

There are opportunities in all areas of the construction industry, and there is scope for development projects in all the property investment areas mentioned in this chapter.

Finding property

Estate agents

In Poland there has generally been a certain amount of property in private ownership. The property broker or estate agent tended to operate alone from home. As the property market evolves the situation is changing and there are now a few firms employing a number of staff. There is currently no form of regulatory body although suggestions have been made that a chamber should be established.

An agency is likely to be staffed by lawyers, economic advisers and sales people. As the staff in the type of agency described are multi-disciplinary a full service can be provided from finding a property to dealing with the purchase. A common service provided by the agency is the supply of a car and bodyguard as many transactions are in cash.

The main business is likely to be residential as at present much of the retail and office accommodation tends to be owned by the state. However, residential property may in certain circumstances be used as office space, and privatisation should increase the business accommodation available to the private sector.

Fees are usually charged to both parties, often as a percentage of the purchase price. Estate agents advertise their services in various newspapers.

Advertising and other means of finding property

It is common practice to place an advertisement in a newspaper or other publication specifying requirements as a means of obtaining property. There are a number of English language publications such as *The Warsaw Voice* and the *Polish Business Voice*. Enquiries may also be made of the various local authorities. There is of course no substitute for a network of contacts.

Surveyors

It is not usual practice to carry out a survey and in fact there is no equivalent profession to that of the Western surveyor although the need will develop as the market expands. Certain firms may be licensed by the Polish government to carry out official valuations of property. Practitioner training courses in valuation and surveying methods are being introduced.

Doing the deal

Advisers

It is necessary to find professional advisers at the outset. The growing interest in the Polish market has resulted in the growth of consulting companies offering legal, economic and financial services.

Costs

As in the UK, the costs of the transaction are likely to include fees for permits and registrations, plus professional fees for agents, notaries and lawyers.

What are the risks?

There are two main risks to the investor's rights: expropriation and the possibility of reprivatisation.

1. Expropriation is only permitted for public purposes and on payment of compensation at market value. The decision to expropriate and the amount of compensation offered can be challenged in the courts. It is important to check the relevant development plans on purchase.
2. It is not yet clear how those who were dispossessed when their property was nationalised will be treated. Pressure groups have been formed claiming the return of property or compensation. Various proposals as to methods of compensation have been put forward but no decisions have yet been taken.

Protection against risk

A foreign investor may be able to ask the Ministry of Finance for guarantees in respect of investment. Insurance may be available in respect of certain types of investment.

CONCLUSION

The idea of price differentials is still relatively new. With the increase in properties available and the interest in development to meet the demands of the new economy, the property market will be likely to expand and the interest of potential investors aroused.

There are undoubted difficulties such as:

- finding property and ascertaining its ownership;
- the lack of infrastructure; and
- the general problems associated with doing business in Poland such as poor telecommunications.

Successful transition to a free market economy should outweigh these risks, and so the opportunities must be worth exploring.

14

The Commercial Code

Frere Cholmeley

INTRODUCTION

Civil Code and Commercial Code

The commercial legal framework in Poland is based primarily upon the Civil Code of April 1964 and the Commercial Code of June 1934. There are a number of laws which are concerned with matters not covered by these Codes such as bankruptcy and unfair competition, or which override or modify their provisions (for example on foreign exchange or foreign investment).

Broadly speaking, the Civil Code covers contracts and other commercial and trading relations. The Commercial Code covers companies, partnerships and equivalent business structures.

This chapter outlines the general provisions of the Civil Code, particularly concerning contracts for sale. It then summarises the insolvency regime.

GENERAL CONTRACT LAW

In the reforms to the Civil Code of 28 July 1990 a new Article 353 was introduced which emphasised the change in direction occurring in Poland from a centrally planned economy to a market-driven economy.

The new Article establishes clearly the freedom of the parties to conclude a contract and to arrange its terms according to their wishes unless the contractual terms fail to:

- reflect the essence of the relationship; or
- abide by the principles of social co-existence; or
- comply with the law; or

- provide for obligations that are capable in principle of being performed.

What constitutes the principles of social co-existence is not stated in the Civil Code. In practice these principles are not applied to normal commercial transactions.

Unless stipulated otherwise in the Civil Code or other laws, the parties to a contract can negotiate contractual terms contrary to the provisions of the Civil Code.

The businessman looking to commence trading in Poland will find few surprises in the laws of Poland governing the negotiation and conclusion of terms of contracts regulating common commercial relationships. However, unlike courts in common law jurisdictions, Polish courts will tend to interpret the terms of a contract by looking to determine the underlying intentions of the parties and the commercial aim of the contract, rather than interpreting its literal meaning. The main rules are these:

1. Unless specified in the Civil Code or other laws, there are no formalities applicable to the formation of a contract other than a sufficient expression of the parties' declaration of will to contract. The main formality is a need for writing for the making and amending of contracts for the transfer of property rights, patent licences, and certain other contracts.
2. Unlike English law, a quote or offer which is said to be open for a specified period cannot be revoked before then. If no period is specified, a reasonable one is implied.
3. Announcements, price lists, advertisements and other information aimed at the public or at particular individuals are usually non-binding invitations to negotiate.
4. A contract may be made through a representative.

General powers of attorney must be in writing to be valid. A limitation on the agent's capacity does not necessarily invalidate a transaction concluded by him in the name of the principal outside that limitation. The Civil Code still regulates the terms of agency agreements. This is dealt with in the chapter on agencies in Part III.

Other rules are as follows:

- The limitation period for most claims is ten years but in the case of business activities the limitation period is three years. A shorter period applies on claims for defects on sale (see below). These limitation periods cannot be reduced or prolonged by contract.

- In domestic relations all contracts must refer to the zloty but in international contracts any currency may be stipulated.
- A person in breach of contract is obliged to pay damages on a similar basis to English law, including loss of profit, and may also be able to claim specific performance.
- If an interest rate for delay in payment is not fixed in the contract a statutory rate of interest is due automatically.
- Liquidated damages can be provided for.

The Civil Code also imposes liability for tort which is similar in general terms to the English law concept. The time limit for claims is three years from awareness of the loss, with a longstop of ten years from occurrence for undiscovered losses.

Particular rules on sale of goods include:

- Putting an item on display at the place of sale with a price attached to it is regarded as an offer for sale.
- The seller is responsible for safe delivery unless otherwise agreed.
- As with English law, unless otherwise agreed, ownership passes immediately on sale for specific items and on delivery for non-specific items. Retention of title clauses are permitted if in writing, and are effective against the buyer's creditors subject to certain additional formal requirements being satisfied.
- Risk of loss passes on delivery unless agreed otherwise.
- The buyer must warrant that he has good title to the goods and that they are free from defects unless these have been specifically pointed out to the seller. This liability cannot be excluded by contract, which is a rather more onerous situation for the seller than under English law.

If the goods have defects then the seller must offer to exchange the defective goods immediately for goods free from defects, or to rectify the defects. Only if he does not can the buyer cancel the contract or ask for compensation. This gives the seller a statutory right to correct defects which English law does not include.

Statutory rights for defects are lost unless a claim is made within a month of discovery by the buyer (or sooner if a shorter period is normal by trade custom). Subject to these notification obligations, claims under a warranty for physical defects cease to exist after a year in most cases (three years for defects in buildings) calculated from the day of delivery/hand over to the buyer. The limit does not apply to fraud.

INSOLVENCY AND LIQUIDATION

Rules governing insolvency and liquidation in Poland are scattered throughout the Commercial Code of 1934, the Bankruptcy Law of 1934, the State Enterprises Act of 1981, the Law on Economic Activity of 1983, the Insolvency Law of 1990 and the Privatisation Law of 1990. These laws have been subject to amendments and in some areas there is overlap. Until recently, the laws were rarely applied in practice.

What enterprises can be liquidated?

Certain state enterprises are still outside the scope of the insolvency laws, in such sectors as transport, forestry and telecommunications. All other enterprises may be made insolvent.

A state enterprise may be liquidated if:

1. its profits after tax are insufficient to pay a dividend; or
2. it has substantially ceased trading; or
3. the Anti-Monopoly Office requires it to be liquidated; or
4. for the purposes of privatisation.

Liquidation of companies

As in the UK, a private company may be liquidated if:

1. its constitution provides for liquidation in the relevant circumstances; or
2. the shareholders resolve to put the company into liquidation; or
3. a declaration of bankruptcy is made against the company.

A business is obliged within two weeks of becoming insolvent to file for liquidation unless it has applied for an arrangement with its creditors, failing which directors can be made liable. The definition of insolvency is unclear but includes negative net assets and ceasing to pay debts.

Owners and creditors of businesses may also file for liquidation or insolvency. If liquidation is ordered, the appointment of a liquidator and subsequent realisation and distribution of any assets follow a similar course to the UK.

15

Competition

Frere Cholmeley

BACKGROUND

In Poland the free market economy is still in its infancy. An overwhelming share of the economy is still controlled by monopolies, accounting for 90 per cent or more of the potential market. As a result, Poland tends to lack small and medium-sized firms which will help to balance the market. It was recognised therefore that it was essential to implement modern anti-trust legislation to facilitate the creation of a free market economy and help fulfil the conditions of certain international financial aid packages.

On 24 February 1990 the Monopolistic Practices Act (the Act) was passed to:

1. ensure the development of competition;
2. protect businesses from anti-competitive practices; and
3. safeguard the interests of consumers.

ANTI-MONOPOLY OFFICE

On 13 April 1990, pursuant to the Act, the Anti-Monopoly Office (AMO) was founded. The prime aim of the AMO is the promotion of competition. Its duties listed in the Act are wide-ranging and cover:

- policing and counteracting anti-competitive practices;
- monitoring prices in markets with limited competition;
- shaping the organisational structures of businesses;

- registering businesses having a monopolistic position in the home market;
- researching concentrations in the economy and proposing actions to attain a balanced market; and
- advising the government generally on matters concerned with competition.

Overall, the AMO can be seen as having two complementary functions of equal importance: one function is concerned with the structure of the economy which involves it in deciding upon mergers, transformations and incorporations of businesses together with assessments of the anti-competitive effect of state and privately owned enterprises holding dominant positions; and the other function is to regulate anti-competitive practices.

ANTI-COMPETITIVE PRACTICES

The Act identifies a variety of forms of conduct which may be prohibited. The Act differentiates between on the one hand forms of conduct which are prohibited outright and, on the other, practices that are prohibited unless they are necessary to conduct the economic activity concerned and do not result in a substantial restriction of competition.

Outright bans

The practices banned are:

1. charging extremely high prices;
2. delaying sales with a view to increasing prices;
3. artificially curtailing production, sales or the purchase of commodities, thus causing price increases; and
4. abusing a dominant position by market sharing, discriminating unfairly between customers, refusing to supply, and dumping.

This complete prohibition applies to businesses holding a monopolistic or dominant position. The Act interprets a monopolistic position as being one where an entity does not encounter any competition on the home or local market and defines a dominant position as one where the entity does not encounter substantial competition on the home or local market. A business will be deemed to hold a dominant position where its market share exceeds 30 per cent.

Potential bans

The forms of monopolistic practice which may be prohibited unless justified on economic and competition grounds include:

- imposing unreasonably onerous contract terms;
- tying arrangements;
- agreements between competitors which fix prices or other terms;
- agreements dividing up a market according to geography, product lines or groups of customers;
- agreements controlling volumes for the production, sale or purchase of products; and
- agreements preventing new entrants to a market.

These bans apply to all businesses, not merely monopolies.

POWERS OF THE AMO

The AMO has power to conduct inspections to establish whether the business concerned is complying with the provisions of the Act, or decisions of the AMO, or court orders.

The AMO when investigating a business may:

- enter its premises;
- inspect any of its documents and demand copies and extracts of such documents;
- demand explanations, including written statements from its employees;
- gather data and information on its activities from any other sources without any additional consents;
- order the protection of documents and other evidence; and
- use the opinion of experts.

Information gathered in the course of an investigation is secret.

Notifications to the AMO

An enterprise intending to merge or transform a business (for example by converting one type of company into another) must notify the AMO. Notification must also be made where it is intended to establish a business which could command a dominant position in the market or where one of the parties to the venture already holds such a position.

The AMO may issue within two months of the notification a decision refusing to allow the transaction where the consequence would be a dominant position. Otherwise the transaction may proceed.

Decisions

Where the AMO finds that any prohibited practices are being operated it issues a decision to that effect together with instructions to cease and desist. Consequential orders, such as price reductions, may be made.

Where it is established that a business holds a dominant position the AMO may limit the activities of that business or order the breaking-up or dissolution of the business.

Decisions of the AMO can be appealed against within two weeks.

Penalties

The AMO may impose:

1. Fines for anti-competitive practices of 15 per cent of the income of the penalised business for the preceding tax year (excluding sales tax). A fine cannot be imposed more than one year after the end of the year in which the use of the prohibited practice is discontinued.

2. Default fines if a business fails to comply with a decision of the AMO or a court order, for each month of non-compliance, of one per cent of the highest monthly income, after sales tax, of the business in the tax year in question. This fine may be imposed within three years from the original decision.

3. Default fines for non-compliance with decisions concerning dissolution and merger are the same except that the fine must be between one and ten per cent of the relevant income.

4. Default fines on individuals for non-compliance by companies they manage of up to six months pay.

WORK OF THE AMO

During 1990, the AMO reviewed some 1500 cases. From these reviews approximately 70 AMO decisions were issued, the majority being concerned with the prevention of monopolistic practices but a significant number with the shaping of organisational structures. The AMO also received around 120 notifications.

The most common monopolistic practices are the imposition of unfavourable conditions and tying.

The AMO has been extremely busy in its inaugural year and no doubt will remain so for the foreseeable future.

16

The Fiscal Framework

Touche Ross & Co

The system in operation in Poland at present is based on the separate taxation of public and private sectors, and it is the private sector regime which will be described here. Separate subdivisions of taxpayer operate within the two sectors and thus income tax, which is primarily charged on business activities in the private sector, may be subdivided between corporate income tax and the income tax levied on individuals.

Every legal entity earning an income is subject to tax. The legal entities liable for corporate income tax include limited liability companies and joint stock companies. Partnerships and companies established under the civil law (essentially limited partnerships) are not legal entities and therefore participants are separately taxed on their individual shares.

The principal route for foreign participation in a Polish enterprise is the joint venture, a legal entity that can for all practical purposes be regarded as a company.

Poland has for some time sought to provide a favourable legal and tax climate for foreign investment, primarily through the medium of joint venture companies (although the tax holiday given to joint ventures is being withdrawn in 1991). A number of bilateral conventions to avoid double taxation have been concluded and proposals have been advanced to establish enterprise zones.

In this chapter, after introductory sections on the Polish tax authorities and proposals for restructuring the tax system, the taxes applicable to individuals and business entities are explained. Where applicable, the effect of Polish taxation on non-resident entities and expatriates is highlighted.

The principal taxes covered are:

- corporate income taxes;

- taxes on individuals;
- turnover tax;
- salary tax;
- salary increase tax; and
- surtax.

The principles of social insurance contributions, and of taxes on inheritance, gifts, real property and agriculture are also set out.

THE TAX AUTHORITIES

The supreme tax authority is the Ministry of Finance, but taxpayers will normally deal with Tax Offices, which:

- calculate and collect taxes from individuals and from state and private sector enterprises (except for local taxes and charges and farmers' tax obligations);
- accept or reject tax liability returns;
- investigate tax-related financial criminal cases;
- act as a court of first instance in tax cases;
- enforce administrative decisions regarding financial liability.

Fiscal Chambers are a higher authority than Tax Offices. *Inter alia*, they supervise the functioning of the Tax Offices, prepare central budget resource plans, verify annual financial reports of state enterprises and other state bodies, and carry out tax, currency and finance control.

The tax authorities may demand the submission of corporate plans, balance sheets, profit and loss accounts and any other information and materials necessary to check that tax payments have been correctly made. As tax liabilities are limited to five years from the date on which they were due, accounts need only be retained for the previous five years.

Annual inspections are carried out at the end of each fiscal year (which runs for the calendar year) with the purpose of checking that accounts have been properly kept, assessments calculated according to all the specific tax provisions, and all payments of tax were properly made. Annual inspections are generally carried out for each taxpayer, except for those entities whose accounts have been verified by an accountant acting on behalf of the Fiscal chamber. Preliminary inspections would be carried out in the Tax Office on the basis of documents submitted by the economic entity. On-the-spot inspections are also carried out at the company headquarters.

The authorities verify tax liability before making an assessment. They not only consider returns rendered by the taxpayer but information that other persons are obliged to supply by law. Taxpayers obliged to keep accounts must forward an annual balance sheet, enclosing an appropriate declaration approving the balance sheet and a copy of the auditor's certificate. The tax authorities inform taxpayers of their tax obligations by a notice of assessment.

Taxpayers are obliged to give the authorities access to their accounts and other documents. Failure to do this may lead to assessment on an estimated basis. There are financial and custodial penalties for tax offences.

Income tax is paid in advance each month and adjusted at the end of the year.

PROPOSALS FOR RESTRUCTURING THE TAX SYSTEM

Proposals for introducing changes to the tax system are being prepared. It is expected that VAT will be introduced in 1991, and that two VAT rates will be established - an 18 per cent normal rate to apply to almost all goods, and a 5 per cent reduced rate to be applied to agricultural and food products and to publishing. Some essential goods such as vegetables, milk, fish, and agricultural, scientific and forestry services would be exempt. It is also planned to introduce a universal personal income tax from 1992 onwards. In March 1991, an annual income exceeding Z36 million is subject to surtax. This was Z16 million in 1990 and Z3.6 million in 1989. Surtax rates increase proportionally with income (from 10 to 40 per cent).

CORPORATE INCOME TAXES

A Polish resident legal entity is liable for corporate income tax (*podatek dochodowy*) on its income from all sources (except foreign-source income, which will usually be exempt if the income is subject to the same kind of tax in the foreign country and the foreign country applies reciprocal principles). An entity is regarded as resident if its legal seat or place of management is in Poland, although there is no precise definition of residence. (Note that joint ventures are treated for the purposes of corporate income tax in the same way as non-resident companies, see below.)

Corporate income tax is levied at the rate of 40 per cent.

Dividends must be paid out of post-tax profits. There is a basic withholding tax of 30 per cent from dividends paid abroad by resident and non-resident companies, but this may be reduced by treaty. In the case of the UK the rate is 5 per cent (15 per cent if the payee owns less than 10 per cent of the payer). Poland has double taxation treaties with most developed countries. Most agreements follow the OECD model.

Net receipts from all taxable sources, including capital gains, are aggregated for income tax purposes. The income or deficit from each separate source is the difference between the sum of receipts from this source, both in cash and in kind, and allowable expenses.

Taxable sources include income from economic activities, leasing and renting, capital and property rights, and the sale of securities, commodities, property rights, intellectual property rights, and other sources such as subsidies, grants, subventions, and any other benefits gained free of charge. Interest on savings accounts is not included. Income is usually determined from the annual accounting records.

Inventories are required to be valued at their 'real value'. This is not defined in Polish law, but cannot be lower than purchase or manufacturing cost.

Gains on the sale of fixed assets are generally taxable, and related expenditure and capital losses on the sale of fixed assets are deductible. Gains from selling land more than ten years after purchase or buildings more than five years after purchase are not taxable.

Expenses incurred in earning the related receipts are deductible from those receipts. Deductions are made in the year in which the expenses are disallowed. There are regulations covering capital expenditure on buildings, plant and equipment.

Rates of depreciation have been fixed for all taxpayers. There are 60 different rates ranging from 1.5 to 50 per cent. The straight-line method is applied. It is likely that in the future these rates will be changed and made more flexible.

There are regulations covering disallowable items of expenditure and the treatment of losses (but note that there are no provisions concerning the carry-forward or carry-back of annual losses).

Taxation of non-resident entities

As foreigners mainly operate in Poland through the medium of a joint venture, it is dealt with here as if it were a non-resident entity, although strictly it is not. Joint ventures are liable for corporate income tax at the rate of 40 per cent of net profits from Polish enterprises.

They are exempt for the first three years of their operations. (The date of commencement is the date of the first sales invoice, not the date of registration.) An additional period of tax exemption of up to three years may be granted when such enterprises operate in priority sectors of the economy. This exemption is being removed in 1991. The exemption allowed does not apply to the withholding tax that must be charged on distributions to non-resident shareholders.

TAXES ON INDIVIDUALS

Around 1992, it is planned to introduce a universal personal income tax, but the present form of income tax (*podatek dochodowy*) is charged only on the specific sources of income, described below. All individuals, including foreigners, are theoretically liable, but in practice foreigners are not charged because they must conduct economic activity through a legal entity liable for corporate income taxes.

Resident individuals are subject to income tax on their world-wide income from taxable sources. An individual is normally regarded as resident in Poland if he has a residence or customary place of abode there, or stays there for six months or more.

When both husband and wife earn income, their aggregate income is taxed. Income earned by children and grandchildren is aggregated with that of the parents or grandparents, as the case may be, when the latter have the use of this income.

The income tax scale is progressive and the marginal rates are between 20 and 50 per cent on all income in excess of Z3.6 million. However, the total tax must not exceed 40 per cent of total income.

Income tax is charged on:

- income from business activities;
- income from scientific, research, artistic, literary, publishing

and educational activities that are not subject to salary tax;

- income from real estate;
- lease and rental income;
- income from capital in money and property rights;
- income from the sale of commodities, property rights, real estate, businesses, securities, rights to use a property in perpetuity, and any other property rights; and
- income from other specified sources, such as subsidies.

Chargeable capital gains are included in income for the purposes of the charge to income tax.

Income tax is calculated as a percentage of the surplus of income earned over allowable expenses.

As with companies, income is usually computed on the basis of annual accounting records. In keeping with the general rule for income tax purposes, income-connected expenses are deductible, including allowances for depreciation, expenditure on research and development, etc.

Note that income from employment is liable for separate taxes (salary tax, salary increase tax and surtax).

There are regulations covering exempt income (for example, alimony, interest on savings accounts) and deductions and reliefs. Also exempt is income from foreign enterprises and enterprises with foreign participation for the first three years of operation, commencing with the start-up of production or service provision, or, in the case of trading companies, the first purchase of merchandise, provided that not less than one-third of the income for the three years is reinvested in those enterprises.

Salary tax is accounted for on a monthly basis by employers. Employers must also calculate and account for surtax, as a rule, annually.

Special position of expatriate employees

Expatriate employees are liable for salary tax in the same way as Polish employees, except that the rate applying is 30 per cent instead of 20 per cent.

An expatriate resident in a country with which Poland has a tax treaty is normally exempt from Polish taxes on employment income, if employed by a foreign employer and present in Poland for not more than 183 days in a calendar year.

TURNOVER TAX

This tax represents the only form of taxation on turnover currently in force, but it should be noted that Poland is planning to introduce in the near future a value added tax.

Turnover tax (*podatek obrotowy*) is charged on individuals and corporate entities in relation to any economic activity connected with industry, trade or services carried out within Poland. A single sale of goods may produce liability. The turnover tax may also apply to imports of goods.

The tax is charged at only one stage in the production system, on the sale of finished goods. It may be necessary to furnish the authorities with a certificate confirming that goods are not for on-sale to ensure that tax is not levied on raw materials, semi-processed goods and spare parts sold.

The tax is imposed on gross turnover and normally based on consideration receivable, rather than consideration received. In the case of imports, turnover tax is based on the value of imported goods.

Turnover tax is paid each month or quarter, and, if necessary, adjustments are made at the end of the year. There is a basic turnover tax rate for domestic and imported goods of 20 per cent that is charged on individuals and legal entities other than state enterprises. Rates in general range from 20 per cent to 50 per cent, but those applied to alcoholic drinks range from 60 per cent to 95 per cent.

No tax is chargeable in the case of foreign trade activities. Also exempt are activities subject to the salary tax, activities of a cultural or social nature, and small-scale activities such as the casual sale of privately grown products.

SALARY TAX

Salary tax (*podatek od wynagrodzeń*) is a tax on employees borne by employers. It must be accounted for by all economic entities, including joint ventures with foreign participation.

The tax is calculated as a percentage of total cash expenditure, but on a net pay basis. Thus, at the current rate of 20 per cent, tax of Z20 would need to be accounted for on pay of Z100.

Exemptions include those granted for state-owned companies, disabled employees, farmers paying agricultural tax, and severance payments.

SALARY INCREASE TAX

As part of government measures to control wage and salary increases a salary increase tax (*podatek od ponadnormatywnych wynagrodzeń*, known as the 'popiwek') is in force. The tax applies most notably to state-owned companies, but does not apply to private companies or joint ventures with majority foreign participation. Also, all joint ventures trading before 1991 are not liable.

The starting point for calculating any charge is the level of earnings in September 1989. The level is adjusted each month using a formula based on the rate of inflation. Tax will be charged if wages and salaries are increased by more than the officially calculated amount. If the latter is exceeded by up to 3 per cent the tax is levied at 200 per cent on the amount of the excess. If the limit is exceeded by more than 3 per cent the rate is 500 per cent on the amount of the excess.

SURTAX

Individuals living in Poland who earn income from employment are liable for surtax (*podatek wyrównawczy*) when a statutory threshold (Z36 million in 1991) is exceeded and their income is not liable to income tax. There is no definition to indicate what constitutes living in Poland, but it can be assumed that the tax does not apply to foreigners employed and working in Poland unless a double tax treaty stipulates otherwise.

There are exemptions for various types of income including awards, interest and bonuses on savings accounts, and income from the sale of securities. Deductions are allowed for salary tax, tax-deductible expenses and various other items. The tax is charged at progressive rates ranging from 10 per cent to 50 per cent, but the overall charge is not to exceed 40 per cent of total chargeable income.

REAL PROPERTY TAX

Real property tax (*podatek od nieruchomości*) is chargeable on individuals and all economic entities, including state enterprises and joint ventures. Real estate subject to the tax includes buildings not used in connection with agriculture and undeveloped real estate.

The tax rates vary according to the type of property being charged. They include the following:

- apartment buildings liable for statutory insurance, 0.05 per cent of the insured value;
- other apartment buildings, Z200 per square metre;
- buildings used for business purposes, Z8000 per square metre;
- other buildings, Z300 per square metre;
- real estate used for an economic activity, Z220 per square metre;
- real estate not otherwise charged, Z10 per square metre.

AGRICULTURAL TAX

Persons (including joint ventures) engaged in normal farming activities are liable for agricultural tax (*podatek rolny*) on the basis of the number of 'conversion hectares' being farmed. Conversion hectares are a function of the land area, class of agricultural land (derived from its historic use), and the tax district in which the land is situated.

The tax rate is the value of 125 kilograms of rye for each conversion hectare.

Specialised farm production, such as poultry, horticultural, and mushroom farming, is charged on the basis of specified standards laid down for such production. Alternatively, profits may be taxed on the basis of normal income and expenditure accounts.

There are reliefs for investment in livestock, buildings, land improvement, and equipment for protection of the environment. Twenty-five per cent of sums invested may be deducted from the tax due. Applications for relief must be made to local administrative authorities and accompanied by invoices.

SOCIAL INSURANCE CONTRIBUTIONS

All employers, including foreign employers, must pay social security contributions (*składka na ubezpieczenia społeczne*) for their employees in Poland at the rate of 43 per cent, and make a further

2 per cent contribution to the unemployment fund. These percentages are applied on a net pay basis in the same way as for salary tax.

INHERITANCE AND GIFT TAX

The recipient of a gift or inheritance is obliged to pay tax (*podatek od spadków i darowizn*) at rates varying between 5 and 40 per cent on the net value of the property received. The rates vary according to the relationship between the recipient and the deceased or donor as do basic tax-free amounts.

Exemptions are available for household goods, farms, gifts and inheritances from abroad, and dwellings. Non-residents are liable if property rights are transferred in Poland.

ROAD TAXES AND SPECIAL TRANSPORTATION FEES

Vehicles and trailers are liable for local road tax (*podatek drogowy*) at rates of between Z10,000 and Z440,000, depending on vehicle type.

The special transportation fees (*specjalne opłaty transportowe*) are applicable to foreign buses and lorries engaging in international traffic in Poland. The rate is arrived at by multiplying a special index by the exchange rate of the US dollar against the zloty. The special index is based on the number of places on the bus or the capacity of the lorry.

FISCAL DUTIES

Fiscal duties are levied on the transfer of property rights with a value in excess of Z200,000. The rates are 5 per cent for movable property, 10 per cent for immovable property, and 5 per cent for other property rights.

Fiscal duties are also levied by a number of government bodies for administrative proceedings of various kinds, including the issue of business licences, and the consideration of official applications.

OTHER TAXES

Simplified forms of taxation are levied on particular types of activity. These forms generally relate to small traders and include market duty and a lump-sum turnover and income tax.

There are many kinds of taxes levied for various services provided by government, including water duties and environmental duties.

17

Telecommunications and Post

British Telecom

TELECOMMUNICATIONS

National and international telecommunications in Poland are currently the responsibility of the *Polska Poczta Telegraf i Telefon* (PPTT - Polish Post, Telegraph and Telephone), a state-owned enterprise operating under the aegis of the *Ministerstwo Łączności* (Ministry of Posts and Telecommunications). Further information about services discussed in this chapter and about acquiring equipment approval can be obtained from the PPTT (for address see Appendix 4).

The Ministry of Posts and Telecommunications has recently been restructured and plans are advanced for the PPTT to be restructured prior to the proposed separation of the post and telecommunication services due to be completed by 31 December 1991.

While the postal service will remain in full state ownership as a public utility enterprise, the telecommunications service 'Polish Telekom' will be restructured as a joint stock company, with the Polish government holding 100 per cent of the shares for an initial period. This chapter looks first at telecommunications and then at the postal service.

The Communications Act of 15 December 1990 which came into force on the 15 January 1991 encourages private participation in most fields of telecommunications activity and which will greatly enhance the development and availability of telecommunications services. (The provision of international basic public services will, however, remain under the exclusive control of the PPTT.)

Quality of service

Telecommunications services within Poland as well as the international services to and from Poland are currently poor by Western European standards. This has been due to two major factors:

1. Telecommunications in Poland has been given a low priority over the past 40 years which has resulted in under-investment by the Ministry of Posts and Telecommunications, the PPTT and equipment manufacturers. Inevitably this has led to the rundown of the Polish telecommunications network resulting in telephone exchanges that are equipped with out-of-date analogue technology and insufficient equipment to be able to cope with the increasing traffic demand. The current position is that there are only 3.2 million telephones for a population of 39 million (ie 8.23 telephones per 100 of the population) whereas the comparable average figure in Western European countries is 50.

2. The export of specified high-technology equipment, particularly telecommunications equipment, from the West to Poland has for the past five years been subject to licence controls applied by the Nato 17-nation Co-ordinating Committee on Multilateral Export Controls (CoCom). This has prevented major modernisation and digitalisation of the network although certain items of equipment can now be exported to Poland. The CoCom restrictions may be further relaxed as Poland is now moving towards democracy.

Fortunately due to the new world order, the enlightenment of the Polish authorities and the new communications law, steps are being taken to revitalise Poland's ageing telecommunications infrastructure.

A higher priority is now being given to telecommunications as a result of sweeping economic reforms, intended to bring about a change from a command to a free market economy. The Polish authorities have realised that if they are to attract Western businessmen and investors (necessary for the success of the Polish reform programme), good national and international telecommunications are essential. The major aims to improve the telecommunications network are:

- a planned increase in the number of telephone subscribers from 3.2 million to 10 million by the year 2000;

- a total investment in telecommunications of US$23 billion over the next 10 years. (An amount equal to half the current Polish national debt.)

The Ministry of Posts and Telecommunications and the PPTT have high aspirations to extend and modernise their telecommunications network but lack the necessary finance. The Polish government is trying to attract the involvement of foreign companies and capital in Polish telecommunications. The World Bank and the European Investment Bank are expected to loan US$200m and US$250m respectively over the next few years towards the development of the telecommunications network.

The international telephone service to and from Poland has already shown signs of improvement particularly for those customers in Warsaw connected directly to the KOMERTEL business overlay network. This network has a separate digital microwave network in Warsaw together with a separate international exchange by-passing the existing congested and overloaded international telephone exchanges. [A new digital international telephone (5ESS) exchange entered service in April 1991.] KOMERTEL numbers can be recognised as they occupy a unique numbering scheme within the Polish network ie +48 3912 XXXX. Ordinary Warsaw telephone numbers (ie area codes 2 or 22) cannot be accessed via the KOMERTEL network.

The service to the other Warsaw (non-KOMERTEL) customers should have shown signs of a significant improvement by the time this book is published. The installation of a new undersea optical fibre telephone cable from Poland to Denmark plus a digital microwave link from the Baltic Sea landing point to Warsaw, and a new digital international telephone exchange in Warsaw will greatly reduce traffic congestion and improve reliability. The quality of service offered to and from the other cities in Poland will steadily be improved as a major investment programme in the Polish long-distance trunk network gathers pace over the next few years in the framework of a three-year development project realised with World Bank and European Investment Bank loans.

ADDITIONAL TELECOMMUNICATIONS SERVICES

This section outlines the various basic and value-added telecommunications services that are available although some of the services may not be fully available in all parts of Poland in the immediate future. As the basic telecommunications network is improved the services offered will be extended and the reliability/availability of each of the services will steadily improve.

Telegram

The telegram service is currently the most reliable and most widely available of all the services offered, although it may take one or two working days for delivery.

Telex

The coverage of the telex service is very extensive in Poland and major investments have improved the service over the past three years. The use of telex is currently the most reliable way of passing large amounts of information both internationally and within Poland other than by using postal or courier services.

Most of the main hotels in the major cities have telex facilities, that can be used by visiting businessmen.

The charge for national and international telexes is made according to the call duration but in cases of emergency calls within Poland, a fixed surcharge is levied. The cost of an international telex call from the United Kingdom to Poland is 23p per minute.

Telephone

Apart from the KOMERTEL network the availability of telephone lines is poor and the length of time the customer must wait for connection to the telephone network tends to vary widely based on individual localities and on a combination of available exchange capacity and of spare local cable pairs. There is a waiting list of approximately 2.6 million and potential customers can wait several years for connection. The easiest way to obtain a telephone line is to purchase or rent an office that already has a line connected.

The national telephone service is extremely poor even for calls made across Warsaw. The existing analogue telephone network cannot cope with the excessive demands placed upon it, especially at peak hours when the call failure rate becomes extremely high. Where new digital exchanges have been installed the quality of service has shown signs of improvement.

The quality of the international telephone service to Poland (except for the KOMERTEL network) is not currently as good as the service provided to and from countries in Western Europe. International Direct Dialling (IDD) calls to Poland may be made with varying degrees of success to all of Poland, with one call in ten, on average, succeeding at the first attempt. However, IDD calls from Poland to the UK can only be made from selected large cities, with one call in twenty, on average, succeeding at the first attempt. During the summer of 1991 dramatic improvements in the quality of service are expected as the new international digital facilities are brought into service.

To minimise the number of call attempts it is advisable to make international calls between 2300 and 0600. The use of Voice Mail, automatic telephone answering machines or facsimile machines will make the best use of this period whereby recorded messages can be accessed by the recipient the following working day.

The quality of service achieved on international calls to and from the KOMERTEL network is that the majority (80 per cent) of calls are successful on the first attempt.

IDD calls to Poland from the UK are charged at 51p per minute during the cheap rate and 61p per minute at the standard rate including VAT. The country code for Poland is 48.

Local telephone calls within Warsaw can be made using type-A pre-paid tokens or jetons in public payphones. These tokens can be obtained from newsagent kiosks and main post offices. A local call without any time limitation is charged at Z300 (approx 2p).

On long distance calls within Poland there are cheap rates between 1600 and 0600 on Monday to Friday and all day at the weekends. Calls are charged according to distance, ie up to 25 kilometres, from 26–100 kilometres and above 100 kilometres. Calls can be made using type-B pre-paid tokens which can be obtained as described above.

IDD calls cannot be made from the existing public payphones at the present time. The number of public payphones is to be increased by 19,000, out of which 12,000 will be phonecard payphones which will allow local, long-distance and IDD calls to be made. The phonecards will be available at main post offices.

International calls from Poland to the UK are charged at Z28,560 per minute for urgent calls via the operator, Z14,280 per minute for non-urgent calls via the operator and Z6,050 per minute for IDD calls. Calls made from hotel bedrooms may incur a surcharge. The international access code is 00.

Telephone Operator Services

Business visitors from the UK may make an arrangement whereby the cost of international telephone calls to the United Kingdom made by them in Poland may be charged to their company in the UK by previously obtaining a BT Chargecard. The visitor may also use the reverse charge (collect) call service via the Polish international operator whereby calls are paid for by the customer receiving the call. Appreciable delays (one to three hours) are often encountered when using the operator service although this should improve once the network modernisation gathers momentum and further international operators are employed.

Mobile cellular radio systems

A mobile cellular telephone network operating at 450MHz will become available in the autumn 1991 initially covering the Warsaw region but it will cover the whole of Poland within five years. The service will be run by the PPTT as a joint venture with a foreign partner who has yet to be selected.

Facsimile (Fax)

The use of facsimile in Poland has risen dramatically over the last few years but the quality obtained will depend on the condition of the telephone network. The cost of the facsimile call is the same as for calls dialled over the public switched telephone network. Facsimile messages can be sent and received at most major hotels for a fee.

Bureaufax

A public facsimile service is available in Warsaw at the main Post Office. (See Appendix 4.) The service is also available in larger post offices in the main towns. A charge is made by the PPTT to both transmit and receive facsimile messages.

Switched data transmission services

Data can be transmitted, nationally and internationally either over the public switched telephone network (PSTN) or via the PPTT's new packet-switched data network known as POLPAK.

Data may be passed over the PSTN network using data modems approved by the PPTT. The speed of transmission obtained will depend directly on the quality of the connection offered by the telephone line. A maximum transmission rate of 2400bps is possible but not guaranteed. The cost is charged as a normal telephone call on a call duration basis.

POLPAK will enter service in summer 1991, initially, in Warsaw but will cover the whole of Poland over the next three years. Leased line connections giving an X28 asynchronous service at 300bps and 1200bps as well for X25 synchronous service at 2400bps, 4800bps or 9600bps will be offered. X28 dial-up access will also be available at 300bps and 2400bps.

The cost of calls using dial-up connections will be based on call duration and the volume of data transmitted. Connection to the POLPAK network can be authorised through the PPTT.

Paging

A paging system is to be available in Warsaw in summer 1991. The POLPAGER service will be run by the PPTT.

Electronic Mail

Two competitive nationwide electronic mail services will be available in summer 1991 with access being provided through the PSTN telephone network using personal computers. One of the services will be run by the PPTT and the other rival service by the TESA Company.

International Private Circuits

International private circuit services are available to Poland from the UK to various specifications depending upon the user application and the location of the customer terminal in Poland. Circuit rentals are charged on the basis of two half-circuits; a UK-end and a Polish-end. Charges will be higher for circuits terminating in cities other than Warsaw. At present only analogue services are available but after the installation of the new Polish digital trunk network and the availability of additional satellite earth stations, digital private leased circuits will be available offering a limited coverage of Poland. Orders for these circuits can be placed with either the PPTT or BT who will offer more convenient 'one-stop-shopping' arrangements.

TELECOMMUNICATIONS EQUIPMENT APPROVAL

Any telex, telephone, facsimile and modem equipment obtained by the customer must all be approved for connection to the Polish telecommunications network by the Ministry of Posts and Telecommunications. Approved equipment should be obtained from well-known suppliers and potential users are advised to seek local sourcing to ensure technical compatibility and availability of maintenance, service etc.

POLISH POSTAL SERVICES

The Polish Post Office provides various services including the following:

- postal services for letters, parcels and Datapost the Express Mail Service;
- subscriptions to newspapers;
- newspaper delivery to subscribers in rural areas.

There is approximately one post office every 45sq kilometres and for every 4,500 inhabitants (in the UK there is approximately one post office for every 2,842 inhabitants). The ratio in Poland is satisfactory, although lower than the European average.

Poland has the highest exchange of postal traffic with the following countries, in descending order: Germany, USA, USSR, France and the UK. The Polish Post Office handled 1.1 billion items in 1989.

Quality of service

The Polish Post Office serves a country which is fairly densely populated and where the distances to be covered are manageable. However, quality-of-service monitoring shows the processing time of mail within the country to be lengthy. International outgoing airmail letters, for example, spend 4.8 days, on average, within the Polish postal service before leaving the country and incoming airmail letters spend 3.4 days in the system before they are delivered.

The Polish postal service at present has to rely on a complex railway network for routeing its mail around the country. The development of road networks, the use of internal flights and the reorganisation of rail networks are pre-requisites for an improved quality of service.

The mechanisation is, at present, insufficient but the Polish Post Office plans to modernise much of its equipment in order to accelerate the processing of mail.

The mass media and the general public in Poland are quite critical of the quality of service offered by the Polish Post Office. The latter is concerned to develop the services it provides and is collaborating with experts from the Universal Postal Union (UPU) in order to improve efficiency.

Quality of service objectives

Resolving the problems outlined above will enable the postal service to attain its service standard aim of delivering all letters by the second day after posting and all parcels by the third day after posting.

Access to postal services

Post office opening hours

Post offices are open from Monday to Friday between 8.00am and 4.00pm in rural areas and between 8.00am and 8.00pm in large towns. On Saturdays post offices close at 1.00pm. Postage stamps are also sold at street kiosks.

Delivery and collection

One delivery per day is made in the mornings from Monday to Friday. Only mail for PO Boxes, urgent mail or mail to private addresses in Warsaw is delivered on Saturdays. In large towns there are separate deliveries for parcels and urgent or registered letters. Delivery is made to the door or to PO Boxes. (PO box numbers are obtainable, depending on availability, by making an application on the relevant form at a local post office.)

Mail is posted at the Post Office or in pillar boxes. The times of collections are indicated and there are several in a day.

Freepost/business reply

Freepost facilities are not usual but it may be possible to come to an individual agreement with the Polish Post Office regarding the provision of a reply paid service. Further information can be obtained from the Polish Post Office (see Appendix 4).

Guaranteed express service

Domestic service

The Polish Post Office provides an express service *Super-Expresz* between 12 large towns that guarantees next day delivery.

International service

Poland introduced an international Express Mail Service (EMS) in

1987. Inward items only were accepted until 1989 when an outward service became available. The service is known as *EMS Pocztex.*

Inward International Datapost

International Datapost items can be sent from the UK to many areas of the country and are delivered two days after posting. Deliveries are made every day except Sunday to the door or to the PO Box. Postcodes must appear on Datapost items.

Outward EMS

Coverage and time guarantees Items are accepted to 34 international destinations and this figure is likely to grow. EMS items are accepted in 18 major towns in Poland and it is envisaged the service will be extended to a further 7 towns. Items are handed in at the post office since collections are not yet available. At Warsaw 3 Office there is a separate counter for the posting of EMS items. The customer is informed of the expected delivery time at the time of posting. In the case of a delay, the EMS fee is refunded. The quality of service objective for items to Europe is to attain delivery the day after posting.

Fee The EMS tariff is based on five regions in the world and on 500 gram weight steps. The price for a 2 kilogram item to Europe is US$26.

Business users The Polish Post Office is considering introducing a collection facility and contracts for regular EMS users following recommendations made by an expert from the UPU (Bettineschi, 1990). An EMS collection service is currently undergoing trial in Warsaw.

Preparing mail for posting

The following points should be noted when preparing mail:

- The postcode should always be used, appearing in the final line of the address.
- Envelopes may be purchased at stationery shops or at post offices. The latter sell envelopes with stamps pre-printed on them.
- Packets and parcels for international destinations are checked by counter staff at the post office before acceptance. Therefore, posters should take items to the post office

unwrapped, together with packaging materials, in order to pack them after they have been checked.

Services and tariffs

Mail travels by surface within Poland and by surface and air from Poland to international destinations.

The high rate of inflation results in frequent tariff changes. The following postage rates were charged in January 1991:

Inland

■ Local letter up to 20 grams	Z700
■ Long distance letter up to 20 grams	Z1000
■ Printed matter up to 50 grams	Z700
■ Registration	Z1500
■ Express service	Z1500
■ *Super-Expresz*	Z12,000

- Insurance service is also available for valuable items

To other European countries

■ Surface letter up to 20 grams	Z2000 (for airmail, Z200 for each additional 10 grams)
■ Registration	Z5500 (in addition to postage)
■ Express	Z5500 (in addition to postage).

18

Transport

Touche Ross & Co

Introduction

Poland covers an area of 312,683 square kilometres (120,728 square miles), 28 per cent larger then the area of the UK, and considerably larger than Czechoslovakia and Hungary. In comparison with other Eastern European countries it has a well developed railway system, which is the most intensively used European rail system west of the USSR. There is also a well-developed road network, although there are few dual carriageway roads, and minor roads are poor. To the north, Poland has a 600 kilometre coastline on the Baltic Sea with a number of important sea ports, notably Gdańsk and Gdynia to the east and Szczecin to the west. The country's only international airport is at Okęcie, about eight kilometres (five miles) from Warsaw.

In November 1990, the Polish government announced that the country's transport infrastructure would be one of three top priorities for investment over the next years.

This chapter is organised into two main sections: goods transport, covering freight traffic to, from and within Poland; and passenger transport within Poland; covering air, rail and road communications.

TRANSPORT OF GOODS

Freight transport to and from Poland

The British International Freight Association (BIFA) recommends road transport as the most efficient and cost-effective method of transport for most cargo to Poland. Transport is usually arranged on an *ad hoc* basis and the journey from London to Warsaw normally takes three to four working days.

Most freight forwarders will be able to arrange for freight transport both to and from Poland. *Lloyds Loading List* publishes a weekly guide which specifies companies specialising in transport services for Poland.

No permits are needed to transport freight to or from Poland, although permits may be necessary to cross transit countries in Western Europe. Details are available from the International Road Freight Office (see Appendix 4).

Freight transport by rail is possible through the rail freight arm of British Rail - Railfreight Distribution. No regular services currently exist, but arrangements can be made for a negotiated price by contacting Railfreight Distribution directly. Transit time is approximately six days.

Air freight to and from Warsaw can be arranged through British Airways, or through the Polish national airline LOT.

Sea freight from the UK centres on the Polish container port of Gdynia and can be arranged through Polanglia, a joint venture between Polish Oceanlines and the UK company Unit Baltic Corporation. Polanglia has a roll-on, roll-off (roro) operation with facilities to handle all types of cargo.

The freight sector in Poland

There are a number of both state and privately owned freight forwarding companies in Poland, specialising in both full load traffic (FTL) and less than full load traffic (LTL), or groupage. Private sector companies have been established both by Polish nationals or as joint ventures linked with Western European freight forwarding or transport companies. It is expected that, as a result of the Polish government's privatisation policy, the private sector will grow significantly at the expense of the state sector.

Currently, the major road groupage operator to Poland is the state-owned Pekaes International, which runs 60 driver-accompanied units per week, to and from the UK. Pekaes operates Western trucks and trailer combinations, most of them under five years old, and can provide 12-metre trailers, drop frame trailers, clothing vehicles and low loaders. There is a weekly groupage service from London to Warsaw, and similar arrangements exist in Warsaw, where a weekly groupage service is organised to London.

Most export and import activities are co-ordinated in Warsaw (by ministries, state export/import companies or by private companies), although there is an important groupage depot at Słubice on the Polish border with Germany. In general, Polish exporters prefer to include the costs of FTL in their quotations.

Polish importers now generally want consignments delivered freight-paid to final destination (in contrast to the former insistence by Polish importers that UK exporters sell on an ex-works or FOB basis). For full load and part loads this presents no great difficulty. However, for small loads and groupage BIFA currently advise UK exporters to deliver to the Polish border at Słubice, or warehouse in Warsaw, as internal distribution within the country is not yet considered to be up to Western standards. All invoices and accompanying documentation should contain the telephone number, contact name, region number and terms of delivery of the Polish importer, otherwise cargo will not be cleared promptly through Polish customs.

Domestic freight transport

The Polish domestic freight market is currently undergoing considerable change with haulier licences being issued to a large number of small private operators. The state-owned Polish Domestic Freight Forwarding Company (PSK) continues to dominate the market using the state-owned domestic carrier PKS (not to be confused with the similarly pronounced Polish international carrier, Pekaes International).

At the time of writing, PKS continues to use Eastern European vehicles for road haulage. As equipment shortages can often delay delivery, and there may be a reluctance on the Polish side to use alternative transport, BIFA advises UK companies to insist on the right to organise their own transport within Poland. It is probable that, in time, the dominance of the state-owned hauliers will be reduced by competition from private operators, Western companies and joint ventures using modern vehicles and more efficient distribution techniques. For the time being, however, UK companies are advised to seek expert advice and stay abreast of developments in a market which is undergoing major restructuring.

Freight transport regulations

A liberal agreement exists between Poland and the UK which allows UK hauliers to operate to Poland without permits, although normal permit rules apply to transit countries. The maximum permitted height of a vehicle travelling in Poland is four metres. The maximum gross laden weight of an articulated truck with more than four axles is 42 tonnes.

Courier services to Poland

The major companies such as DHL, TNT, Federal Express and UPS all offer express parcel, document and freight services to Poland. A 48-hour service is available for documents to Warsaw. Deliveries to other major Polish cities take 72 hours, with an extra day necessary to reach outlying areas. (Freight deliveries may take an additional day to clear Polish customs control.) Price structures vary, but start at £16 per half kilogram for a door-to-door service including customs clearance. Any local office of these companies will be able to deal with enquiries and make arrangements for transport to Poland.

PASSENGER TRANSPORT

Air travel

There are international flight connections between Warsaw and most major European cities, but the only daily direct flights from the UK are those from Heathrow to Okęcie (Warsaw's airport). The Polish national carrier, LOT, also operates scheduled flights to Kraków and other Polish cities.

There are currently two daily direct flights between Heathrow and Okęcie, with services provided by British Airways and LOT. (There is an additional BA flight in the summer months.) The flying time is approximately two hours, with a one-hour time difference between London and Warsaw. Flight times in summer 1991 are as follows (all times local):

From London Heathrow	*Departs*	*Arrives*
LOT	10.50	14.00
British Airways	11.30	14.55

From Warsaw Okęcie	*Departs*	*Arrives*
LOT	08.15	09.30
British Airways	16.00	17.30

Travellers to and from UK regional airports usually have to route via Heathrow in order to fly direct to Warsaw, although there are direct flights from European mainland cities. KLM, Sabena and other international airlines operate indirect flights from London and Manchester for transfer connection in Amsterdam, Brussels, Paris, Prague or Vienna. There is no airport tax. The current (summer 1991) business class return flight from London Heathrow to Warsaw Okęcie costs £641; the economy class fare is £534.

Warsaw Airport

There are at present two terminals operating at Okęcie, with international flights at Terminal 1 and domestic flights at Terminal 2. The two terminals are connected by bus and taxi services. There is a hotel operated by a French chain within two kilometres of the airport. There is a new Warsaw airport under construction, with work scheduled for completion in 1992.

There are internal air services between Warsaw, Gdańsk, Kraków, Poznań, Wrocław, Szczecin, Rzeszów, Katowice, Koszalin, Częstochowa and Bydgoszcz. Schedules and particulars of flights on Polish and foreign routes are available at the Warsaw office of LOT (see Appendix 4).

Getting to and from the airport Okęcie is about eight kilometres (five miles) from the centre of Warsaw. The easiest way of travelling between the airport and the city centre is by taxi. The journey takes approximately 10 minutes and costs about £5. Alternatively, there is a bus service (tickets cost about 10p) which operates every 10 minutes during peak periods and takes half an hour to reach the city centre.

Car hire arrangements can be made either in the UK or at Warsaw Airport. Avis, Budget and Hertz operate through Orbis, Poland's state-owned tourist service, and the normal European conditions for car hire apply. The March 1991 cost of hiring a Ford Scorpio was £56 per day, plus £4.60 a day for insurance, the weekly rate for the same car being approximately £300 with unlimited mileage. Most major credit cards are accepted. Car hire services, with or without a driver, are also available in the main towns in Poland through the Orbis offices.

Transport within Warsaw

An underground metro system is under construction in Warsaw, and is scheduled for completion in 1993. At present, the only means of transport available are state-owned trams, buses and taxis. There are regular bus and tram services, and local and long-distance coach services. Taxis may be hailed in the normal way, and operate from taxi ranks around the city and at the main railway stations. It is customary to tip taxi drivers 10 per cent.

Parking may be difficult in the centre of Warsaw, but is relatively easy elsewhere in the city.

The road network

There is no motorway system in Poland, although a number of partly constructed motorways and dual carriageway highways do exist. Seventy per cent of public roads are classified as main roads, and are generally in good condition, although minor roads in Poland are usually of a lower standard than is found in the UK. Visitors entering Poland by private car require an International Driving Licence and an International Insurance Certificate (Green Card).

The following speed limits apply on Polish roads:

Built up areas	50 km/h
Other roads	90 km/h
Highways	110 km/h

Emergency telephone numbers throughout Poland are:

Ambulance	999
Fire	998
Police	997
Polish Automobile Club (in Warsaw)	954

In June 1990, the Polish Ministry of Transport announced a major investment programme to upgrade the road network. Priority is to be given to links considered important to east-west trade. These include a 564 kilometre north-south motorway from Gdańsk to the Czechoslovak border, and two east-west major routes to link Germany and the USSR. Petrol stations are to be found along the main roads in Poland, although they can be few and far between. The new investment will also be directed, in part, to improving roadside facilities.

Railway services

All railway lines in Poland are owned and operated by the Polish State Railways (PKP), with Warsaw and the Baltic sea ports well served by international rail links.

There are twice daily services from London to Warsaw, the journey taking approximately 33 hours. Trains leave every morning from London Victoria via Dover – Ostend – Brussels – Cologne –

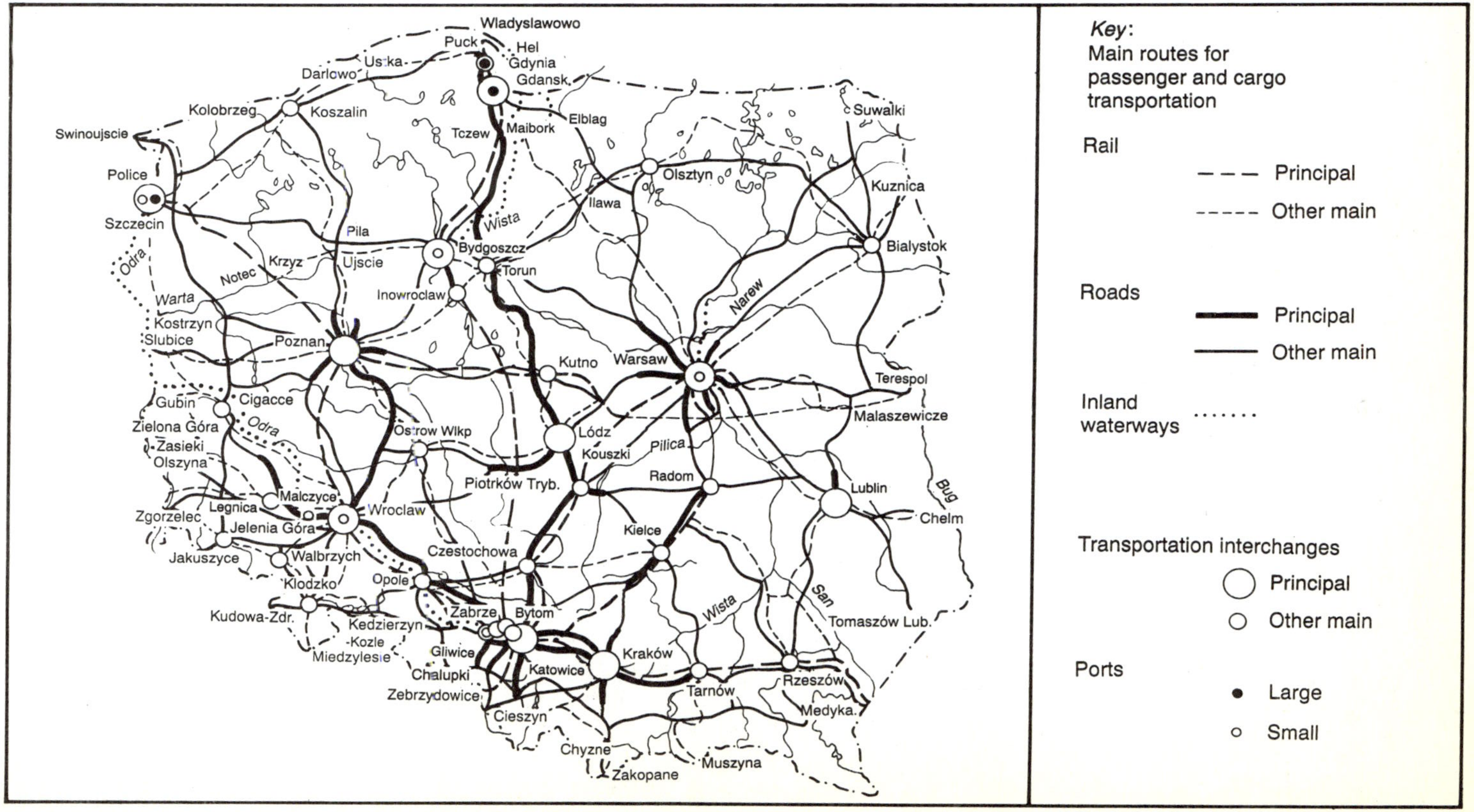

Map 18.1 *Infrastructure in Poland*

Hanover - Berlin - Poznań - Warsaw; or from London Liverpool Street via Harwich - Hook of Holland - Hanover - Berlin - Poznań - Warsaw. The first class return fare is approximately £350, or £212 for second class.

Poland has an extensive and, in relation to other Eastern and Central European countries, well-developed domestic rail network. Over 80 per cent of the rail network is electrified, although speeds are still quite slow.

Second class carriages are spartan and, for the small additional cost, first class presents an altogether more comfortable way to travel.

The main station in the capital is Warsaw Central from which travel plans for other parts of the country can be made and seats booked in advance.

In May 1990 PKP received US$153 million in loans from the World Bank to put towards a US$216 million investment programme. The money is to be spent on upgrading rolling stock and improving signalling and telecommunications equipment.

Plans currently exist to upgrade the north-south rail link to Budapest in Hungary and to modernise the east-west link to take 120 km/h trains. Future projects over the next 15 years include upgrading of the lines from Warsaw to Gdańsk, and Warsaw to Katowice for 160 km/h trains (designed to allow for speeds of 200 km/h) and represent a major commitment on the part of the Polish government to improve the country's railway network with the help of aid from the West.

19

The Environment

Frere Cholmeley

THE BACKGROUND

Polish environmental law and policy must be set against the background of a country dominated for the last 40 years by an ideology which encouraged the growth of heavy industry without due regard for the environmental damage associated with that growth.

The result of inefficient low technology industrial development regardless of the environmental cost, combined with a rigid centrally planned economy has resulted in a country severely polluted in certain parts, especially Upper Silesia. Particular problems include:

1. The discharge of waste into rivers as a result of which 80 per cent of water from rivers and lakes is undrinkable.
2. Pollution of the air, especially by sulphur dioxide causing acid rain and damaging both forests and beautiful ancient cities such as Kraków. Over 77 per cent of Poland's power comes from coal and much of the coal used is 'brown coal' which emits high levels of sulphur dioxide when burnt. Existing coal-burning facilities are inefficient and need replacement with modern systems.
3. Degradation of the land by open cast mining.
4. Incorrect management of industrial and municipal waste.
5. Over 60 per cent of food produced around the region of Kraków is inedible because of the amounts of heavy metal found in vegetables.
6. Trans-boundary pollution (for example, air pollution from the burning of poor quality lignite in East German power stations

close to the Polish border). The pollution of the River Odra on the Czechoslovakian-Polish border with heating oil in 1986 remains a subject of controversy. There have also been cases of waste dumping in Poland by enterprises in neighbouring states.

Poland's environmental problems have not been caused by the absence of an environmental regulatory scheme. A legal framework does exist for the protection of the environment but laws are rarely enforced.

Part of the difficulty concerns a lack of independence between the regulated and the regulators. Often a state administrative body is responsible for regulating a state-owned industrial plant, the former being powerless to control the latter in a political climate which encouraged economic development and production targets at the expense of the environment.

The year 1987 saw the creation of the Ministry for Environmental Protection and Natural Resources which, in 1989, became the Ministry of Environmental Protection, Natural Resources and Forestry. It has overall responsibility for environmental policy in Poland.

Poland has substantial legislation in the environmental sphere. The most important law is the Environmental Protection Act 1980 ('EPA').

THE AIMS OF THE EPA

The EPA was designed to protect:

- land and mineral resources;
- water and marine environment;
- air quality; and
- green areas in towns and cities.

It was also to protect people against:

- excessive noise;
- irresponsible management of waste; and
- radiation.

How to achieve the aims

Charges

The EPA establishes a scheme of charges to be levied on those conducting polluting activities. Fees are charged in respect of air pollution, liquid emissions and waste storage.

Fines and offences

A polluter can be fined for exceeding set limits in respect of liquid emissions, air pollution, noise and storage of waste.

The EPA and related legislation impose criminal responsibility for pollution.

Penalties

Very serious offences under the Polish Criminal Code of causing public danger to life as a result of pollution can result in 10 years imprisonment if the act was intentional, or 5 years if it was due to negligence.

Offences under the EPA carry up to three years imprisonment. Fines can be imposed in addition to imprisonment though they are generally very low.

Compensation

The EPA requires a polluter to pay for the cost of restoring the environment or, if this is not possible, to pay compensation. This provision is very rarely invoked.

Further features of the EPA

Land use and planning

The EPA requires environmental protection to be considered by local authorities as part of land use planning.

Rights of environmental associations

Environmental associations have the right to take legal action against a polluter. An administrative authority, in considering a planning application for a development likely to have a major environmental impact, has to inform environmental associations and consider their objections before granting a permission. At present environmental associations are not strong and rarely exercise such rights. Changes are proposed which may also grant individuals equivalent rights of action.

Environmental impact assessments

If a new development is listed by the Minister for Environmental Protection as especially hazardous to the environment, then the developer is required to carry out, prior to the development, an environmental impact assessment setting out the likely effects of the proposed development and indicating how harm can be minimised.

Waste disposal

The EPA deals only generally with this topic. However it does set out special categories of waste, including radioactive waste. Disposal of such waste requires the consent of the Voivodeship concerned. A ban on the import of all kinds of waste from abroad was introduced in 1989, partly in response to scandals involving Austrian companies dumping waste in Poland.

National Parks and Landscape Parks

Poland has designated certain areas as National Parks and Landscape Parks. Landscape Parks are more extensive and serve touristic and recreational purposes as well as the protection of the environment. There are development restrictions on both, but light development, for example for the purposes of tourism, may well be permissible in Landscape Parks.

LIMITATIONS OF THE CURRENT REGIME

The system of environmental protection based on the EPA has been unsuccessful in preventing serious pollution in Poland:

- Fines are too low. They do not compensate for environmental damage and are a cheaper option than the cost of reducing pollution.
- Prosecutions have rarely been brought to court. Those that reach the prosecutor's office have often been discontinued on the grounds of 'economic necessity'.
- The resources for finding and measuring pollution are very limited.
- In Poland only individuals and not companies can commit crimes. It is often difficult with a large organisation to find the individual responsible for a pollution offence.

CHANGING ATTITUDES

As Poland becomes more open to the West and as it develops a market economy, so it is eager to implement lasting solutions to its environmental problems. There is developing across Eastern

Europe a growing awareness of the interdependence between the environment and the economy. New legislation to deal with environmental protection is currently being drafted and is expected to reflect the influence of US and EC environmental law.

Publicity

One means of contributing towards better management of the environment in the West has been the use of adverse publicity. Until very recently, this was not available to Polish environmentalists. However this is changing. In 1989 a list of the country's 80 largest polluters was published in the government newspaper, and environmental information is no longer subject to censorship.

Independence

An independent commission for environmental impact assessment has been set up. The barriers to creating independent non-government organisations have been abolished. As industry is privatised this will result in greater independence between the regulated and the regulators.

Emissions trading

Proposals for 'emissions trading' are being considered whereby a company may be allowed to exceed limits in respect of one process in return for savings on others.

Corporate criminal liability

Legislation may be introduced which imposes criminal liability on companies for acts of pollution. There is a specific proposal to require companies to appoint environmental directors on German or Japanese models, who would have personal responsibility for any breach of environmental regulations by their companies.

THE EFFECT ON THE OUTSIDE INVESTOR

Opportunities

Factories may be able to obtain grants from the Environmental Protection Fund to assist in the installation of pollution reducing equipment. However, the amounts available are likely to be restricted.

Legislation passed on 12 January 1991 abolished the use of tax incentives and credits to encourage particular activities, but it may be that subsequent environmental legislation will reintroduce them for projects benefiting the environment.

Foreign aid or assistance from the World Bank may be available to joint ventures for the purchase of pollution reducing equipment. Last year the World Bank granted Poland a loan of £9 million aimed at providing technical assistance, training and specialised scientific equipment.

Existing heavy polluting factories and installations will come under increasing pressure to improve their environmental performance or face closure. New industrial and manufacturing plants which incorporate state of the art pollution control techniques are likely to have a competitive edge and could benefit from positive publicity for an environmentally friendly stance. Foreign companies utilising Western technology should be at an advantage in this regard.

Poland offers an expanding market for pollution reducing equipment and techniques. An international environmental equipment trade fair was held in Poznań in November 1990 at which foreign firms participated.

The EC has established the PHARE programme which can provide finance and assistance for specific environmental projects. Opportunities may be available to take part in such projects.

Western consultancy firms are currently operating in Poland. They are often asked to carry out environmental clean-up studies for companies considering investing in Polish industry particularly as part of Poland's privatisation plans.

The risks

Increasingly stiff fines and penalties can be expected for breach of environmental regulations. Polluting factories can expect to face closure more readily in the future. Therefore, it is essential to be clear about the potential environmental impact of a proposed activity. Frequently, a joint venture or business acquisition may involve the purchase of land and existing industrial plant, including the risk of substantial liability for pollution.

New and tougher environmental legislation may impose liability in respect of an operation which was previously in compliance. It is very hard for a foreign investor to avoid this risk except by accurately forecasting the changes that will undoubtedly be made.

Investors should be aware that obligations may be imposed on them by provincial planning authorities to clear up previously contaminated land as a condition of allowing a development to proceed. However, under existing legislation the prime responsibility for the clean-up of land rests with the state. There are no current proposals to alter this.

THE FUTURE

Expect new and tougher laws, perhaps combined with more rigorous enforcement. Also, look out for incentives encouraging environmentally friendly developments.

Poland has indicated its eventual goal of becoming a member of the EC. Part of the realisation of this goal will consist in the harmonisation of Polish environmental law with EC environmental law. This is likely to lead to the gradual adoption of EC standards in the environmental field and potential investors should be aware that eventually they are likely to be required to meet those standards.

20

The Labour Market

Touche Ross & Co

Introduction

Overall, the Polish labour market must be seen as favourable. This is especially so for the new investor seeking to establish a joint venture. Wages are comparatively low, and even the high employers' social security obligations and employment taxes will only be of minor consequence to a Western employer.

Skills are abundant and labour is plentiful. There are certainly rigidities in the system, although the trend is towards their reduction. Joint ventures currently have a favoured position and should be able to attract the best workers.

The starting age of employment in Poland is 18 and the retirement ages of men and women are 65 and 60 respectively. Between those ages, there are roughly 22 million people, whereas the active labour force amounts to some 18.5 million (10.5 million men and 8 million women) of whom 1.3 million were unemployed in the spring of 1991, with unemployment expected to rise further as the 'shock treatment' of the economy continues. Unemployment sits uneasily with the right to work of every citizen enshrined in the Constitution of the former Polish Peoples Republic, but it must be remembered that the hitherto full employment was illusory and maintained artificially – absenteeism, moonlighting and unofficial second jobs were common, and work attitudes were generally poor, epitomised by two sarcastic sayings which had wide currency: 'whether you're standing up or lying down, the pay is still Z2,000' (this was some time ago: the average monthly wage at time of writing is Z2,000,000) and 'we pretend to work and they pretend to pay us'.

During 1990, employment has fallen steadily with registered unemployment increasing from a negligible level at the beginning of the year to about four per cent of the labour force mid-year and six per cent at the end of the year. In the state sector, the biggest fall in employment has occurred in industry, with trade and construction also registering large falls. The private sector, however, is booming, although agriculture and crafts have fared badly.

Problems in labour relations are more likely to occur in the declining heavy industrial sector, which is likely to remain state owned for some time.

About 60 per cent of the labour force is employed either in the state-owned companies or cooperatives. The remaining 40 per cent are employed in the teaching profession, the civil service, the health sector, etc. – as well as in the private sector. Of those employed in the private sector, half are small farmers while the rest are employed mainly in trade, services, manufacturing and handicrafts.

At present, there are favourable conditions in the supply of labour. More and more students are leaving further education colleges (they represent the blue collar workers) and universities, and these numbers continue to increase. By offering higher salaries than those offered by state-owned companies, foreign companies are being successful in attracting the best employees.

In this chapter, the framework of employment legislation is outlined. The information given is up-to-date at March 1991 but the position on individual rules may change and should be checked.

PAY RATES

In Poland, wages are regulated by collective labour agreements, decrees issued by the Council of Ministers and individual contracts.

Basic pay may be determined by:

1. piece rate (per item), or lump-sum piece rate (per number of items), determined on the basis of work standards and piece rate payment principles currently in force; or

2. time rate (per hour, per day or per month).

In addition to their basic pay, employees are also entitled to the following benefits:

- functional benefits (for administrative personnel who receive bonuses on the basis of a points system with each type of job attracting a specific number of points);

- special payments for shop-floor workers who act as foremen;

- extra payments for overtime, dangerous or strenuous work, shift-work and night work.

In addition, employees in the state sector also receive the following:

- pay rises according to their length of service (usually one per cent for each year, with certain limits);
- anniversary awards (usually granted after 20, 25, 30, 35 and 40 years of continuous employment); and
- severance pay for those retiring from their jobs.

Following legislation in 1984, many enterprises have developed special systems for paying their staff. The basic features of these enterprise-based systems are that:

- Employees are entitled to basic pay, calculated according to their 'work category'.
- Basic pay rates are determined separately for manual, blue collar workers (hourly rates) and for white collar workers (monthly salary).
- Basic pay rates depend on the points allocated to the particular work category – these points depend on the complexity of the duties performed, the responsibilities held, etc.
- The value of each point in money terms is based on the specific resources earmarked by the enterprise for pay increases in a given year.

There are 22 such work categories, the first equivalent to 20 points or less, and rising in bands to the 22nd category, of 391 to 420 points.

Table 20.1 *White collar workers, monthly basic pay*

Work category	*Points*	*Monthly salary (zloty)*
1st	0 to 20	120,000–150,940
2nd	31 to 35	152,487–197,350
3rd	36 to 50	175,692–197,350
21st	366 to 390	686,202–723,330
22nd	391 to 420	724,877–769,740

Note: Work category 22 would be the Director of the Enterprise, and additionally he would obtain functional benefits for his professional qualifications, university degrees and professional experience.

Table 20.2 *Blue collar workers, hourly basic pay (at an average 42-hour working week)*

Work category	*Points*	*Hourly wages (zloty)*
1st	20	848
2nd	35	978
3rd	50	1,109
4th	62	1,213
11th	176	2,204
12th	199	2,404

Note: For example, a welder would be in work categories 6 to 12 (94 to 199 points) and a bricklayer in work categories 4 to 10 (62 to 158 points).

The basic pay in the first (lowest) category cannot be lower than the lowest pay in the national economy (Z120,000 per month at January 1990). Examples are given in Tables 20.1 and 20.2 of basic pay rates in 1990 from a Warsaw industrial building enterprise.

As can be seen from the tables, Polish employment law on the payment of workers is still highly regulated. The emergence of private companies will almost certainly force a more flexible approach - at the moment, pay rises offered by private companies are subject to the swingeing salary increase tax. Thus, together with joint ventures established before 1991 and joint ventures with majority private capital, they have the freedom to pay their employees at whatever levels they wish - which gives them a significant advantage in recruiting the best staff.

WORKING HOURS AND HOLIDAYS

The total number of hours worked may not exceed 8 hours per day and 42 hours per week for state enterprises and 46 hours per week for others. From the beginning of 1991, a 42-hour week has been introduced for all enterprises.

In certain cases - as for example in factories operating continuous processes, the retail trade or transport - working hours may be extended to 10 hours per day under certain circumstances, although the total number of hours worked may not exceed the general norm of 42 hours per week. Also, night shifts may be refused by anyone who is under 18 or pregnant.

Where there are unhealthy working conditions or particularly strenuous work, working hours may be reduced. The principles for making such reductions are determined by the Council of Ministers in agreement with the trade unions.

Sundays and Polish national holidays are officially work-free days. There has, in 1990, been a comprehensive reorganisation of official holidays, with a general return to the traditional holidays observed in Poland before World War II - notably 3 May (Constitution Day, commemorating Poland's liberal constitution of 1791), 11 November (Independence Day, commemorating the regaining by Poland of her independence from the partitioning powers in 1918), and 15 August (the feast of the Assumption and Soldiers' Day, commemorating the defeat of the invading Red Army at the gates of Warsaw by the Polish army under Piłsudski in 1920).

Enterprises in sectors such as transport, retailing or the health services may require employees to work on official holidays but must grant them other days off in lieu. Working on Saturdays used to be usual, but it is now rare for more than one or two Saturdays to be worked per month.

Each employee is entitled to a continuous paid holiday each year. This is worked out at:

- 14 working days after the first year of work;
- 17 working days after 3 years work;
- 20 working days after 6 years work; and
- 26 working days after 10 years work.

The period on which the length of vacation is calculated also includes the time spent studying after graduating from primary school. Seasonal workers are entitled to one day's vacation per month of work. If an employee does not use his vacation, he may be granted a financial equivalent according to provisions laid down from time to time by the Minister of Labour and Social Policy.

In addition, employees may request unpaid maternity leave (16 weeks at the first birth; 18 weeks at each subsequent birth; and 26 weeks upon giving birth to more than one child at the same time). Leave for child care is as follows:

- A female employee who has been employed for at least six months may take three years child care leave in order to take care of her child personally until it is four years old.
- During this period of leave the employee is entitled to a family allowance, depending on the family's overall income.

- An employee whose children are less than 14 years old is entitled to 2 extra paid days holiday per year.

With regard to leave for professional training, employees who are sent by their employers on professional training courses are entitled to paid training leave of between 2 and 28 working days, depending on the level of the training. Special leave of two paid working days is payable on the occasion of the employee's wedding, and one or two paid working days is payable on the occasion of the death of next-of-kin.

OVERTIME AND BONUSES

Work carried out in excess of normal working hours constitutes overtime. It is only permitted in the case of a rescue action to save someone's life or health or in order to protect property, to carry out emergency repairs, or when the employing institution has a specific need for extra work. In the latter case, overtime may never exceed 120 hours per employee per annum unless the Council of Ministers determines otherwise. For overtime work, the employee is paid an overtime bonus in addition to his regular salary or wages. This is worked out at 50 per cent of the basic salary for the first two overtime hours on a given day and 100 per cent of the basic salary for any further overtime hours and for overtime worked at night (9.00pm to 7.00am), on a Sunday or on an official holiday.

SOCIAL SECURITY AND OTHER BENEFITS

The social security system in Poland requires the following obligatory contributions:

- the employers' insurance contributions;
- independent insurance contributions (from individual farmers, members of farmers' cooperatives, artisans, agents, artists, etc.); and
- state pension insurance contributions (for soldiers, disabled soldiers and policemen).

Social security is dealt with by the Social Insurance Institution (*Zakład Ubezpieczeń Społecznych* - ZUS). It operates through local branch offices and inspection offices. Labour and social insurance courts, which constitute separate organisational units of district courts, have the authority to resolve any disputes on social security matters.

All employers, including foreign employers, must pay social security contributions (*składka na ubezpieczenia społeczne*) for all their employees at the rate of 43 per cent, except on behalf of disabled persons, for whom the rate is only 5 per cent. These percentages are applied on a net pay basis (in the same way as for salary tax).

The social security rates paid by individuals engaging in business activity and by persons cooperating with them, also amount to 43 per cent of income.

Polish social security benefits can be classified as either short-term or long-term benefits. Short-term benefits comprise:

- Sickness benefit, paid for up to six months if an employee is unable to work because of illness.
- Salary differentials, paid if an employee is forced to accept a different job at a lower salary due to his state of health.
- Childbirth benefit, paid on the birth of a child.
- Maternity allowance, paid during periods of maternity leave.
- Family care allowance, paid when an employee must personally look after an ill child or other ill member of the family and in consequence is temporarily unable to work.
- Child care period benefit, paid during periods of child care leave.
- Funeral allowance, paid in the case of the death of an employee or of a member of his family.

Long-term benefits (pensions) comprise:

- retirement pension;
- disability pension;
- dependant's pension, paid in case of the death of the family bread-winner.

To receive an occupational pension an employee must fulfil both the following requirements: reach retirement age (65 and 60 years respectively for men and women); and reach retirement age during a period of employment, or no later than five years from the termination of employment. A woman who has been employed for

35 years or a man who has been employed for 40 years may retire earlier, regardless of their age, if they have been dismissed by their employer because the enterprise employing them is undergoing problems.

There are also benefits for accidents at work and occupational diseases. Unemployed people who are granted professional training benefits during apprenticeship or training periods for new jobs are also entitled to family allowances and to public health services, even though no social security contributions have been paid in respect of them.

TERMINATION OF EMPLOYMENT

A contract of employment may be terminated in the following ways:

- by mutual agreement;
- by a statement to this effect made by one of the parties, having observed the statutory notice period;
- dissolution of contract without notice (for example after prolonged inability to work, or dismissal because of the employee's fault);
- automatically, when the period of time covered by that employment contract runs out; or
- on the completion of the task for which the contract was drawn up.

An employment contract made for a trial period may be dissolved at the end of that trial period, or before its end if 13 days notice has been given. A trial period must last for a minimum of two weeks.

The statutory periods of notice for a normal permanent contract of employment are:

- two weeks for an employment period not exceeding one year;
- one month for an employment period of at least one year;
- three months for an employment period exceeding ten years.

The employment period is defined as the total time that the individual has worked, and not the time that he has worked for that particular enterprise.

During a period of notice, an employee is entitled to two paid working days for one months notice, or three paid working days for three months notice, during which he can look for another job. Within five days of a planned termination of a contract being notified, the local trade union may make representations to the management about the individual concerned.

An employer may not dismiss a worker with less than two years to go before retirement, during pregnancy or maternity leave, during a vacation or other justified absence from work, or if the employee is a member of the local trade union board or (in a state-owned enterprise) of a workers' council. The Appeal Commission for labour disputes resolves problems arising out of such dismissals and may award compensation to an employee for unjustified or illegal dismissal. However, in the case of the bankruptcy or liquidation of the enterprise, this principle is no longer valid.

GROUP DISMISSALS

Employers may lay off groups of workers for economic, organisational, or technological reasons. A group dismissal is defined as the simultaneous dismissal of at least 10 per cent of the staff of an enterprise employing up to 1,000 people, or at least 100 employees of an enterprise employing more than 1,000 people.

In cases of group dismissals, the management must notify the trade unions at least 45 days before the dismissal is due to occur. Both parties should reach an agreement and determine the criteria and the schedule for the dismissals within 30 days after such a notification. In practice, individual dismissals are frequently used because they enable management to avoid the obligation of negotiating and concluding an agreement with the trade unions.

When group dismissals occur, employees are entitled to severance pay and salary differential benefits where applicable. Severance pay is dependent on the duration of employment, and is worked out as:

- one month's salary for an employment period which has lasted less than ten years;
- two months' salary for an employment period which has lasted from ten to twenty years; and
- three months' salary for an employment which has lasted more than twenty years.

An employee is entitled to receive the salary differential benefit if he takes a less well-paid job in a different enterprise. The benefit amounts to the difference between the salaries of his new and previous jobs. It is paid by the new employer for a six-month period.

On dismissal, all employees must receive severance pay and, where applicable, salary differential benefit, if the dismissal occurred because of the enterprise's economic weakness, or because of restructuring or the introduction of new technology.

THE UNEMPLOYMENT FUND

The Unemployment Fund was introduced by the Employment Law of 29 December 1989, and is the responsibility of the Minister for Labour and Social Policy.

It is financed by means of an obligatory levy, paid by all enterprises, which is calculated at two per cent of the amount of an employee's income on which social security contributions are calculated. The Fund may also earn income from its own investments and financial dealings and, if necessary, acquire funds from the state budget.

The Fund resources the following:

- apprenticeships and training schemes for the unemployed;
- training benefit for the unemployed (this amounts to between 40 and 80 per cent of the individual's previous wages) to which he is entitled for a period of up to six months;
- loans for the creation of new jobs or for the start-up of new businesses by the unemployed;
- public works; and
- unemployment benefit.

Unemployment benefit amounts to 70 per cent of the person's previous salary during the first 3 months of unemployment, 50 per cent during the next 6 months, and 40 per cent thereafter.

Unemployed university graduates, who have not been in employment since graduating, are entitled to unemployment pay amounting to 200 per cent of the lowest state sector salary during the first 3 months; 150 per cent during the next 6 months, and 100 per cent thereafter. Otherwise, only people who have been employed for at least 6 months within the previous 12 are entitled to unemployment benefit. Those without a right to unemployment benefit may apply to the local social aid organisation for a temporary allowance.

THE UNIONS

According to the Trade Union Law of 7 April 1989, employees have the right to create and associate in trades unions according to their needs and wishes.

Trade unions are autonomous and independent of the state and of the enterprises where their members work. Their activities must be based on internal statutes which should be consistent with the terms of their constitutions and with Polish law. Their purpose should be to defend the rights and interests of employees and represent them in negotiations with management.

Trade union membership is voluntary. An employee who does not belong to a union may nevertheless nominate a trade union to represent him providing that the union has given him permission to do so. Serving soldiers and the employees of certain bodies under the control of the Ministries of Defence and of the Interior do not have the right to associate in trade unions.

Trade unions must be legally registered on the basis of their statutes which must be established by the union's founding committee. In order to apply for registration, a union must have at least 10 members or, if another trade union is already operating in the same enterprise, 30 members.

The basic organisational unit of any trade union is the work-place. The scope of a union's activities in the work-place includes the following:

1. Forming opinions on all individual matters in which workers are involved (there is considerable worker participation in Polish management).

2. Forming opinions on the management and workers' bodies of the enterprise, particularly in discussions on wages and salaries, labour regulations, awards and bonus systems, holiday schedules and social issues.

3. Collaboration with management on the training and education of workers and the exploitation of any inventions devised by them.

4. Ensuring the observance by management of regulations concerning labour as well as safety and hygiene at work.

If, in a work-place, there is more than one trade union, then the trade unions present must work out a common position on the issues listed above. This is particularly necessary when wages, salaries, awards, bonuses and labour regulations are being discussed.

Relations between trade unions and management in a work-place often result in disagreements. Any such disagreement should be resolved within seven days by a six-member commission (all parties involved being represented). If this period expires without a settlement, the Social Arbitration Board of the Regional (voivodeship) Court acts as a mediator. If no solution is then found, a strike may be organised. Management should be notified of a strike at least seven days before it begins.

The Social Arbitration Board of the Supreme Court settles disputes between trade unions and government bodies if such disputes exceed the scope of an individual enterprise and if the parties have not reached an agreement within 10 days. Strikes of a political nature are not allowed by law.

In the present social and political climate in Poland, the role of trade unions is very important. In particular, the independent self-governed trade union Solidarity, which is the direct power base of the present government formed under President Lech Wałęsa by Prime Minister Jan Bielecki, has much influence. This situation, and also the considerable personal prestige of President Wałęsa among working people, has so far allowed the government to implement socio-economic changes and in particular, an economic programme, the result of which has been an enormous decrease in the real standard of living for most Poles.

However, there are clear indications that the patience of the people is running out. There was the extraordinary showing by the hitherto unknown expatriate Pole Stanisław Tymiński in the presidential elections in November 1990, displacing the former Prime Minister Tadeusz Mazowiecki from the second round of voting. There are also strikes, some breaking out independently of trade union organisations, as well as workers' protests. Protests are also being organised by farmers (their main organisation is the ISTU - the Solidarity of individual farmers). It must be expected that trade unions will respond to pressure from their members and become more aggressive.

At present, one of the major causes of strike action is the threat of group dismissals (as well as union pressure to increase wages and salaries) associated with the financial situation with which Polish firms now have to cope as a result of operating in a market economy - difficulties in selling products in a free market, decreases in production, high interest rates, and so on. In such situations, most trade union organisations are blaming management for incompetence in co-ordinating production and for their lack of operational strategies.

On the other hand, inefficient and undisciplined workers can no longer rely on the strong support that they used to receive from trade unions in previous years, when, in practice, there was no way to dismiss them. In addition, there is now competition for jobs (and a large, and growing, number of unemployed), so it is easy to find and employ qualified workers of all specialities to replace trouble-makers. The dismissal of inefficient workers will usually only be hindered where there is competition to recruit workers between different trade unions existing in one work-place, and each union is trying to enhance its reputation by flexing its muscles.

21

Management and the Professions

Touche Ross & Co

BACKGROUND TO THE POLISH MANAGER

Most management positions are occupied by university graduates. They usually work in a company for many years and their promotion is gradual. The majority of top management posts in production companies is made up of engineers. Lawyers and economists are also well represented among senior management.

At present, one can observe a tendency for economists, particularly those specialising in finance, to play a greater role in company management. Until 1989, political factors had been of great importance in promotion. Although highly skilled professionals could and did hold senior positions, in general members of the Communist Party were favoured for promotion to managerial posts, and they were not necessarily required to have any particular skills or management abilities.

Towards the end of 1989, at the beginning of the process of transformation of the centrally planned economy into a market economy, there was a shift towards recognition of specific managerial skills and abilities, with the accent on proven results, experience, specialist skills and knowledge of foreign languages. For instance, many companies now employ managers for marketing and advertising.

Candidates at interview are usually asked to present a sound and clear programme of their business development. However, managerial ability per se is still not regarded as an important issue, probably because of the difficulties of measurement against a track record established in entirely different circumstances.

TRAINING FOR INDUSTRY AND COMMERCE

During the early part of 1990, many new schools and training centres for industry and commerce were established. The following three institutions specialise in training managers:

- International Business School in Warsaw;
- International Management School; and
- International Management Centre of Warsaw University.

There is also a very good department of Organisation and Management at the University of Łódź.

Towards the end of 1990, the total number of institutions offering training in management, industry and commerce had grown to over 30, including management schools with links with other countries (eg, the Polish-American Business School or the Polish-German Business School). Most of their training is oriented towards business management, although some of the schools specialise in capital markets, securities, privatisation of the economy, corporate restructuring, etc.

Recently, schools specialising in training in specific fields have also been founded. For example, there are now schools training management specialists in agriculture, construction, environmental protection, accounting and so on. There are also regional training centres throughout the country carrying out training for graduates from secondary education and preparing them for work in blue collar positions.

THE PROFESSIONS

Law

The prerequisite for following a law career in Poland is to obtain a law degree. After graduating, there are four options. One may become:

- a judge;
- a public prosecutor;
- a legal adviser (usually working for a specific company); or
- an independent solicitor.

At present there are about 5,000 solicitors in independent practice and upwards of 20,000 legal advisers.

Both legal advisers and solicitors have their own professional bodies at the national level (ie, the National Council of Legal Advisers and the National Bar Council), as well as at regional level.

Currently legal advisers, who may only work for companies, are striving for unification of the legal profession. This would give them the right to offer legal services to individuals on a professional basis, which at present is only open to solicitors.

The universities whose law faculties have the highest reputation are Krakow, Warsaw, Gdansk and Wroclaw.

Accountancy

In order to become a professionally qualified accountant in Poland, the following requirements need to be fulfilled:

1. Possession of, at least, a secondary school diploma.
2. Completion of a specialised course in accounting.
3. Completion of the requisite minimum work experience (ie, for law or economics university graduates three years, one year to be spent in either a managerial or an independent post, and for high school graduates six years, of which three years are to be spent in a managerial or an independent post).
4. Passing a state exam (most candidates attend a two-year course in order to prepare for this - candidates are given three opportunities to take the final exam).
5. A declaration under oath.

As the number of independent accounting and auditing businesses is increasing, and in view of the rapid growth of the private economy and the related increase in the demand for accounting and auditing services, significant changes are planned, commencing in 1992. The Ministry of Finance, which is the supervisory body for accounting and auditing, plans to follow the Western patterns of organisation of the accounting and auditing professions. It is expected that there will be a significant shift towards an independent accounting profession.

Engineering

The engineers' professional body is the Supreme Technical Organisation (*Naczelna Organizacja Techniczna*), which comprises some 20 associations of engineers and technicians of various disciplines (eg, Association of Electrical Engineers, Association of Mechanical Engineers, Association of Mining Engineers and Technicians, Association of Communication Engineers, etc.).

The Supreme Technical Organisation grants the titles of the first- or second-level engineering specialisation. In order to obtain the title and the appropriate diploma, one has to present the results of some original work, have worked for at least five years, and have knowledge of at least one foreign language. The system encourages engineers to develop by granting them professional status.

The engineering courses at the Polytechnics of Warsaw, Wrocław, Kraków, Łódź, Gdańsk and Szczecin are highly regarded. Warsaw Polytechnic has a specially high reputation for electronics and electrical engineering, Wrocław for chemistry, Łódź for chemistry and textiles, and Gliwice for mining.

The process of transformation of the economy into a market system is now obliging engineers to create new organisational links. Currently, depending on the demand from certain sectors, engineers are not only working as employees of companies, but are also establishing small engineering businesses offering professional services.

Medicine

Polish physicians are established under their own self-regulating body, the Medical Chamber, which is responsible for the registration of medical doctors (who are only allowed to practise after registration), medical ethics, issues relating to legal responsibility of doctors and the professional development of physicians.

Physicians develop their skills through a process of specialisation. A physician who wants to specialise in a given field of medicine has to work as a doctor for at least two years and, after approval of his candidacy by the Regional Chief Doctor (*Lekarz Wojewódzki*), he receives training in specialised clinics (in both theory and practice) and then has to take examinations.

Most doctors practise in state-owned hospitals or out-patients clinics. Some doctors have private general practices or work in partnerships.

In the future, the state-owned medical complex will also constitute the core of Poland's public health service.

HIGHER EDUCATION

The principal universities offering engineering and law degrees have already been mentioned. Very many managers in industry and commerce, as well as in government, are economists by training, and there are also a number of mathematics and sociology graduates.

The prestige higher education establishment training economists is the *Główna Szkola Handlowa* (the Principal School of Commerce) and its elite department is the faculty of foreign trade, which apart from giving its graduates a good grounding in economics also gives them a knowledge of foreign languages. The faculty of finance and statistics also has a high reputation. The *Głowna Szkoła Handlowa* had been known in the years since the war as the Principal School of Planning and Statistics - SGPIS. Outside Warsaw, the Economics Academy in Poznań is acknowledged for its excellence.

The University of Wrocław is famed for its mathematics faculty, and the Catholic University of Lublin (the only private institution of higher education in Poland) for sociology. There are also excellent sociology faculties at Warsaw and Kraków.

Part III

The Options for British Business

22

Planning

Touche Ross & Co

As with any venture, whether it be in Poland or the UK, there is a need for a clear strategy and a sound business plan. There will very probably be some guesswork required - more than in the West - so more flexibility and slack should be built into the plan. Also, Poland presents specific features to the UK businessman which need to be considered, and they form the bulk of the subject matter of this book. Otherwise, the questions which need to be asked are all familiar:

- What is the maximum financial exposure and minimum acceptable return?
- Does the Polish venture fit with the overall business strategy?
- What human resources need to be committed and for how long?
- Using conservative planning, when does break-even occur?
- What are the risks and are they acceptable?

Answers to these questions will in turn influence the investment decision, and also the choice of the eventual entry strategy. With the possible exception of the first, all will be affected by specifically Polish factors. Particular points to consider are highlighted in the following sections.

WHY POLAND?

Undoubtedly, the return of free market economics, national sovereignty and democratic politics to the countries of Central and Eastern Europe, after 50 years, presents extraordinary opportunities, not least for the Western businessman. In deciding how to exploit those opportunities, and which markets to trade in, it is useful to stand back and make comparisons of the countries' potential.

There are political and economic factors to consider:

1. How stable is the country politically, are economic reforms likely to continue and are they likely to achieve their desired results?
2. What are the government's policies towards foreign trading partners, can profits be got out, is the currency stable, is it convertible?
3. Is skilled labour available and reliable, are local management skills available, what are the employment costs?
4. Is the supply of raw materials, components, distribution services and utilities available and reliable, and at what cost?
5. How good is the transport infrastructure, communications, the media?
6. What is the population, how fast is it growing, how does it break down by age, what is the proportion of town to country?
7. What is the nation's wealth, what is the GDP and the GDP per head, what is the spending power, how many cars, televisions, washing machines are there?

Answers to these and similar questions will be interpreted and ranked differently according to each potential investor's business requirements and particular plans and expectations.

Poles themselves, so often in their history the victims of their geopolitical situation, now realise that they have the chance to make their geopolitics work for them. They are situated between highly developed and wealthy Germany and the backward but potentially fabulously wealthy USSR. Another question which may well be asked is how this situation can best be exploited.

TIMESCALES

It is important to plan entry into the market carefully. Branches need one to one-and-a-half months and joint ventures two to three months to establish, so work needs to start early to allow for the necessary bureaucracy before legal permission for the branch or joint venture can be obtained - and without this it is not possible to trade legally.

FINANCIAL POINTS

When making costing calculations in respect of products or services it is important to include all costs, such as turnover taxes on entry of goods into the country. Having ascertained a profitable selling price, the question must be asked, if aiming at the local market, whether people will actually pay this selling price.

When estimating cash flows, make allowances for the delays in the banking system - up to three weeks to transfer funds from the UK to Poland.

MARKET ENTRY STRATEGY

The absence of comprehensive business intelligence has been referred to elsewhere in this book - there is a lack of ready information and what information exists is often not wholly reliable. As it is essential to know one's own market, this suggests that rather than rush full-scale market entry, the first moves might be exploratory and possibly in cooperation with a local business. This would build up knowledge of the local conditions and opportunities on which decisions on the best entry strategy could be based.

One of the basic decisions is whether to 'go it alone' or to 'go with locals'. Poland currently presents unique market conditions and almost inevitably locals will have to be used to assist. This does not, however, mean that one should automatically go into a full-scale joint venture.

There are five principal options for market entry:

- agency;
- cooperation agreement/technology transfer agreement;
- branch;
- joint venture
  - 100 per cent owned
  - part-owned with Polish partner;
- buying a privatised enterprise.

The decision on which is best should take into account the following factors:

- the level of control required - for example, in an agency, the foreign investor will not be able to exercise full control, in a branch he can; and in a branch exchange risk can be minimised because payments can be remitted direct to the UK in sterling;

- the type of activity - for example, a joint venture may find it difficult to get permission to import and sell if it is not undertaking production in Poland; it may be easier to get permission for this type of activity for a branch;
- the tax situation - for example, a sale from the UK into Poland may not attract turnover taxes but it may if the sale is made in Poland.

Many investors are attracted to the idea of a joint venture because of the availability of the three-year tax holiday. (This exemption is to be removed in 1991.) However, the joint venture may carry disadvantages which should be evaluated so that any trade-off is worth it.

For example, the potential joint venture partner may:

- have little concept of profit or efficiency - what are the costs of any additional overheads incurred, as opposed to starting from scratch?
- be used to working to a plan - which may not be harmful if the plan is realistic and geared to demand, but otherwise there may be excess stock incurring extra storage costs - what is the cost of tying up this additional working capital?
- not be used to working in a competitive environment, and may have poor price controls;
- be significantly overmanned as a result of the guaranteed right to employment - what is the cost of this overmanning?

It is important to evaluate these factors and the risks attaching to them before making decisions.

LOCATION

One of the fundamental questions is which location is best? Many entities choose Warsaw because it is the capital, and for many ventures this is the obvious option, but an open mind should be kept. Depending on the activity, other major towns may be better - for example, the clothing industry is centred on Łódź, which is only one-

and-a-half hours from Warsaw; heavy industry is concentrated in south west Poland, and locating there would mean that customers would be nearer. With regard to the availability of premises, these are now probably also easier and cheaper to find outside Warsaw.

SALARIES

In Poland wages and salaries are paid under a net pay scheme, and it should be noted that wage and salary costs will usually be referred to net. It is thus important to bear in mind that for every Z1 million paid to an employee, a further Z650,000 is paid in taxes - by the company. For example:

	Zloty	
To the employee (net)	1,000,000	
Salary tax	200,000	(20%)
ZUS (social insurance)	430,000	(43%)
Unemployment fund	20,000	(2%)
Total salary cost	Z1,650,000	

Alternatives which may be considered in some cases are sub-contracting, or employment on a contract basis - where payment depends on results. In either case, ZUS (Polish social security) will be saved, so this can be a worthwhile consideration. Additionally, salary taxes are slightly lower at 17½ per cent compared with the 20 per cent when there is a full contract of employment. For example:

	Zloty	
To the employee (net)	1,000,000	
Salary tax	175,000	(17½%)
ZUS (social insurance)	—	(nil)
Unemployment fund	—	(nil)
Total salary cost	Z1,175,000	

REPORTING

There is a need for regular reporting so that activity can be monitored. The key reporting features required need to be ascertained, and then planned into the Polish system of financial reporting from the start. The Polish system of accounting, up to now, has been geared to satisfying the tax authorities and the generation of statistics, not to the production of management information. There is a need therefore to adapt Polish reporting systems so that problems can be identified at an early stage and remedied.

23

Marketing

Saatchi & Saatchi Advertising Worldwide

INTRODUCTION

Under a planned economy there was no real necessity for marketing in its Western sense. Production and distribution were determined centrally by the State. So companies were not interested in sales, but in producing and fulfilling their set production schedules. In some cases, even the consumer was told how much he had to consume. Even now the process of marketing and forward strategic planning is not fully established in Poland. Equally, there is little understanding of the need for flexible and fast reaction to rapidly changing market conditions, particularly among senior managers in state-run enterprises.

Of course, the inability of Polish managers to react quickly to new situations is often the result of the ineptitude of the public administration.

Among the 500,000 entrepreneurs and private sector managers who have appeared in the past 18 months however, there is an acute awareness of how much they have to learn about business; marketing is the magic word that most will volunteer as being the most important thing they wish to learn.

Western businesses will play an important role. They should provide the Polish economy with experienced managers as joint ventures develop and also should help to erode some of the more traditional bureaucratic obstacles to change.

The free flow of information, integral to the operation of a market economy, is by no means sufficient. The need for market research as a sophisticated marketing tool was just not understood in the full commercial context and statistical information was available only for government purposes. Since 1988 several market research companies have opened up, attempting to work to Western standards - it is too early to evaluate their quality as yet.

The present market situation in Poland is characteristic of an economy in transition. In many areas, state intervention and control is still in evidence (mainly in areas essential to the country's economy such as coal, agricultural fertiliser and transportation). However, there are now several products groups (such as cosmetics, clothes, household goods, audio and video equipment) where normal market rules are in force.

POLISH CONSUMER MARKETS

After many years of acute and persistent shortages, 1990 brought widespread stability to consumer markets. It came about as a result of a sharp drop in demand - the financial resources of the population decreased, in real terms, in December 1990 by 26.7 per cent in comparison to December 1989. At present, supply of basic food and other raw materials or products is just sufficient to meet demand. It is estimated that in 1990 imports of consumer goods accounted for 15 per cent (8 per cent in 1989) of the total value of goods on the market.

Twenty-four per cent of the Polish population lives on or below the minimum subsistence level. They have just enough money for food and clothing. Only 12 per cent of the population has what could be described, in economic terms, developed Western standards of living. Officially, the average Polish salary for a state enterprise worker in a medium-sized company is about US$150 per month. It should be noted that about 50 per cent of the population has a secondary source of income, boosting the national average by at least 25 per cent. In addition, Poles have US$10 billion in savings of cash in zloty and foreign currency accounts, according to the government.

Care should be taken in quoting averages in rapidly changing circumstances, since in some private companies Polish managing directors can even earn as much as US$10,000 per month. To give some comparison of prices, Tables 23.1 and 23.2 show the approximate costs of consumer items.

Practically all goods found in the West are available in Poland. Industrial electrical machinery (39 per cent) and petroleum products (18.5 per cent) accounted for the greatest proportion of imports in December 1990. In the electrical and machine product

Table 23.1 *Consumer item costs*

Item	*US$*
Packet of Marlboro cigarettes	1.00
Packet of locally produced cigarettes	0.40
One kilo of average quality sausage	3.50
One litre of petrol	0.43
Colour TV (locally produced)	500.00
Colour TV (imported brand)	600.00
Jar of jam	0.60
Imported car (eg new Renault Clio, basic model)	11,200.00

Table 23.2 *Average income disposal*

Item	*Approx %*
Food (excluding alcoholic beverages)	39
Rent	10
Household goods	14
Consumer goods	15
(alcohol)	(9)
Clothes	10
Transportation	9
Other	3

group the most frequently imported products are colour TVs and computers, as well as the spare parts to service them. In the food category the greatest share of imports are for coffee, confectionery and citrus fruits. Thirty per cent of all cigarettes are imported. Cosmetics, detergents and personal hygiene articles account for the largest share in chemical industry imports. Forty per cent of clothes are imported, which accounts for 10 per cent of total imports.

A new phenomenon on the consumer market is the declining significance of Polish producers: foreign goods are cheaper and of better quality, even if they do appear unsophisticated or out of date by normal Western standards. This applies particularly to audio-visual equipment where such companies as Sony, Sanyo, Philips, Hitachi, Samsung compete for the Polish consumer not with Polish manufacturers but among themselves. Such items are brought in by specialised distributors who provide guarantees and authorised after-sales service. This form of after-sales support was previously not formally available to the Polish consumer.

DISTRIBUTION

For the past forty years the distribution system in Poland has accorded with the ideology of the centrally planned economy. The main suppliers were in charge of distribution as well as retailing. Private trade used to function only in street markets and accounted for only a small share of total retail sales (in 1989 a mere 5 per cent). As a result of the transformation towards a free-market economy, the national distribution system is undergoing significant change and many of the present outlets can only be thought of as offering short-term solutions. To date, in the wholesale/retail industry, only small shops and warehouses have undergone privatisation (the number of private retail outlets increased fourfold in 1990 to 272,000). In 1991 large retail networks and wholesalers will undergo the privatisation process. The elimination of the old monopolies from the distribution structure has forced trading companies, and in some cases the manufacturers themselves, to assume the traditional role of wholesalers, thus filling the void.

Currently, one of the greatest obstacles facing effective distribution is the lack of modern, functional organisations having a network of nationwide storage points, transportation fleets, IT-led stock control systems and warehouses. Wholesaling in the past has been completely disorganised - state-owned enterprises have had the largest base but have been totally ineffective by Western marketers' standards.

Modern and often foreign-owned forms of distribution are now operating on the market. Such an example is the Swedish home furnishings company IKEA whose successful formula of manufacturing, wholesaling and retailing (even the in-store presentation) does not differ in Poland from their shops in other countries.

The unrestrained development of the retail trade as a whole has not been accompanied, to date, by an improvement in services provided by the shops themselves, ie displays, choice, etc. The siting of shops is also very irregular - residential areas of large towns are still practically devoid of shops. The retail trade is also characterised by a lack of specialisation (everyone sells everything) and many of the smaller shops sell mainly imported products - to ensure quick turnover. For all practical purposes a planned distribution system or policy does not exist and there is as yet no sensible grouping or segmentation of product categories at any stage in the distribution chain. Foreign trade companies, eager to extend their ranges and diversify into new areas, are duplicating imports instead of filling gaps in the market. This means that retailers are selling identical, imported goods, which results in price wars and the lowering of margins.

Many Western companies recognised this weakness early on in 1990 and serious efforts are already underway to provide distribution systems to meet the needs of the free commercial market of the future.

PRODUCT POSITIONING

At present, the process of launching new or even established products and creating their brand image differs considerably from Western standards. Many Polish producers, although realising the importance of advertising, produce and place the product on the market without any form of systematic market research and certainly without any promotion strategy, or even the help of a professional advertising agency, marketing or communications specialists. Communications support materials are minimal and relatively pedestrian, such as basic product folders, simple posters, or even calendars with just the manufacturer's name overprinted. TV and press advertising (which often simply contains the basic commercial information without any product image or branding) is frequently in the most primitive form.

Many foreign companies bringing their products into Poland produce promotional campaigns while remaining unaware of the lack of advertising literacy of the Polish consumer. There have been instances when advertising has been literally translated (mainly in TV commercials), insensitive to the local conditions, and has been so misleading to the consumer as to be totally negative in effect. In the case of both Polish and foreign companies, one can confidently state that the majority have so far failed to realise the use of branding as an effective device to promote consumer choice.

Broadly speaking there are two traditional views about the effectiveness of advertising in Poland. One is that every company, service or brand which advertises will be noticed, regardless of content, because of the relatively small volume of advertising. The other is that there is no point in advertising a good product, because it will sell anyway.

The younger generation, many of whom have access to satellite television, enjoy watching Western commercials and assume that Western brands are of a higher quality than their Polish counterparts. The fact is that the Polish consumer, of whatever age, has not learned to discriminate between one Western brand or another. So whether Adidas is better than Nike, or any other Western sports shoe manufacturer, is where, in the future, advertising has a very important but sensitive role to play.

ADVERTISING

Advertising, merely as a form of communication, has been recognised in Poland for a long time, but not in the form required to meet the demands of a market economy which is a completely new phenomenon, formerly regarded as propaganda. Now, however, more and more local manufacturers, due to their declining share of the market and the growing competition of imported products from foreign companies, appear to understand the role and significance of advertising. Nevertheless, the amount of money spent on advertising is still incomparable to the level of expenditure in the West - indeed such sums are just incomprehensible to local companies.

Due to current tax laws, only a small proportion of advertising expenditure can be allocated as a legitimate business cost, so Polish companies see advertising not as an investment but as an on-cost from which they gain no benefit.

Moreover, there is also a considerable shortage of professionals and specialists in the advertising business in Poland, and there are certainly not yet enough agencies possessing sufficient skills and experience to offer world standards of services to their clients and especially to foreign companies.

There are only a handful of agencies of reasonable size active on the Polish market which deal, more or less exclusively, with advertising. They have developed, in part, out of advertising departments of former state-owned concerns or enterprises. Furthermore many staff from these state organisations seeing new entrepreneurial opportunities, have left and founded their own independent agencies. These are generally very small and inexperienced compared to professional Western standards.

In 1990 only a very few international advertising agencies had opened offices in Poland. By summer 1991 only about five of the world's largest agency networks will be represented. A vital consideration for the development of Western agencies is the need for training and know-how transfer into the local advertising community.

By way of comparison, the breakdown of advertising expenditures in 1989, as against the first half of 1991, was estimated as follows:

Table 23.3 *Advertising expenditure*

	1989	*1991 (6 months)*
Fairs/exhibitions	30%	15%
Newspapers	20%	25%
Literature, brochures	10%	10%
TV	7%	20%
Window displays	7%	5%
Radio	5%	8%
Neon advertising	2%	2%
Miscellaneous (cinema, outdoor, direct mail and sponsorship)	19%	15%
	100%	100%

Some companies are making an effort to introduce direct marketing services but because of the inadequacies of the Polish postal services (lack of punctuality and insufficient infrastructure) and the unavailability of any commercially and professionally compiled lists, this form of advertising cannot be said to exist currently in Poland. In Warsaw there is a brand new 'postal advertising agency' which claims to offer this form of marketing service but, like many of the new entrepreneurially minded start-up companies, this agency has not yet got the appropriate experience of sophisticated direct marketing.

Transport advertising and roadside posters are now available in the seven major cities in Poland. The transport advertising concessions are in the process of being granted by the local authorities to a number of different contractors. Western contractors, such as UK's Arthur Maiden Limited now offer sophisticated, illuminated billboards (see Case Study 5, page 299).

One significant result of the fragmentation of the Polish market and decline in importance of Foreign Trade Enterprises (FTEs) is the necessity to provide sales literature in Polish. Although a proportion of the Polish population speaks some German, French or English the depth of this knowledge is not enough to allow for buying decisions to be taken simply from foreign language materials. Firms, offering their sales literature in Polish will therefore naturally have a significant competitive edge.

MEDIA

1991 will be of crucial importance for the Polish press, radio and television media. Hitherto this was not the case as a result, mainly, of the extent of state control and financing of TV and radio.

Television

Ninety-nine per cent of households (just over 12 million) have a TV set; 47 per cent have a colour TV, though in some areas, particularly Western Poland, the percentage is higher. Until the end of 1990 state television (PRT) had a monopoly, broadcasting on Channels 1 and 2, but several private stations are already awaiting a permit to start operations.

The largest part of Polish TV's revenue has historically been made up by state subsidies and licence fees. However, the licence fee is not legally enforceable and the state subsidies have been cut dramatically.

To make up for the shortfall in revenue PRT has been forced to increase its advertising rates by around 100 per cent. Further increases are expected before the end of the year, although this will still only represent 10 per cent of the station's revenues. Owing to the dramatic increase in prices, demand for commercial airtime has dropped considerably. Barter deals are no longer accepted and deals previously struck are being renegotiated by advertisers and their agencies to secure more favourable terms. None of these regulations, however, are definitive as the legislation is still continually being redrafted.

A broadcasting reform commission is currently making recommendations to parliament and the final bill is expected to be passed before autumn 1991. The recommendations are expected to produce a third national channel and an undetermined number of local stations. Over 200 applications for broadcast licences have been received so far.

Commercials are shown in blocks between 8am and 3pm and in spots during the afternoon and evening.

Polish TV has a very high level of penetration compared to its Western counterparts. There is a tradition of family viewing and little audience fragmentation; the main edition of TV news at 7.30pm reaches 55 per cent of all adults. There is also a comparatively high level of overspill into both the USSR and Czechoslovakia. Channel 1 is a general, family channel, whereas Channel 2 offers more cultural programme content (comparable to BBC 2 in the UK).

In keeping with the international accord for free access to information, there has been a marked relaxation of bureaucracy surrounding the installation of satellite TV dishes. An increasing number of dishes is to be seen, but it is difficult to quantify this trend since the majority of dishes in use are not registered. Most new housing developments have a commercial dish built in for use by all residents. Nevertheless, it constitutes a considerable audience for international commercial satellite channels such as CNN, MTV, Superchannel, Sat1, Sky 3, RAI UNO, Teleclub. In 1990 there were 87 cable networks in Poland and further networks are planned in the major cities by *Polska Telewizja Kablowa* and the Amsterdam-based Poland Cablevision.

TV at present is the most significant medium shaping public opinion, particularly for the middle and lower classes who tend to read fewer papers, than the more educated classes.

Radio

Ninety-six per cent of Polish families have *at least* one radio (less than TV penetration) and one driver in every two has a car radio. PRT runs the four state-owned nationwide radio stations broadcasting on channels 1-4 - Channel 1 is the most popular with 58 per cent reach, Channel 2 has 12 per cent. Radio 'Solidarity' (sponsored by the trade union Solidarność, see Case Study 3, page 291) and Radio Gazette, heard within a 50 km area around Warsaw, are the most popular independent stations. Radio 3 reaches all areas of Poland and targets young listeners who are very loyal to the station. Over one hundred new small independent radio stations are awaiting a permit to transmit. Over 70 per cent of listeners tune into radio for at least 10 minutes daily.

Press

In January 1990 AGPOL, the state-run Foreign Trade Publicity and Publishing Enterprise, lost its monopoly on placing foreign advertising in the print media. AGPOL used to take foreign orders and place them with *Prasa-Książka-Ruch (RSW)*, formerly owned by the Communist Party, who process all domestic sales orders. From there they would be distributed among the 21 publishing houses also run by RSW. RSW is now in the final stages of liquidation. However, AGPOL continues to survive alongside the increasing number of new small local agencies selling media space.

The restructuring has created upheaval and a state of instability in the press market. A great number of press titles have ceased publishing, particularly among high-circulation colour weeklies and regional newspapers. On the other hand, there has been a plethora of new launch initiatives and applications to the county courts for publishing licences. The scale of this phenomenon is demonstrated by the fact that since June 1990 the Warsaw County Court alone has received 160 applications for registering new publications (some of which are former titles resurfacing under a new publisher). At present there are about 2,000 press titles registered in Poland.

Among the most popular nationwide daily newspapers are: *Życie Warszawy* with a circulation of 240,000 copies; *Gazeta Wyborcza* with a circulation of about 430,000; *Rzeczpospolita* (business broadsheet) read by all top and middle managers with a circulation of 250,000 and *Express Wieczorny* between 150–200,000 (depending upon the day of the week). Among the general news weeklies are *Polityka* with a circulation of 350,000 copies and *Przegląd Tygodniowy* with 130,000, but they are dropping in popularity and have low technical standards. *Kobieta i Życie* which circulates 400,000 copies and *Przyjaciółka* 1,400,000, are both successful women's weeklies, but are now dropping in popularity due to their low reproduction standards and the introduction of better quality titles from publishers such as *Burda* in Germany. Additionally, there are many local daily newspapers with circulations of up to 150,000 each. These are very important in reaching regional markets and are often more popular than the national dailies. Two new business magazines have been introduced which have a most important influence on Polish management: *Gazeta Bankowa* (weekly) which circulates 40,000 copies and *Businessman* (bimonthly) 30,000.

FAIRS, CONFERENCES AND MISSIONS

Traditionally, trade fairs have been an important means of selling foreign goods to Poland. The most important is the Poznań International Trade Fair which is held annually and opens on the second Sunday in June. The duration of the fair is eight days and usually some 50 countries are represented, with foreign participation being organised on a national pavilion basis. For a number of years the UK has been one of the principal exhibitors with a collective commercial display organised by the Birmingham

Chamber of Commerce. The Poznań Fair Authorities also organise a series of specialised international fairs which take place in the spring and autumn. The areas covered include mining, energy, metallurgy, agricultural and medical equipment.

In addition there are both many established and new fairs organised in Poland. The Warsaw Book Fair and the International Computer Exhibition are among the best known. Dependence on fairs, however, will diminish as other mainstream media develop, offering alternative means to promote products, services and brand image.

Conferences, lectures and small exhibitions may also be useful. Many foreign companies (including computer, medical products and cosmetics producers) organise such events, usually in hotels. The Marriott hotel in Warsaw is one of the most popular, although other hotels in Warsaw, Kraków and Poznań are acceptable and a number of new 5-star hotels are being developed.

Finally, another opportunity for businessmen to market their products is to take part in trade missions. These may be led by government ministers or prominent industrialists and are accorded a lot of attention in Poland. The CBI is planning, as part of the Initiative Eastern Europe, to organise such missions into Poland.

24

Export and Import

The Polish Investment Company

BACKGROUND

The liberalisation of foreign trade has been fundamental to the creation of a new economic reality in Poland. The principal changes have been:

- the abolition of the monopoly of Foreign Trade Enterprises;
- the establishment of the right of all Polish companies and individuals to conduct foreign trade;
- the introduction of the internal convertibility of the zloty.

Under the previous regime it was obligatory to have a licence in order to import or export but now it is only necessary to have such a licence in a few specific cases. The basic philosophy of the new customs regulations is that the prime control over imports will be tariffs.

It was envisaged that, during Poland's transition period from a centrally planned economy to a free market economy, if certain restrictions were not applied, then disastrous consequences could follow. This is why restrictions have been applied to the trade in particular commodities namely those essential for the functioning of the economy and domestic market. It is hoped that these restrictions will be gradually lifted.

The whole way of trading with Poland has changed. The market has become very fragmented and the reliability of payments and deliveries less certain. Recently some Polish businessmen have been committing themselves to contractual obligations which they cannot fulfil. In some instances they are willing to agree several sales contracts which, in total, amount to more than their production capacity. As yet there has been no successful prosecution of non-performance of contractual obligation.

THE CHANGING ROLE OF FOREIGN TRADE ENTERPRISES

Prior to the beginning of 1990, foreign companies had relatively easy and secure methods of trading with Poland. Polish Foreign Trade Enterprises (FTEs) were the only institutions legally entitled to deal with international trade. The advantages to foreign exporters to Poland were:

- Single point of contact.
- No translation requirements.
- Security of payments.

However, the monopoly of FTEs has now been dismantled. Recent reforms have made it legal for any Polish enterprise or private individual to engage in foreign trade. In addition, all joint ventures with foreign firms receive automatic permission to engage in foreign trade by simply registering.

As a result, several thousand private and state enterprises have become active in foreign trade. Unfortunately, most state-owned companies often lack the skills and experience to conduct foreign trade. As a result a significant quantity of trade is still being handled by FTEs.

The organisation and practice of Poland's FTEs are also changing. No longer attached to specific ministries, they all now operate under the general authority of the Ministry of Foreign Economic Relations. As the FTEs were being required to act as separate profit centres, they too have set out on the privatisation route. The first privatisation has already been successfully completed (Universal has already issued shares to the public) and several other organisations are now planning to follow in its footsteps.

Although in the short term FTEs are still an important link in Polish foreign trade, their present role will have to diminish with time as Polish manufacturers open their own export departments. In order to survive, FTEs will have to restructure, probably into holding companies with some manufacturing subsidiaries.

Finally, UK companies wishing to deal with FTEs should note that there are significant variations in their strengths. Some (usually when their Polish partners are small and fragmented) are still very strong, while others (dealing with larger Polish enterprises) have mostly lost their franchise.

EXPORTING TO POLAND

Customs tariffs on imports to Poland

Poland's system of tariffs has been constructed according to the Harmonised System of Commodity Description and Coding of the Customs Co-Operation Council in Brussels. It specifies what are termed the 'conventional rates' of duty applicable to goods originating from countries to which Poland provides Most Favoured Nation (MFN) treatment which includes goods originating from countries that are members of the General Agreement on Tariffs and Trade (GATT). Poland is a member of GATT and has been accorded normal tariff treatment under its rules. For countries that are not members of GATT or with which it does not have MFN arrangements, Poland applies what are termed 'autonomous rates' that are generally 100 per cent higher than conventional rates.

The average tariff incidence is about 8 per cent, with duty rates on investment goods ranging from 10–25 per cent, and those on raw materials and unprocessed products in the range of 0–100 per cent.

The Polish customs system was revised in July 1984, and a new system of import duties was introduced on 1 January, 1989. Subsequently, the levels of import duties have been modified to keep up with devaluations of the zloty. The most recent case involved the introduction of a 25 per cent tax on the import of textiles (as a result of significant pressure from Polish textile manufacturers). Import duties are usually dealt with by the importing organisation, but this may change as Polish enterprises become more familiar with Western trading practices.

Customs clearance usually takes place at the border. However, owing to the small number of crossings and large queues of trucks forming on Polish borders, some customs clearances have been moved to major towns.

Due to the forthcoming transition to the EC-approved eight-digit customs classification, a new customs tariff is expected to be introduced as of July 1991.

UK businessmen exporting to Poland are advised to research carefully not only the current customs tariffs but also the degree of pressure under which the government is being put to increase some of the rates. A sudden increase in tariffs can make long term contracts unprofitable. From 1 January 1991 turnover tax is payable on importation, rather than sale.

Import Licensing

On 1 January 1990 all quantitative restrictions on imports entering Poland and paid for in convertible currency were eliminated. With very few exceptions such imports can now be made without import licences.

The goods that currently require import licences are:

- inflammable materials;
- isotopes;
- military and police equipment;
- arms;
- industrial waste;
- alcohol (vodka and spirits).

CoCom, the Co-ordinating Committee on Multilateral Export Controls placed restrictions on the export to Poland of certain strategic goods and advanced technology. The UK regulations are contained in the Export of Goods (Control) Order 1989 and subsequent amending orders. With the general improvement in relations between East and West, many of these restrictions have been lifted. However, some are still in place and exporters of high technology equipment should make sure that they do not fall foul of these.

Documentation

The requirements for trade-related documentation may vary according to the goods involved but the importing enterprise should always state what is necessary. A normal requirement is that commercial invoices be legalised by the Polish Commercial Counsellor's Office in London (see Appendix 4). There is no charge for this service. A declaration of origin on the invoice or a certificate of origin should also be provided.

Commercial samples

Commercial samples may be imported free of duty when of negligible value, otherwise the temporary import procedure must be followed.

Temporary import procedures involve obtaining a letter from the enterprise, for production to customs, confirming that the sample is in the possession of the enterprise and that it was left without charge. The temporary import or export of goods is allowed only under customs supervision and requires an application to be made to the Supreme Customs Office in Warsaw. A written undertaking is required to confirm that the goods will be sent out of, or returned to, Poland by the dates specified.

Alternatively, samples may be imported under an ATA Carnet. This is an international customs clearance document which allows samples to be temporarily imported without duty, or without the need for raising bonds or depositing duty with customs posts in different countries. Under this procedure a deposit of a percentage of the total value of the goods, or a guarantee for the amount of the deposit must first be lodged with the issuing chamber of commerce. HM Customs and Excise have approved the London Chamber of Commerce and Industry and certain other chambers of commerce as issuing and guaranteeing bodies for these Carnets. Further information about the issue of the Carnets, together with details of the fees charged, may be obtained from these bodies. A Carnet cannot be used for goods being despatched by post.

Agents and rep offices

Traditionally, UK companies looking for agents to represent them in Poland were restricted to negotiating with one of the 11 state agencies. The only alternative was to deal with one of a number of Austrian agents which carried out regular business in Poland on behalf of Western companies.

Recent reforms in Poland have allowed other public and private companies, as well as private individuals, to act as agents for foreign companies. Western companies are now able to hire Polish citizens to represent them in their sales and marketing efforts or after-sales support.

Poland has adopted one of the most liberal regimes for foreign agencies of the East European countries. No prior approval is required and a Polish citizen or company need only register his or her intent with the Ministry of Foreign Economic Relations.

UK companies seeking to find an agent in Poland are advised to exercise caution. Owing to the relaxation of rules, there are hundreds of potential agents currently registered, of which only some will have the necessary qualifications. It is, therefore, advisable to check carefully their competence and experience before engaging them. (Agencies, distributorships and franchises are discussed in more detail in Chapter 27.)

Getting paid

The new legislation introduced in January 1990 gave all Polish importers equal and unlimited access to convertible foreign exchange. Banks are obliged to accept and execute payment orders for all imports in convertible currencies, if they comply with the existing import regulations. The National Bank of Poland must provide an adequate amount of foreign currency to commercial banks to secure liquidity of the system of internal convertibility.

It is, therefore, now possible to receive payment in convertible currency for sale of products to any Polish company or individual. However more than usual caution should be exercised in selling on credit. Some Polish entrepreneurs, as well as large companies, are facing severe liquidity problems. Short-term cover is available from ECGD where payment is secured by an irrevocable letter of credit confirmed by a bank outside Poland.

IMPORTING FROM POLAND

Finding suppliers of goods

Liberalisation of exports from Poland has been accompanied by a major deregulation of the export trade regime. The producers are free to choose the channel through which they export their products. It may be one of the former FTEs (they are dealing mainly in commodities, for example copper, coal, sulphur, oil, grains, meat) or any firm selected from the diversified network of new specialised private traders. The decision whether to use these established channels or export independently is left entirely to Polish firms.

As a result of demonopolisation of foreign trade, the number of registered firms and persons directly engaged in foreign trade has been steadily growing. It includes manufacturers of industrial products, farmers' organisations, construction firms, trading companies, and a great number of private ventures selling their own products.

A UK firm seeking to buy Polish products might end up dealing with the relevant FTE, a smaller private trading company or directly with the manufacturer. The approach differs between different products. In commodities it is still the FTEs which have the dominant position. However, certain consumer or industrial goods can now be imported directly from the manufacturer. There are as yet no equivalents of UK reference works which give a quick guide to the manufacturers of goods in Poland. UK companies have to either use their own contacts or they can obtain relevant information from the Polish Embassy in London, the DTI or specialist UK advisory companies.

A further investigation has to be made of the reliability of supply from the Polish company. The timing and quality of shipments was and still is one of the main problems of buying from Poland. Furthermore, some companies are on the brink of bankruptcy and thus they might not be able to fulfil their commitments.

Export licensing and restrictions

While imports paid in free currencies are fully deregulated, the authorities still exercise a number of controls over Polish export.

Exports of 22 goods are subject to quota. Nineteen of them, such as coal, coke, paper, copper, sulphur, silver, meat, butter etc serve to prevent the re-export of raw materials imported from the Comecon countries, or to ensure adequate supplies in the domestic market. The quotas on textiles, shoes and steel products are applied however, as a reciprocal consequence of quotas imposed by other industrial countries on the imports from Poland of these goods.

The raw materials which require export licences are:

- petrol fuels for engines;
- fuels for self-ignition engines;
- fuel oil;
- peat and products made of peat;
- non-ferrous scrap;
- lead;
- aluminium;
- nitrogenous fertilisers;
- phosphatic fertilisers;
- polyethylene;
- potassium fertilisers;
- polypropylene;
- copolymer ethylene-propylene;

- polyvinyl chloride;
- synthetic rubber;
- synthetic fibre;
- chipboards;
- wood cellulose;
- waste paper;
- crude hides, conserved and half-tanned hides for tanneries;
- cheese;
- flour;
- cereals, feedgrains, oilseeds.

The Council of Ministers is currently reviewing the possibility of reducing the above list to just six items. Poland has also entered into Voluntary Restraint Agreements with the EC for several products. These limit the volume of exports of steel, textiles, and agricultural products.

Customs duties on exports of Polish goods

There are no export taxes levied by Polish customs for any goods except selected brands of coal and on engine fuels.

With regard to taxes levied by other countries, Poland has been granted Most Favoured Nation status by the EC and also benefits from the EC's Generalised System of Preferences (GSP), whereby tariff preferences for a range of goods are granted unilaterally on a non-reciprocal basis. However, products must be sold at market prices with recourse, in case of disagreement, to arbitration under GATT rules. The agreement to co-operate covers not only the fields of trade expansion and diversification but also economic and industrial cooperation in petrochemicals, shipbuilding, food processing, agriculture, mining, environmental protection, management of natural resources, health and service industries (especially banking and insurance).

OTHER REGULATIONS

Duty-free zones

The new customs laws have allowed for the creation of duty-free zones in Poland. Enterprises operating in these zones are allowed to take goods into or out of them without licences or paying customs duties. Currently sixteen duty-free zones have been formally established. These are at Darłowo, Kołobrzeg, Szczecin, Świnoujście, Goleniów, Gryfin, Kolbaskowo, Brody, Sulechów, Wrocław, Kędzierzyn-Koźle, Gliwice, Ustka, Terespol, Poznań and Cieszyn.

Provision has also been made for the establishment of bonded warehouses. Commercial activities carried out within these zones and warehouses are considered as activities carried out abroad. Trade between these zones and warehouses and other countries is duty free unless such trade is in contravention of international agreements made by Poland or where the goods concerned are restricted such as in the case of drugs and dangerous or noxious substances.

Polish, foreign and multinational enterprises may operate within duty-free zones but only Polish enterprises may operate bonded warehouses. Goods may only be stored in bonded warehouses for up to four years and may be a useful storage facility for supplying Polish enterprises that cannot afford to carry large stocks of imports. Applications for a licence to establish and operate a bonded warehouse should be made to the President of the Main Customs Office. The application should contain the following information:

- name of the applicant;
- commercial activities presently carried out by the applicant;
- the commercial activity to become conducted in the bonded warehouse; and
- name and location of the bonded warehouse.

The applicant should send with the application a certified copy of its or his entry in the commercial register or a certificate of his registration for economic activity and the licence issued by the Minister for Foreign Economic Cooperation.

Anti-dumping

The provisions of the new customs law comply with the regulations of the anti-dumping code negotiated by GATT which covers, among other things, circumstances when dumping occurs, the determination of what constitutes injury for Polish domestic industry and the assessment of anti-dumping duty.

25

Trade Finance

The Polish Investment Company

This chapter discusses various aspects of financing trade between the UK and Poland. The topics covered include letters of credit, the forfait market, export credits available in Poland, export credit insurance and, finally, countertrade.

LETTER OF CREDIT AND OPEN ACCOUNT TRADING

Financing exports has become more difficult as a result of the weakening financial position of Polish companies and the high interest rates charged in the country.

Currently most Polish enterprises opening letters of credit for imports to Poland have their funds blocked immediately by the bank. In cases of smaller companies, advance payment is a common form of settlement.

Polish companies exporting goods are finding it increasingly difficult to offer credit terms. The cost of three months' credit in Polish currency might be as high as 30 per cent. To avoid this cost and still offer credit a few Polish exporters have agreed discounted LCs from Polish banks. This however still is a novel idea in Poland and it is advisable for British importers to assist their Polish counterpart in arranging such a facility.

Securing non-LC based settlement like cash against documents has become very difficult since the traditional relationships have deteriorated. Polish Foreign Trade Enterprises (FTEs) which traditionally were 100 per cent secure are now often in financial difficulties and also a significant proportion of trade is carried out directly with local Polish companies. As a result trading in Poland without LCs is perceived to be risky.

FORFAIT MARKET

Poland has traditionally been a user of the forfait market. This market was really developed in the 1950s on the back of West German exporters selling capital equipment to Eastern Europe. In Germany the interest rates were much more stable and the export credit system was less flexible or did not exist. Basically a forfait consists of an exporter selling the importer's promissory notes, bearing interest at fixed rates, guaranteed by the importer's bank. Very often, if a transaction were payable over say five years, this would involve 11 promissory notes as each semi-annual repayment would be covered by a separate promissory note. This type of finance was extensively used in Eastern Europe. The promissory notes were normally guaranteed by the foreign trade bank of the importing country concerned - in the case of Poland, by Bank Handlowy.

Recently the market has more or less dried up because either the Western banks have not been prepared to purchase the notes and accept the risk or, quite often, because they were not aware of what was happening in Eastern Europe. In order for the market to advance it is necessary for some of the new Polish commercial banks to make themselves known in the market so that their names will be accepted as guarantors. At the present moment it is only easy to place Polish paper for up to two years, but this period is expected to increase considerably as details of the improvement in the Polish debt service position become well known.

CREDITS AVAILABLE IN POLAND TO UK EXPORTERS

The list below describes the most important credits which Polish financial institutions have recently received. These are offered or guaranteed by international financial institutions or governments.

1. US$260 million, from the World Bank.
   Credit line opened on 8 May 1990, interest rate variable, duration 17 years.
   The borrower is the National Bank of Poland.
   The line of credit is administered by seven participating banks and will be used to finance projects stimulating the growth of export-orientated industrial production in Poland.
2. US$100 million, from the World Bank.

Credit line opened on 7 May 1990, interest rate variable, duration 17 years.
The borrower is the National Bank of Poland.
The credit is administered by seven participating banks and will be used to finance food industry development projects.

3. US$18 million, from the World Bank.
Credit line opened on 3 July, 1990, interest rate variable, duration 17 years.
The borrower is the Ministry of Natural Resources, Forestry and Environment Protection.
Distributed by the National Bank of Poland to finance Environment Protection projects.

4. US$145 million, from the the World Bank.
Credit line opened on 11 September 1990, interest rate variable, duration 17 years.
The borrower is the Polish State Railways.
Distributed by the National Bank of Poland to finance projects improving the transportation system in Poland.

5. US$250 million, from the World Bank.
Credit line opened on 3 October, 1990, interest rate variable, duration 17 years.
The debtor is the Polish Oil and Gas Mining Organisation.
Distributed by the National Bank of Poland to finance projects improving production of various fuels.

6. ASch500 million, from the Fund for the Recovery of East European Economy.
Available from 1 September 1990, interest rate five per cent, duration eight years.
Credit is available for Austrian firms investing in East Europe.

7. A$200 million, from Australian and New Zealand Banks.
Available from 29 May, 1989, market interest rate, credit time 240 days.
The borrower is the Commercial (foreign trade) Bank. The credit is available to finance the exports of Australian raw materials to Poland.

8. US$500 million, from the Export-Import Bank of the United States.
Not available till the end of negotiations on Polish debt.
Prime rate, duration 15 years.

The credit will finance any business initiatives which will be reviewed case by case.

There are also several other credit facilities available for trade and investment in Poland. They originate from Belgium (Bfr100 million), Canada (C$20 million), Denmark (Dkr40 million), France (more than Ff3 billion), Finland, Germany (DM2.5 billion), Italy, Korea (US$450 million), Spain (US$165 million), and Switzerland.

It has been announced recently by the Paris Club that Polish debt will be reduced by a minimum of 50 per cent. Assuming that this is implemented, Poland should resume repayment of interest. This will enable Poland to receive many new credit facilities and thus the list of credits given above will be enlarged.

TRADE INSURANCE

British companies trading with Poland are able to access the ECGD facilities for investment insurance and short-term credit insurance.

Investment insurance provides cover for new equity investment against the political risks of war/civil war, expropriation and restrictions on remittances. The remittance risk is conditioned to a joint venture's ability to earn from exports sufficient convertible currency to fund remittances. However, there is a new foreign investment law currently going through the Polish parliament which in time may result in removal of this restriction.

Short-term credit insurance cover (ie for exports paid for within 180 days) is available provided that payment is secured by an irrevocable letter of credit (ILC) opened by an acceptable Polish bank. (Although for large ILCs Bank Handlowy is still favoured, smaller ILCs might be accepted from other banks. Export Development Bank and Bank Pekao SA have already issued ILCs which have been acceptable to the ECGD.)

Credit insurance cover for *medium-term* business (ie on terms in excess of 180 days) is not available in view of Poland's current debt position. Although at present the Paris Club has committed itself to reducing the debt, the ECGD is not planning an immediate review of this policy.

There are also other providers of trade credit insurance cover in UK apart from the ECGD. Trade Indemnity for example provides up to 90 days and in certain instances up to 110 days cover for exports to Poland. Until very recently Poland had no insurance company offering export credits similar to the British ECGD, French COFACE or German Hermes. The transition to the market economy has made it necessary for the Polish government to establish a financial institution of this type. In addition, the position of Polish companies dealing with countries of the 'first currency area' has weakened. (The first currency area consists of the Soviet Union, the Comecon countries and non-European communist countries except for China.) Deliveries to this area were historically invoiced in transferable roubles, but starting from 1 January 1991, this trade is now invoiced in convertible currencies. The shortage of convertible currency experienced by these countries makes trading with them risky.

The new insurance act passed by parliament authorised the creation in early 1991 of The Corporation for Export Credit Insurance (*Korporacja Ubezpieczeń Kredytów Eksportowych* - KUKE). KUKE is modelled on the French COFACE. The decision to model KUKE on COFACE is the result of initial assistance by the French company and some know-how assistance promised for the future. The export credit will be insured against the trade risk by the corporation itself but in case of very large transactions and political risk the insurance will be backed by the Treasury.

The WARTA Insurance and Reinsurance Company was for many years the state monopoly insurance company dealing with foreign visible and invisible trade. The new Insurance Act enables any firm which is licensed by the Ministry of Finance to carry out insurance operations but it seems quite possible that WARTA will keep its leading position for some time yet.

The shareholders of WARTA are the Treasury (60 per cent of the capital, represented by the Minister of Finance) and the transportation firms, Polish Airlines, Polish Ocean Lines, Pekaes road transport enterprise; and FTEs, Polimex-Cekop and Rolimpex (agricultural produce). The issued capital is only Z2 billion (US$10.5 million). Until 1990 the company was under government control. However, there are now plans for putting it into private hands. Until KUKE was started, WARTA has performed some functions of an official export credit insurance company but has now ceased such activities.

There are also a number of American and French insurance companies which plan to start operations in Poland including foreign trade insurance business.

The leading domestic insurance company has, for many years, been the State Insurance Establishment.

COUNTERTRADE

This is a much changed situation. The bad news for the British businessman thinking of doing business with Poland is that he can no longer use the excuse that he cannot cope with countertrade demands as a reason for failing to secure sales contracts. Countertrade requirements have not been part of the Polish government's foreign policy for well over 18 months. In the days when foreign trade was monopolised and centrally planned, and meagre foreign exchange resources were inefficiently distributed to effect imports, there were attempts to increase foreign exchange earnings by imposing a variety of countertrade requirements. These would vary in style and severity depending on the desperation of the FTE. Now, so far as Poland is concerned, switch transactions, escrow accounts, and the like have effectively passed in to the economic history books of the period.

The recent economic changes have brought about the demise of countertrade as an instrument of foreign trade. While it was expected that the new liberal policy of non-interference would stop the use of countertrade with the foreign private sector, it has been somewhat surprising that new thinking has also been quick to bring an end to both the rouble clearing payment mechanism and to official bilateral clearing arrangements. The latter encompassed trade with such countries as India, Bangladesh, Pakistan, China, Brazil and Colombia. Bilateral trade with Iran, Libya, Iraq, where oil was the main motivation, has also ceased.

The clearing arrangements were, at the peak of their activity, a very useful tool for the agile foreign export manager to secure sales to Poland. He could accept payment in a clearing currency which could be sold on at a discount, or could sell kits or components to the clearing country for assembly and re-export to Poland. The sale of Rank Xerox photo-copying machines to Poland via India is a classic example of this mechanism.

The single largest blow to countertrade in Poland was the currency reform which gave internal convertibility to the zloty. This reform, helped by the US$1 billion IMF stabilisation fund, ended the system of centrally planned foreign exchange allocation. From that date, all Polish importers could import what they pleased, when they pleased, provided that they had access to sufficient local currency funds.

Countertrade is still being put to specialised use where the Polish importer, for reasons of poor cash-flow or the high cost/unavailability of hard currencies, wishes to delay his payment. In which case, the obligation, for example a 180-day term letter of credit drawn on a Polish bank, which may not be so readily acceptable, can be replaced by an obligation from a leading Western corporation. In essence, the Polish payment risk is being substituted by the Western company payment risk, which, in many cases makes for faster and cheaper payment, as its obligation is more marketable to banks.

THE FUTURE

With sufficient foreign exchange reserves from a healthy $4.5 billion trade surplus in 1990, aided by the tight monetary policy which is visibly forcing idle dollars out of households into the banking system, it seems that there is no need for a policy review at present. However countertrade may make a comeback in certain specialised areas.

With regard to project finance, while there is no shortage of finance for major capital investments available to Poland today, there is a reluctance by Polish investors to make use of these funds due to an uncertain economic environment, a recession in the OECD countries and lack of good investment management and marketing skills in Polish enterprises.

There is room and need for a greater readiness on the part of the foreign co-investor or business partner to commit other resources to the financing package. The style of financing of the Marriot Hotel in Warsaw or the purchase of Boeing aircraft by LOT, the Polish national airline, and the building of the new LOT terminal at Warsaw Airport by Hochtief of Germany, where income from hotel, airline or airport services was tapped abroad or directly allocated and held in escrow to repay the loans, is not the format of the future. Indeed in today's environment it would be unacceptable. However a commitment by the foreign partner to provide a wide-ranging trade support programme, or offset programme as it is commonly called, may well become a feature of doing business with Poland.

Offset programmes are implemented by numerous governments (eg Spain, Portugal, Greece, Switzerland, Israel, Belgium, Finland and Canada) to maximise government purchasing power by extracting additional commitments from the foreign supplier which will assist the purchasing country's economy. These programmes are primarily limited to government procurement. In Poland's case the main areas would be infrastructure development, especially in the telecommunications field, where billions of dollars will have to be invested over the next few years. Non-government imports, for example car imports, could be an area for consideration and the Austrian method of dealing with massive car imports from Japan and Germany could serve as a useful model. British contractors may well look at these models to formulate their strategic thinking when competing for major contract awards.

Private sector investors in Poland may well require their foreign suppliers to enter into long-term purchase contracts, to give marketing and design assistance, and to make technology updating commitments, as prerequisites to doing business. Being competitive in price may not alone be enough; the foreign supplier should seize the opportunity to enhance his offer with buy-back arrangements and the like.

INTERNATIONAL TRADE

Since the disbanding of the clearing payment arrangements, the Polish government has left a large segment of Polish industry without access to such markets as the USSR, India, Bulgaria, Romania, Pakistan and China. These important markets are suffering badly from foreign exchange shortages and demand countertrade. Hence the Polish exporter will either have to comply or forgo doing business there.

The Soviet Union is a special case and the Polish government is giving it due consideration. Polish companies have an excellent starting point for countertrading with the USSR. They know the markets well, have good access to enterprises and people, accept the difficult local conditions and have an ability to deliver their goods quickly in exchange for Soviet products.

The decentralisation of foreign trade will continue to develop as the numerous Soviet republics gain greater autonomy, but for countertrade transactions Moscow still maintains control. A recent Polish sale of wheat to Uzbekistan against the import of Uzbeki cotton could only take place with the approval of the central authorities in Moscow. Countertrade is the main feature of Polish-USSR trade and its future format and payment structure is being negotiated at government level. However, Polish companies are not idly waiting around but are finding their own solutions. Whether Polish trade with India, China and Brazil can survive without government support or intervention remains to be seen. In any case it will be a matter of having to comply with and adjust to the buying countries' needs. Not being able to comply is no excuse. Solutions will need to be found.

26

Leasing

The Polish Investment Company

A recent headline in the business section of *Rzeczpospolita*, the leading daily Polish newspaper, confidently declared that leasing was the saviour of business. That view may be rather too optimistic. Nevertheless, leasing offers many advantages that should be considered when doing business in Poland.

Although many Polish businessmen and Polish banks view leasing in the same favourable light, many would freely admit that they do not really know exactly what leasing means or precisely how to go about transacting a lease. In order to fill that gap one or two of the more enterprising Polish banks are already planning to establish leasing departments of their own, with the help of western leasing experts.

SOME OF THE BENEFITS

UK manufacturers who are trying to sell their goods in Poland potentially have help at hand in the form of Polish domestic leasing operations. These can pay for Western goods in hard currency, yet leave Polish credit risk with Polish banks, where it belongs. And a lease will undercut any loan, however subsidised, because lease rentals are fully deductible against corporation tax (currently 40 per cent) whereas only the interest portion of a loan enjoys this benefit. On the other hand the lessor obtains accelerated depreciation not available to the lessee.

Furthermore the tax benefit is immediate (providing the customer is paying tax) as tax is paid monthly in Poland, so that cash flow is immediately improved. As mentioned later in this chapter, the tax system is to be overhauled generally, and leasing will doubtless undergo further review in this context.

Contrary to most Western opinion, Polish banks have been very profitable. The banks have substantial funds available for financing capital equipment to which Western financial leasing lends itself. However Western financial leasing is not widely available in Poland. The concept of the transfer of economic benefits without ownership has hitherto been confined to well-established hire and rental agreements (*dzierżawa* and *najem*). These are not suitable forms on which to base Western leasing because of the greater protections they afford to the lessee, and the onerous responsibilities placed on the lessor. Nevertheless, the key benefits of Western leasing are well-understood by Polish banks and potential lessees.

As owners of the equipment, lessors can reduce the potential loss on a credit default: and leasing offers cash flow benefits as well as being tax-effective by accelerating tax depreciation.

Credit risk has suddenly become a major issue with Polish banks. The move to a market economy has exposed the unprofitability of many established companies. Ironically, entrepreneurs with good start-up ideas are considered to be just as risky in Poland as they would be anywhere else in the world.

It would be true to say that leasing can only be arranged for good credit risk customers, who could qualify for a Polish bank guarantee or a Polish bank's endorsement on a bill of exchange. It would be wrong to assume that the role of leasing is to bolster poorer credit risks with the disposal value of the equipment involved. Any leasing transaction of a significant size would require bank support of the kind mentioned earlier.

TAX REFORMS

As for taxation, that great friend and foe of leasing, the need for reform has become so pressing that the system will be completely overhauled this year. The result should make the Polish tax system more comprehensible to the Western lessor. Accounting regulations have already been changed: Polish accounting now conforms to the latest EC standards, ahead of most EC members.

The legal system also poses a series of challenges, not least of which is the absence of in-depth specialist commercial advice. In the West, banking lawyers are specialists and it is common practice to use a lawyer with proven experience and ability in leasing. But in Poland, legal advice is more general and faces the need to address novel financial instruments for which no specific legislation exists.

So far, the annual volume of leasing business in Poland is so small as to be negligible, but clearly there is the potential to develop the leasing market to the point where annual leasing volumes match Western European levels (between 10 and 20 per cent of total annual capital expenditure).

There is a certain amount of cross-border leasing into Poland although this is usually quasi-leasing, and essentially is a loan transaction. Strictly speaking, the repayments on those would not qualify for tax relief in many cases, although doubtless customers do try. However, cross-border leasing tends to have even wider creditworthiness requirements than domestic leasing, which gives it a narrow application.

The explosive expansion of Poland's commercial banking operations during 1990 surprised Western participants involved in the process. If leasing is embraced with the same vigour and speed as the other areas of banking, it will soon become a fully developed financial technique.

27

Agencies, Distributorships and Franchises

Frere Cholmeley

Polish law recognises that a business may appoint a representative or agent to act on its behalf in Poland. In certain circumstances the business may even be bound by acts of the agent beyond its authority. However, unlike certain other territories, notably in the Middle East, Polish law does not require a foreign enterprise to operate in Poland through a Polish agent.

Poland does not have any legislation of the kind found in other territories governing the specific terms of agency or distribution arrangements, such as the notice required for the termination of an agency agreement, or the compensation to be paid for termination. Contracts appointing agents, distributors or franchisees are all subject to the general provisions of the Civil Code. Subject to those provisions, a business may negotiate whatever agreement it thinks appropriate. There are registration requirements for agencies, and if intellectual property rights are to be granted to the distributor or franchisee then the agreement should be registered with the Patent Office.

This chapter describes the procedures to be followed for a foreign business which wishes either to establish its own representative office or to appoint a Polish agent, distributor or franchisee.

LOCATING PARTNERS

At present there is no single source able to provide details of Polish enterprises interested in working with foreign partners or principals. The Foreign Investment Agency, the UNIDO office in Warsaw and the Polish Chamber of Foreign Trade each keep records of the

Polish enterprises which are interested in becoming distributors, franchisees or agents for foreign organisations. There are a number of publications coming on to the market where such information is published. It is also worthwhile contacting the British Embassy in Warsaw and the Polish Consulate in London who are able to provide contacts.

AGENCY AND REPRESENTATIVE OFFICES

The appointment and operation of commercial agencies and representative offices in Poland are governed by the Order of the Council of Ministers of 6 February 1976.

Representative offices

Under the Order foreign enterprises may establish representative offices to conduct commercial activities in foreign trade, transport, tourism and commercial services, and other commercial activities which are part of the foreign enterprise's normal business fields.

Polish law differentiates between:

- branch offices;
- technical information offices; and
- supervision offices.

The different types of office are subject to varying operational and taxation provisions.

Branch offices may advertise, conclude contracts and buy and sell goods in Poland. These offices must pay, in addition to corporation tax imposed on all foreign businesses in Poland, a two per cent commission on the value of goods they bring into Poland. Products bought within Poland are exempt from taxation. If the branch office represents other foreigners in addition to the company that established it then a turnover tax of 10 per cent on the commission fee is payable in addition to corporation tax.

Technical information offices are restricted in their activities to providing information on and servicing their company's products. They may not promote their own products, or buy or sell in Poland. Technical information offices are however exempt from taxation. Supervision offices have a similarly restricted role.

To establish a representative office a permit granted by the Minister of Foreign Economic Cooperation or by the Minister responsible for the activity concerned, together with the Minister of Foreign Economic Cooperation is necessary. The permit to operate the representative office will only be granted for a specific period. This period may be renewed. The permit expires automatically if the office is not opened within three months.

Appointment of agents

The Foreign Investment Agency has estimated that foreign enterprises operating in Poland spend on average US$30,000-50,000 annually on each office.

Where a foreign enterprise has limited trade contacts with Poland, or for other reasons does not want to open its own office, it may appoint a local agent. The Polish agent must obtain a licence from the Minister of Foreign Economic Cooperation. The grant of any such licence depends on the likelihood of the agency resulting in commercial activities bringing profits to Poland.

Demand for the grant of licences to enable the provision of agency services on behalf of foreign enterprises has been very great and often comes from Polish entrepreneurs who apply for a licence without previous experience as agents or contacts with foreign companies. Applications are now being allowed which do not identify the foreign enterprise to be represented, although further consent is then needed if a particular foreign enterprise is identified. Great care should be taken in selecting a Polish agent, as the issue of a licence is no guarantee of the experience or skill of the agent.

If the Ministry does not object within three weeks from the date of application then the licence is allowed.

Commission fees for agency services must not be lower than the rate specified by the Minister of Foreign Economic Cooperation, unless his consent is obtained.

Proposed amendments to the law

The Ministry for Foreign Economic Cooperation has produced a new draft law governing the creation of representative offices of foreign enterprises in Poland. The activities of these offices have tended to exceed the activities originally intended due to the vague nature of the Order.

The draft law unequivocally determines that branches of foreign enterprises are considered foreign enterprises in their own right as defined by the foreign exchange laws. It does not require a permit to be issued to open a branch office but merely obliges the office to keep its accounts and records of the agency freely available.

DISTRIBUTORSHIPS

Polish law does not restrict the establishment of distributorships, nor does it impose any particular provisions on a distributorship contract. Again the principle of freedom of contract is applied. There is no prohibition against granting, for example, rights of exclusivity in relation to particular products or geographical areas, subject to general anti-trust laws.

Most distribution networks in Poland today exist either as a result of the previous regime, under which the FTEs, or state monopolies, controlled trade or, more recently, because private enterprises have established their own distribution networks from the ground up. In the present climate many foreign businesses consider it more prudent, in order to maintain control, efficiency and quality, to establish their own distribution network as opposed to appointing independent distributors. Foreign businessmen that do appoint independent distributors should restrict themselves to simple transactions and commercial arrangements that do not require complex documentation or technical co-ordination, as the Polish business culture is not yet accustomed to Western practices.

FRANCHISING

There are almost no franchises in existence in Poland at present. Again, as with distributorships there are no legal restrictions on establishing franchises other than to remember that the licensing of intellectual property needs to be registered at the Patent Office. This, and the protection of trading names and trademarks owned by the franchiser, are dealt with in the next chapter.

However, there is a great deal of interest in Poland at the moment concerning the concept of franchising. It is seen as a suitable technique for facilitating the privatisation process especially for smaller businesses. While franchising is viewed with some caution by potential foreign franchisors, from the Polish point of view franchising has a number of benefits particularly suitable to a developing economy such as Poland's, including:

- aiding the transfer of know-how, technology and management skills more rapidly than other forms of privatisation;
- the provision of training for managers and staff including exposure to the rigours of the market;

- accelerated delivery of reliable goods and services from the Western industrialised countries; and
- encouragement of foreign investment and acceleration of the transition from a centrally planned economy to a free market one.

CONCLUSION

The businessman will find that opportunities to establish agencies, distributorships and franchises are freely available in Poland. However, although there are few legal restrictions it must be appreciated that Poland is only just coming to terms with the variety of trading schemes and arrangements that are accepted as common practice in many Western countries. Poland's economic, legal and physical infrastructures still have some way to go before the business environment is adapted to these more sophisticated forms of trading.

28

Technology Licensing

Frere Cholmeley

The laws governing the field of intellectual property in Poland are comparatively modern and the businessman who deals with such matters will find a great deal of the content of the Polish laws reasonably familiar. Poland is a member of the World Intellectual Property Organisation and has ratified a number of international conventions on intellectual property. UK nationals generally enjoy the same rights as Poles on the basis of reciprocity.

As Poland is keen to encourage foreign investment and construct an economic environment and legal framework which will enable it to join the EC it can be anticipated that the provisions of the Polish laws concerning intellectual property which require amendment to bring them into line with the practices of West European countries in this field will be carried out as soon as practicable.

The concern for a foreign licensor of intellectual property rights, whether by way of technology transfer or distribution of copyright material or franchise, should be the efficiency with which the law is applied rather than its scope.

PATENTS

Governing law

Poland has ratified the Stockholm text of the Paris Convention of Protection of Industrial Property. Poland is also a signatory to the Agreement on the Unification of Requirements of Preparing and Filing Applications and Inventions concluded in Leipzig in 1975. The terms of the Patent Cooperation Treaty came into force in Poland on 25 December 1990.

Kinds of patents

The following kinds of patents are available on the basis of a patent application filed with the Patent Office:

- patents;
- provisional patents (to be abolished);
- dependent patents;
- patents of addition (to be abolished); and
- secret patents under state control.

Patents, dependent patents and secret patents under state control last for 15 years from the filing date. Discussions are taking place to have the period of a full patent extended to 20 years in common with most other European states. The provisional patent lasts for five years from the filing date, but may be transformed into a full patent in the first four years.

Utility models and designs

The Law on Inventive Activity also regulates the protection of utility models and designs.

A utility model is an original technical design of the shape or construction of an object. A design is an original aesthetic design of any object to be manufactured, similar to a UK Registered Design.

The period of protection for each is five years. This protection may be extended for a further period of up to five years.

Applicant

Application for the grant of a patent may be made by the inventor. There are provisions governing employees' inventions, as in the UK. Patentable inventions are defined broadly in line with the legislation in the UK. Unpatentable inventions include plant varieties, computer programs, and food and chemical products.

Rights and obligations

A patent confers the exclusive right to work the relevant invention in Poland. The patent must be worked in Poland by the patentee or his licensee within four years of the filing date of the application or three years from the date of the grant of the patent, whichever is later. The law also provides for compulsory licences and licences of right. However, no incidents of such licences being granted by the Patent Office in respect of patents granted to foreigners have been recorded.

Applications

Under the Paris Convention an applicant may file, within 12 months of filing in another contracting state, an application for a patent in Poland and claim the original filing date as a priority date in Poland.

The procedures for filing, examination, publication and opposition are all conventional.

Particular rights and obligations

Again these are conventional and include:

- Power to license, subject to registration. There are no specific rules on licence terms.
- Power of patentee or exclusive licensee to sue for an injunction, an account of profits, and/or damages. There are also criminal penalties for infringement and false marking.
- Fees on grant and renewal.
- There are no compulsory marking requirements, although patent number marking on products is common practice.

TRADE MARKS

Governing law

In addition to the international conventions mentioned in the patents section of this Chapter, Poland has also ratified the Madrid Agreement 1891 on the Prosecution for the False Use of Trade Marks and the Nice Agreement of 1957 on the International Classification of Products and Services to which trade or producer marks are applicable.

Kinds of marks

The following forms of mark may be registered:

- trade marks;
- service marks;
- collective marks; and
- trade names.

The applicant must have or represent a business and the application must be for goods or services in the field of the economic activity of that business.

What constitutes a registrable mark and the list of unregistrable marks are conventional, as are the rights conferred and the application procedure.

Priority under the Paris Convention is available and must be claimed when filing or within three months from the filing date. A priority document should also be included with the registration in such a case.

Licensing is permitted, but only provided that the use by the licensee is not deceptive and does not cause confusion. Accordingly, goods bearing the mark licensed to the licensee must show the licensee's name and place of origin.

A registered mark must be used in Poland. If it is proved that for three consecutive years the mark has not been used then this can lead to invalidation of the mark's protection. The registration of a mark is valid for 10 years from the filing date and may be renewed for equivalent periods on payment of the renewal fees.

A mark may only be assigned with all or part of the business to which the mark relates.

The proprietor or his licensee can sue for infringement, and may obtain an injunction and damages. The infringer may be imprisoned. Recent examples of the successful prosecution of trade mark infringers have concerned the use of such marks as 'Wrangler' and 'New Man'.

KNOW-HOW

A number of legal problems in relation to know-how arise in Poland. It is unclear what constitutes know-how under Polish law and how it is protected. In the absence of a contractual relationship, the proprietor of confidential know-how or trade secrets is probably protected only against acts that can be classified as torts or unfair competition.

Deliberate misuse is therefore probably grounds for damages and an injunction, but foreign businesses dealing in Poland should not assume the availability of this protection.

Protection may also be available against unfair competition, which is prohibited by statute. It covers passing off, deliberate use of false information, misuse of confidential information and equivalent unfair trading activities.

WHO CAN HANDLE PATENT AND TRADE MARK APPLICATIONS?

To date, the Minister for Foreign Economic Cooperation has

licensed four specialist firms to conduct business and arrange formalities in the field of patent and trade mark applications filed by foreigners. They are Poleservice, Patpol, Agros Holding and Vimex. These same firms handle patent applications filed by Polish inventors with foreign patent offices.

Activity in the registration of industrial property

In 1990 the number of applications for patents increased by some 10 per cent in Poland and for trade marks the number of applications doubled.

COPYRIGHT

Summary

Poland, like the UK, has acceded to the Rome text of the Berne Convention on Copyright, but has only partially acceded to the later Paris text. Various proposals to reform the copyright laws are currently being considered, although no one draft has been agreed on. Until this has been resolved, the scope and operation of copyright law in Poland may sometimes be less satisfactory to copyright owners than in the UK and other Western European countries.

Particular comments of foreign investors under the existing regime are:

- Periods of protection are short by comparison with many other territories.
- Protection for more recently developed categories of work is not clear-cut in law (eg sound recordings and computer software).
- The wide range of model contracts, fixed royalty rates and compulsory licences is inappropriate to a free market economy and potentially damaging to the commercial interests of copyright owners.
- Moral rights are given broader scope than in some countries and may inhibit commercial activity.
- Piracy has been extensive in certain areas, such as sound and video tapes and computer software.

Forms of copyright

The following works are eligible for protection:

1. literary works (this probably includes computer software);
2. scientific works;
3. artistic works;
4. photographs, provided that an express reservation of copyright is indicated;
5. sound recordings, again provided that the year of recording is marked on them.

This list is illustrative only. The law also provides protection for derivative works, new versions and compilations. Originality is required. Newspaper reports and photographs, industrial designs and public decrees and notices cannot be protected.

Save as noted above, there are no formalities for the acquisition of copyright.

The author's rights include the exclusive right to exploit the work commercially and moral rights.

An author's commercial rights expire twenty five years after his death. There is no limitation in time upon the protection of the author's moral rights. Certain works only acquire protection in respect of commercial rights for ten years - namely, photographs, cinema and stage designs and adaptations of a musical work or sound recording.

As in the UK, reproduction, performance and broadcast are all controlled, with limited exemptions for use for news media, and non-commercial cultural or scientific use.

The moral rights of the author cannot be transferred. Commercial rights can be by licence or assignment, but ordinances of the Minister of Culture and the Arts control the basis and rates of remuneration for authors and establish model contracts. The provisions of these terms and contracts are mandatory and contractual provisions at variance with them are void. These requirements have little or no equivalent in the UK.

It is unnecessary under Polish law for works to be marked with any copyright symbol.

29

Establishing a Presence

Touche Ross & Co

This chapter is an attempt to pass on some observations on day-to-day, practical matters which are part and parcel of doing business from a base in Poland. No summary of this sort can be comprehensive, but an attempt has been made to focus on some essential issues in the context of the very particular Polish business experience. The individual sections cover advice on staffing, office equipment, meetings and a miscellany of otherwise unclassifiable points.

STAFF

By March 1991, staff agencies and head-hunters were beginning to be set up, but it is too early to comment either specifically or on the service generally before reputations are established. Consideration must however be given to the most effective ways of finding the right staff. Initially, and as a minimum, a good local manager will most probably be required. There is no shortage of well-qualified, eager, English-speaking candidates and enquiries through contacts and professional advisers should elicit a short list - or at least the best way of compiling one.

Depending on your business and your location, language may be a problem. Although English is being spoken more and more in Warsaw, especially in the business community, this is not necessarily the case in other parts of the country - another reason for a good, bilingual local manager.

Be prepared for staff commitment to be problematic. Staff should be paid enough to ensure 100 per cent, full-time commitment to you and to your business. A not unexpected legacy of the previous artificially cultivated full employment policy, and its consequent overmanning and plethora of non-jobs, is that it is quite common for people to have two or even three jobs, and to flit between them.

Remember also to make clear from the outset your requirements regarding business confidentiality. Pride in one's work and loyalty to one's employer were not exactly nurtured by the previous work environment, although attitudes are changing fast.

The more aware skilled workers and clerical/professional staff recognise that they have some catching up to do on Western Europe in terms of business know-how. Training is thus much sought after and highly prized. In this context, bear in mind that trips to Head Office in the UK to show 'how it should work' are viewed by Poles as an important perk - and hence should tie them in closer to you and your organisation and build commitment.

Special rules on the employment of expatriates

Polish employment regulations apply to expatriate employees in the areas of employment law, conditions of work, social security and trade union activity. The employment of foreigners by non-Polish employers is possible by following the same procedures which apply to Polish employers (on obtaining the consent, at voivodeship level, of the local authority in which the office or factory is based).

The salaries of a company's employees in Poland are determined and are paid in zlotys. Foreign employees are entitled to exchange their zloty earnings for foreign currency after paying all taxes due. The foreign currency sums thus purchased, may be transferred abroad without the need for any further permit.

OFFICE EQUIPMENT

Communications are generally difficult and will remain so until the telephone system is overhauled and modernised. Having telephones installed takes a long time. If you need to make frequent contact abroad by telephone or facsimile, consideration should be given as soon as possible to ordering a satellite line.

Many firms assemble computers in garages! When purchasing computers, or any other office machinery such as copiers and typewriters, try to apply the same stringent purchasing criteria you would in the UK. Service guarantees should always be sought. Choosing a reliable supplier will pay off in the longer term.

Most items are potentially available, but some prices can be surprising. Some things are better imported - for example, for some reason good quality business cards are twice as expensive in Poland as they are in London, even including freight costs - so remember to compare local prices with UK and other European prices.

The waiting period for an order may be frustratingly long and one is often asked to pay money in advance - negotiate!

If placing a large order for furniture and facing a long wait, consideration should be given to cutting waiting time by buying direct from (say) Germany and then hiring someone with a vehicle to drive there and collect - particularly if the local Polish firm is only doing the same thing, and adding on their costs and profit. Their mark up will pay for your transport costs - and no waiting.

MEETINGS

If you are going to speak to ministries, go with something concrete, and be prepared to make serious proposals. The time for general discussions, if there ever was such a time, has passed.

Be very careful when using translators and interpreters. It is not enough for them to merely know the two languages - your interpreter must also understand your business and, more importantly, both business cultures. He will have to be able to put across or explain concepts for which equivalent words are lacking, as the equivalent underlying concepts do not exist.

When in negotiations spanning a series of meetings, make allowances in your timings for going back over ground already covered and which you thought had been agreed at previous meetings.

There is some turnover within ministries at senior level. If you need to establish contact with senior officials, use a locally based professional adviser, who should be up to date with day-to-day movements, to save wasting time.

On the subject of not wasting time, it is important to deal with the people who can actually take decisions - in the Polish business context, this will usually be the director. Among other management, you may come across a reluctance to take decisions - usually because the person to whom you are talking does not have the power to make agreements which will commit his enterprise. Again, use local assistance to appraise whom it is you are going to meet.

OTHER PRACTICALITIES

Be aware that not all insurance you would expect to take out may actually be available – for example insuring the accountant collecting money from the bank. (In this context, note that many transactions are carried out in cash because of the inefficiencies in the banking system.)

Allowance should also be made for the inefficient banking system when transferring funds from overseas into Poland; it can take two to three weeks to effect a transfer. If large sums are involved, then consideration should be given to sending people by air to collect them physically. The rail and air travel costs involved (which are much cheaper when the purchase is made in Poland) should be compared against the potential loss of interest on the funds.

Expatriate staff may require an overseas health package, and it is best to evaluate what is available early.

Vehicle leasing is still rare in Poland. If you wish to lease, consider the possibilities of leasing from overseas.

It is advisable to make someone responsible for collating changes in the law and regulations affecting your business operations as those changes arise, and to maintain an internal library system for reference. Such information on an up-to-date basis is not as readily available (yet) as in the UK.

A legacy of the former way of doing things is the absence of comprehensive business intelligence. Although things are changing fast, there is still a lack of ready information and what information exists is often not wholly reliable. Spend some time getting to know your market before full-scale market entry.

And finally, another legacy of the previous system: two contrasted attitudes which will without doubt eventually wither away, but which currently have to be faced by an employer: 'It's not possible' is a common response from many people when faced with an unfamiliar question. You will find a great demand on your time for day-to-day problem solving – and so training your staff to solve problems becomes vital. The 'No problem' response is the other side of the coin. The author's experience is that for each task which is requested, out of every 100 people who react with 'no problem', no more than 10 will even think about doing anything about it, and only 2 or 3 will actually see it through to completion without continual reminders.

AFTER-THOUGHTS

It is not merely a truism to say that the law is difficult to interpret. Behind the law there will usually be policy guidelines on interpretation for the relevant ministries, and this may give them considerable leeway in the way they deal with individual cases. If you think you have a reasonable case, be prepared to argue it with the ministry concerned.

One of the legacies of the previously centrally directed economy is a generally high level of bureaucracy, which is by and large improving slowly. One of the effects of Poland's espousal of a free market economy is the amount of new, or newly dusted off, commercial legislation. One consequence for the British businessman (as well as for the Polish businessman) is that most matters requiring official input or endorsement generally take much longer to accomplish than their equivalent in the West. For example, one should not expect to form a company in a week! The almost inevitable problems and delays should be anticipated and allowed for in your timetable. They will thus be less likely to be as serious as their unforeseen occurrence, at the last minute, within a tight timetable.

30

Making an Investment

The Polish Investment Company

The Polish government has embarked on an ambitious programme of rapid privatisation for the approximately 7000 state-owned enterprises that make up the bulk of Polish industry. This programme will enhance the flow of opportunities already available to foreign trade investors. When coupled with the progressive liberalisation of foreign exchange and tax regimes it creates an environment where a rapid entry to the Polish and East European market can be best accomplished by the acquisition of a significant stake in a Polish enterprise.

In 1990, the Foreign Investment Agency ('FIA') handled 1800 applications to establish joint ventures in Poland. This was a twofold increase on 1989, when some 850 such applications were made. The total equity value of the joint ventures established in 1990 was US$506 million of which US$350 million was capital invested by foreign participants. According to the FIA, the largest equity input at US$113 milion was from Germany with the United Kingdom in second place with US$106 million.

Historically, these joint ventures have tended to be small and have been financed from the internal resources of the foreign businesses involved. Globally to date, foreign investment has averaged US$280,000 per joint venture, and this average masks the very many joint ventures established at the minimum level of foreign participation (US$50,000) required by the Foreign Investment Law ('FIL').

For example, the average size of joint ventures established by German business amounts to US$188,000. However, joint ventures with the USA are even smaller at an average of US$168,000. Now, with liberalisation of the Polish economy and with clear signs that the economic reform programme is working, it is becoming apparent that substantial foreign companies are increasingly looking to Poland as their stepping-stone into the markets of Eastern Europe.

In particular in 1990, the UK invested some US$106 million in 90 joint ventures, up from 42 the year before. With the notable exception of certain hotel start-up projects, nearly all substantial foreign joint ventures involve the foreign party in a buy-in of an existing Polish (state-owned) enterprise. This trend is likely to be further developed by the stated commitment of the new government to accelerate the privatisation programme and the proposal currently going through parliament to liberalise further the FIL.

MAKING AN ACQUISITION

Having identified a potential acquisition target the first step is to determine its eligibility for transformation into a limited liability company (*Spółka Akcyjna SA*). Some enterprises which are of strategic importance are not eligible for removal from the state sector in total, but part of them may be separable and eligible for foreign participation.

The transformation may be accomplished by statutory reorganisation or by liquidation made under the Privatisation of State-owned Enterprises Act. In turn, the statutory reorganisation may be voluntary on the part of the enterprise management and the workers' council or compulsory, based on the application of the Minister for Privatisation. Any statutory reorganisation (except for liquidation) vests in the workers of the enterprise the right to aquire at a discount up to 20 per cent of the shares of the new limited liability company. There are a number of other legal issues which need to be addressed in the process of creating a legal entity suitable for acquisition and financing. The salient areas are the gaining of all the necessary permissions and the verification of all legal titles to fixed assets.

Having defined the investment vehicle the next step is to prepare a valuation (see page 96) – a process fraught with commercial and political difficulties. The valuation of the Gdańsk shipyard in November 1989 is well remembered as the first signal of differing views between the Polish government and incoming investors. In that case agreement was not reached.

Having convinced the management and work-force that the acquisition is in their interest and having agreed at least some outline of value, the question of funding of the acquisition needs to be addressed. As far as internal funding of the target is concerned, funding availability from Polish banks would probably be maintained and could possibly be increased due to the perceived extra management credibility injected by the foreign investor. However, it should be remembered that Polish zloty borrowings carry an interest cost at the time of writing of about 70 per cent per annum.

It may be possible to consider some form of hedged currency borrowings but any such arrangement has to be structured so as to comply with current exchange control regulations.

EQUITY INVESTMENT

Finally, the question arises of equity investment. From the point of view of the foreign trade investor it is this area which is developing most rapidly. Equity funding is already available from the Industrial Development Agency and might be available from the Polish Development Bank in suitable cases. There are also a number of Western equity funds which either have or are in the process of targeting Poland as an investment focus. For all these institutional investors, a combination of market potential, and sound productive capability provided by the Polish input, together with the managerial know-how of a well-established Western company provide an attractive investment package.

Naturally, as part of any investment proposal and in addition to the above the trade investor will need to provide some prospect of exit for the institutional investor.

The Industrial Development Agency is the main organisation responsible for providing technical and financial assistance to industrial enterprises in the restructuring process. It has been allocated substantial funds of the order of US$200 million which it intends to use to invest in the equity of companies which are being restructured.

The Polish Development Bank, which is still in a formative stage of development, has the task of sponsoring industrial growth through cooperation with commercial banks, primarily in the area of developing long-term lending. Its primary role is unlikely to include direct lending to enterprises unless there are special circumstances such as the size, risk or strategic importance of an investment.

A number of Western institutions have launched or are about to launch investment funds targeted at Poland. MIM and Beta have existing funds in place which include Poland as a preferred location, and a large bank is about to launch a major country fund for Poland.

Investor experience so far is very limited. The only oblique example which can be quoted is the case of Universal SA, a Polish trading company and the largest public share sale to date on the Polish market.

In August 1990, Universal sold shares at the equivalent of US$2 each to the Polish public. Some $20 million were raised by this issue. The shares are currently quoted at the equivalent of $3.40 on a rudimentary over-the-counter market run by Bank IG. The dividend for 1990 was 80 per cent and when aggregated with the increase in the share price, will clearly constitute an attractive rate of return to investors.

In conclusion, Poland has both debt and equity sources of finance of a type familiar to the UK businessman. Although the methods of concluding transactions are rather different and more complex than those practised in the UK, the current pricing of deals, the potential returns and the ability of industrial investors to spread risk by involving institutional capital make such transactions well worth considering.

31

Forms of Investment

Frere Cholmeley

Previous chapters have dealt with the various methods of investing in Poland, including the opportunities and advantages available to the foreign investor under the amended 1988 Foreign Investment Law (FIL) and connected legislation, the alternatives in the form of agency or branch offices and the types of property which may be acquired.

The FIL gives the choice of two company structures, the limited liability company and the joint stock company. The former is more popular and flexible. Joint stock companies are primarily intended for substantial and (in due course) publicly quoted operations. Each form of company can be used either as a joint venture vehicle with at least 20 per cent of share capital contributed by the foreign investor or as 100 per cent foreign-owned subsidiaries, although it is hoped that the minimum contribution requirement will be removed in the near future.

The Commercial Code 1934, as amended, governs their formation, registration and administration. Businessmen who have set up a new company in the UK will find much that is familiar in their basic structure. The considerable time likely to be taken (up to seven or eight months in busy areas) in complying with the formation formalities will, however, be unfamiliar and, as trading prior to incorporation leads to personal liability on the part of those involved, sufficient time should be allowed to establish the company.

Before deciding on a corporate structure, the foreign investor should consider whether an agency or branch office would be more convenient. The formalities may be less detailed. On the other hand a company, even if foreign owned, may in specific cases have preferential treatment, as a Polish entity, by comparison with a branch office.

HOW TO FIND A JOINT VENTURE PARTNER

The first issue to decide is whether or not a Polish partner is needed. Apart from the commercial contributions that a local partner may make (assets, know-how, connections, etc), in certain cases a Polish partner may reduce the need for licences or may enable activities to be conducted that are prohibited to a 100 per cent foreign-owned company. For example the need for a licence to acquire property from the Ministry of Internal Affairs may be avoided.

Whether or not the aim is a joint venture, the Commercial Office of the Polish Consulate in London will be able to help with initial contacts in Poland. The Eastern Europe Trade Council also keeps a list of potential Polish partners. Once in Poland the Foreign Investment Agency (FIA) and the Chamber of Foreign Investors, both in Warsaw, will assist with contacts and introductions to potential partners and economic, legal and other advisers.

PERMITS

The next step is to obtain a permit (the fee is Z1.2 million) from the FIA as required under the FIL, although it is intended to simplify the process so that permits may soon be needed only in certain sensitive sectors or where one joint venture partner is a state-owned enterprise. The permit application will be completed by legal and economic advisers (see Appendix 2 for the layout) and may take up to two months to process. Additional permits may be required to purchase land or undertake economic activities in some sectors such as banking, insurance and mining.

THE COMPANY REGISTERS

There is no national company register. Instead there are about 100 local registers, held by the Polish equivalent of the County Court, which is responsible for the administration and enforcement of company regulations generally. A company must register with the local register responsible for the area in which its registered office is to be situated. The register and the documents filed with it are open to the public and may be inspected by going to the relevant Court. It contains:

1. company name, registration number and registered office address;

2. objects;
3. amount of share capital, how it is to be divided between shareholders and whether paid-up in cash or in kind;
4. full names of board members and details of their authority to represent the company, with specimen signatures (the need to specify the authority of individual directors is an important improvement on the uncertainty that still exists in the UK);
5. term for which the company has been formed (if any);
6. details of the journal in which official announcements regarding the company are to be made.

For joint stock companies it will also state:

1. nominal value and number of ordinary shares;
2. nominal value and number of preference shares and details of any special rights attached;
3. level of paid-up share capital.

It does not show the level of the company's borrowings nor give any details of mortgages. The penalties that may be imposed on a company for incorrect entries include fines or even removal from the register.

CHOOSING THE BUSINESS NAME

Polish business names provisions are similar to those in the UK. A name may be selected freely within certain parameters but the words *Spółka Akcynia* (joint stock company) or *Spółka Z Ograniczoną Odpowiedzialnością* (limited liability company) must appear. The name may include the name of an individual, but only with consent. It may also be descriptive of the business involved, but not if this may be misleading in any way.

It is important to be aware that names cannot be changed without incorporating a new company, and can only be transferred by purchasing the whole of a company's business.

In theory, it is not possible to register a name which is the same or very similar to that of an existing company in the same locality, but in practice this rule has been difficult to enforce. Internationally recognised names may be better protected than others as the registration application contains sufficient information to show whether or not the applicants are genuine. If problems arise with a company name, an investor should inform the FIA and the Registry Court and may be able to start proceedings to obtain an injunction and/or damages for wrongful use of industrial property rights.

LIMITED LIABILITY COMPANIES

Formation

The four consecutive steps for forming a limited liability company are:

1. conclusion of the Charter;
2. calling in and paying up of its entire initial share capital;
3. the appointment of the board and supervisory authorities (if any);
4. registration and incorporation.

Applications to register a company must be made within six months of the conclusion of the Charter or this will lapse and have to be reissued. The board makes the application, which should include:

- the FIA permit;
- the Charter;
- a declaration by all board members that the capital has been paid in and that the assignments of any non-cash contributions have been ensured;
- a list of contributions with details of their interests signed by all board members;
- specimen signatures of all board members authenticated by a notary or the Registry Court;
- (where the first board or supervisory council members are not named in the Charter) a list of these and proof of their appointment;
- a fee of Z20,000 (paid in court fee stamps at the time of registration).

If the local register is a busy one (eg Warsaw), registration could take three months or more. Shelf companies do not exist. Only one shareholder is required to incorporate a limited liability company.

Within two weeks of registration, a copy of the Charter certified by the board must be filed with the FIA indicating the court at which the company was registered and showing the date of incorporation and registration number.

The company charter

The Charter is the equivalent of both Memorandum and Articles of Association and contains the type of provisions one would expect to find in these, namely the rules which govern a company's internal and external organisation. The Charter enables some of the basic administrative provisions found in the Commercial Code to be altered by contradiction. There is no Polish equivalent of the UK's standard Articles of Association. The Charter should specify whether the company is to do business throughout Poland or internationally rather than merely in the area in which it is registered.

The Charter must be notarised and the fees are: 3 per cent of capital up to Z250 million; plus 0.01 per cent above Z250 million.

Capital duty calculated on a sliding scale up to a maximum of Z2 million on capital of up to Z200 million plus 0.1 per cent on capital above that level is payable at the same time. In busy areas it could take up to three months to notarise a charter.

The Charter could be drawn up in a language other than Polish. However, in such a case a certified Polish translation prepared by a qualified translator or a Polish diplomatic mission or consular office must be submitted.

Share capital

The FIL minimum requirement for a foreign investor is the zloty equivalent of US$50,000, although it is intended to remove this, so that all companies, irrespective of foreign involvement, will have to fulfil the lower capital requirements set out in the Commercial Code, which are also under review. Share capital may be divided into shares of equal or unequal amounts and may be contributed in cash or in kind although the FIA may require independent valuations of non-cash contributions.

The Charter should state whether a member may hold more than one share; if only single share holdings are permitted, then the nominal value of each member's share will reflect the actual value of that member's share capital contribution. If any member is entitled to hold more than one share, all shares in the company must have an equal face value (denominated in zloty, minimum Z500,000) and be indivisible. It is possible to pay a premium on shares. They will bear the rights ascribed to them in the Charter and, subject to certain Commercial Code requirements (eg each shareholder must have at least one vote), the shareholders are free to choose what these will be.

FIA permits are required for capital increases or changes in the nature and value of contributions. Capital may be increased by resolution of the shareholders and will involve an amendment to the Charter as well as payment of capital duty (see above).

As in the UK, the procedure for reducing share capital is complicated and involves a series of announcements at specified intervals and the repayment or securing of creditors claims against the company.

Shareholder rights and obligations

The shareholders appoint the board and the supervisory council (if any) and are entitled to supervise the activities of the company. As in the UK, shareholders holding a prescribed fraction of the share capital may exercise special rights (eg, 10 per cent of the share capital offers a right to call a meeting of the company). Shareholder resolutions are required for important transactions such as selling the company's business. They are passed at meetings or in writing signed by every shareholder and the type of majority required at meetings depends on the business being transacted.

An ordinary general meeting, the equivalent of the annual general meeting, must be held within four months of the company's year-end to approve its accounts, the payment of dividends and the activities of the board. This cannot be done by written resolution. The Commercial Code does not specify a quorum for meetings so this may be regulated in the Charter. All meetings should be held at the registered office or in the area where the company is registered and can be attended in person or by proxy. It should be noted that the Commercial Code provides for appeal against resolutions by way of a court action.

Unless otherwise specified in the Charter, existing shareholders have pre-emption rights on an increase of share capital in proportion to their existing shareholdings. Unlike the UK, where there are sufficient net profits, they are entitled to dividends in proportion to the face value of their shares, unless the Charter provides otherwise.

A shareholder may be excluded from the company by court

action on the application of all the other shareholders holding at least 50 per cent of the share capital.

Board, supervisory council and audit commission

Each company must have a board to manage and represent it in its day-to-day affairs, consisting of at least one person who could also be a shareholder. Board members must be reappointed every year at the ordinary meeting but may be dismissed at any time. Their actions are limited by the provisions of the Commercial Code and the Charter. For example a board member may not vote in a matter where there is a conflict of interest between himself or his relatives and the company, which is more restrictive than the corresponding UK position. Board resolutions require a simple majority of members present at the meeting. The Commercial Code does not specify a quorum.

The Charter can establish a supervisory council ('council') or an audit commission ('commission') or both; a company must establish a council if it has more than 50 shareholders and its share capital is in excess of Z250,000,000. Each of these bodies must have at least three members, who cannot also be board members, elected every year at the ordinary meeting. Their duties are to supervise the company's and the board's activities and produce an annual written report. To this end they are entitled to investigate the whole of the company's business and require reports and explanations from board members and company employees. Their powers may be further extended by the Charter.

Continuing registration requirements and changes

The board must keep a shareholders' register. Any changes to this must be filed with the Registry Court. It must also keep minutes of general meetings and copies of all resolutions adopted. Any changes to the composition of the board, council or commission should also be filed. A resolution amending the Charter requires minuting by a notary and will not be effective until registered which could take the court up to three months to process. The fees for filing amendments are minimal.

Transfer/sale, liquidation/dissolution and merger

The transfer of shares may be subject to the requirement of an FIA permit for foreign investment companies, the provisions of a company's Charter, or even the terms of international treaties. Transfers should be in writing and require notarisation and registration, but there is no stamp duty equivalent payable.

Liquidation of a company will take place prior to dissolution, the board usually being appointed as liquidators. Liquidators have much the same function as they do in the UK and can be appointed by the shareholders or the court. Announcements must be made, as for a reduction of capital, and at least six months must elapse after the last of these before any assets can be distributed to shareholders. The process will be different if the company is insolvent. When the liquidation has been completed, the liquidators will apply for dissolution by having the company removed from the register.

The meaning of 'merger' in Poland is narrower than the general term used in the UK and is effected by asset assignment, either from one existing company to another or into a newly incorporated company, in exchange for shares. The Commercial Code sets out the requisite procedure, which again involves announcements and may involve a share capital increase in the acquiring company to enable it to issue new shares to pay for the assets. In all cases the companies transferring assets will be removed from the register and all their rights and obligations will pass to the acquiring company.

Exceptions to limited liability

Individuals who transact any business in the name of a company before incorporation will be personally liable. If shares are issued for non-cash consideration on incorporation, which do not reflect the true value of the assets contributed, and the company becomes insolvent within three years, the contributor and the board members who applied for registration could be jointly and severally liable to make up any difference.

Shareholders may be required to make supplementary payments into the company to cover balance sheet losses; this does not involve an increase in share capital. The Charter may specify the amount and time limit for such payments, which should be in proportion to the relevant member's shareholding; statutory interest may be charged on any late payments. Supplementary payments can be repaid under certain circumstances.

Typical documentation

A separate joint venture agreement is not required but may be entered into. As it need not be registered it may reflect aspects of the venture that are to be kept private (eg further financing, profit distributions, share purchase options and so on). Its contents will be much the same as one would expect to find in a joint venture/ shareholders' agreement in the UK. It could be used to specify a governing law other than Polish law.

JOINT STOCK COMPANIES

Joint stock companies may be formed by public subscription, although this is not essential. The Commercial Code contains complicated formation and valuation procedures where non-cash share capital contributions are to be made or where capital is to be raised by public subscription.

A joint stock company must have three founder members who must sign its Charter prior to notarisation except where it has been formed as a result of a transformation under the privatisation legislation, when all its shares will be held by the State Treasury.

As regards share capital:

1. For an FIL company the minimum share capital is as for limited liability companies. However, if the FIL is changed as currently envisaged the minimum will be Z250 million.

2. Share capital is divided into equal indivisible shares with a face value of at least Z10,000.

3. Shares issued in return for non-cash contributions must have their total nominal value paid-up before registration, cash shares need only be one-quarter paid up, while the whole of any premium must be covered.

4. Special preference shares may be issued; the rights attached to these should be described in the Charter and could be dependant on making additional payments to the company. The Commercial Code does set out some limitations on preferential rights - for example it is not possible to have more than five votes per share.

In contrast to a limited liability company, the first board members may be appointed for a period of not more than two years and thereafter for periods of three years. Minutes of all board meetings must be kept. A joint stock company must have either a council or commission although its Charter may require both; a council is essential where the share capital exceeds Z5 million. Both bodies should be composed of at least five members who will be appointed initially for a term of not more than one year and for subsequent periods not exceeding three years.

Many of the provisions governing joint stock companies are similar to those for limited liability companies although there are often additional safe-guards and procedures to be followed. The shares of joint stock companies may be sold to and subscribed for by the general public; it is intended that their shares, but not those of limited liability companies, may be sold on the stock exchange, once this has been established. Although the only vehicle available for flotation, the joint stock company is more cumbersome and the limited liability company has proved more popular with foreign investors.

TRANSFORMATION OF COMPANIES

The transformation of a limited liability company into a joint stock company and vice versa is regulated by the Commercial Code. It should be noted, however, that in contrast to the UK, such transformations occur very rarely.

OTHER STRUCTURES

Partnerships may be formed by Polish nationals under the Civil Code 1964; limited partnerships are not available as structures under Polish law as these chapters of the Commercial Code have been repealed. It is the intention to reintroduce limited partnerships in the near future, although currently there are no plans to allow foreign investors to use partnership structures.

Foreigners doing business in Poland may come across state enterprises, which are not companies in the strict sense. Nevertheless the legal provisions which govern these provide for registration and management along similar lines to companies. Details of these entities will be found in a separate register kept alongside the company register at the appropriate Court. Another common structure is the civil company, for Polish citizens only, consisting of at least two members. Liability is unlimited and they are registered at the regional financial administration offices under the aegis of the Ministry of Finance, not the company register.

A foreign investor might also find an individual entrepreneur as a potential partner, or even a cooperative. The latter is a separate and private legal entity with limited liability consisting of at least three persons, entered in the Register of Cooperatives kept at the Company Registry Court.

CONCLUSION

To date nearly all companies formed under the FIL have been limited liability companies because formation is simpler, fewer members and no supervisory authority are needed, more control may be retained by members over the transfer of shares and dividend rights may be more easily limited. When deciding which structure to use, the potential investor should consider the size of investment that he wishes to make, the involvement and contribution of a Polish partner and the more stringent and complicated procedures that have to be observed by a joint stock company.

32

Accounting Issues

Touche Ross & Co

Changes in the accountancy laws effected in January 1991 have attempted to bring Poland more into line with EC accounting standards. To many who look at a Polish balance sheet or profit and loss account the presentation, quite apart from the language difference, looks exceedingly complex - and many investors may be led to assume that everything underlying this is also complex.

It is fair to say that, at present, financial statements drawn up in Polish are not particularly useful to a Western investor. This is hardly surprising as the basis for their preparation is totally different. Polish financial statements are drawn up for statistical purposes and are tax-driven. They are thus bound to be different from those prepared in order to provide management information, as in the West.

For example, in Polish accounts, liabilities on the balance sheet will be split into local currency and hard currency - previously a necessary control. We would show one figure. Again, costs are split within the profit and loss account to show overall direct and indirect amounts, rather than splits which can be used to control individual cost categories.

However, there is nothing arcane about Polish accountancy. The same principles of double entry, of debit and credit, are used. There may be some differences in techniques, but the key difference is one of presentation. It is straightforward to represent a Polish balance sheet in UK format and, utilising additional analyses from the books of account, the profit and loss account can also be represented.

Experience has shown that internal controls are much better than in the UK - if anything there are too many controls, not all of which are cost-effective from the UK point of view. However, they are demanded by Polish law, which is very strict in this respect. Documentation, too, is abundant and the standard of books and records is of the highest order.

Polish accountants are extremely good bookkeepers - indeed, historically, that has been their main function. One cannot, however, equate the role of an accountant in the UK with one in Poland. Generally speaking, the functions carried out by a company accountant in the UK will, in Poland, be performed by somebody with the job title of, say, Economic Director.

SOME KEY AREAS IN THE FINANCIAL STATEMENTS

Fixed assets

These will be booked at cost, but are subject to periodic revaluations imposed by the Ministry of Finance. These revaluations represent an attempt to show replacement cost in the balance sheet by taking into account the inflation rate. However, they can lead to serious distortions. For example, the book value of one machine was some US$1 million higher than the cost of importing a new machine. (As it is illegal to overstate the value of assets in the accounts, there is an obvious problem here for the poor company accountant.)

Depreciation has historically been much lower than we would consider reasonable because the system has been tax driven - large depreciation allowances would decrease profits and so lessen the taxation due to the State. While the new regulations now in force have increased depreciation rates, there is still no outright recognition of the concept of an asset's useful life.

Thus from a UK perspective, fixed assets may be stated at a higher cost in Polish accounts than they would be in UK accounts.

Debtors

The concept of collectibility of debts is not always understood by Polish directors as, historically, bad debts have not been a problem. Amounts due have usually been collected, even after one or two years - it is only after court actions that debts are written off.

However, as the new economic reforms will mean bankruptcies for the weaker enterprises, it should be borne in mind that a company owing money may not necessarily be in existence in one year's time.

The introduction of some credit control procedures in your joint venture could save money in the future. If aged debtors listings are not produced, they cannot be used as a management tool.

One feature of the way debts are accounted for in Poland is that the older the debt, the larger it becomes, as interest is charged and added to it. The amounts presented in the balance sheet are progressively increased - this does not, however, mean that the debtor will eventually pay. Because of this accrued interest factor, debts are consistently overstated (in contrast to the UK practice of providing against and writing down old and doubtful debts).

Stocks

These will often be at very high levels because companies will have been used to producing against plan but without much thought to demand - another legacy of the old system of production targets. There will, therefore, often be considerable working capital tied up in stocks.

The new regulations now allow stocks to be shown in balance sheet at cost plus related freight and duty costs. This has not always been the case, so care must be exercised when examining older financial statements. Obsolete stocks, if they are damaged, will be allowed for by reducing the amount stated in the balance sheet. However, slow moving stocks should be scrutinised. With production levels often too high in relation to demand, many stocks could be unsaleable and overvalued - with their net realisable value maybe even close to scrap value.

The 1990 profit and loss account

Great care should be taken when looking at any 1990 profit and loss accounts: the lifting of price control restrictions, together with the fact that stock levels were previously very high has meant that:

- in many cases companies have been selling at higher prices in 1990, but their costs of sales are artificially low because they were using up their cheap stocks, produced when there were still price restrictions; and, therefore
- many companies have made very good profits in 1990 - one should not assume that this performance will necessarily be repeated.

FINANCIAL CONTROL AND MONITORING

As important as the initial planning is the regular monitoring of performance in a format which provides meaningful management information. This information must be such that decisions are capable of being taken at an early stage should managerial intervention be required.

In Poland's constantly changing environment, speed of reaction is crucial. Copies of Polish financial statements will not under normal circumstances be sufficient - at least not for the moment.

It will be advantageous, at the earliest stage possible, to set up the requisite reporting methods: the Polish plan of accounts (which has a minimum number of account headings defined by law) should be further sub-analysed to give sufficient additional categories in order for key management information to be collected for future use.

Remember that Polish accountants are excellent bookkeepers - time spent at the start training and explaining your exact requirements is time well spent. The Polish accountant, depending on his status, may not be capable of taking decisions based on the information but will certainly be more than capable of collating the information needed if properly briefed.

The process of westernising Polish accounts can be set up as a mechanical process using standard formats - cross referencing each Polish account into the appropriate slot within the UK accounts. Simple computer spreadsheets can make this process even quicker.

33

Dispute Resolution

Frere Cholmeley

In law as in medicine, prevention is better than cure. If disputes can be avoided at the outset then time, effort and expense can be saved. Commercial disputes often arise out of conflicting interpretations of a loosely worded contract. In order to reduce the risks of a dispute arising ensure a clearly written contract which deals with potential areas of conflict.

The best approach is to agree terms in advance for settling disputes. For example:

1. Refer any dispute to arbitration either in Poland or in another country.
2. If arbitration is not desirable then specify that the courts of a particular country are to have the exclusive right to hear the dispute.
3. Specify which country's law should apply.

There may be restrictions on how far parties have the choice to specify a particular law and to grant to the courts of one country exclusive rights to hear a dispute. The 1965 Code of Polish Private International Law provides detailed rules. In particular, if the dispute concerns land or buildings in Poland then the Polish courts may claim exclusive rights to hear the case - that is, exclusive jurisdiction.

Disputes can also arise where there is no contract between the parties. Here it will not be possible to specify in advance the means of resolving potential disputes.

If a dispute cannot be resolved amicably then there are four alternative ways of solving it:

1. in the English courts or the courts of another country outside Poland;
2. in the Polish courts;
3. arbitration in Poland;
4. arbitration in England or another country outside Poland.

Additionally mediation services may be used although there is little or no experience of formal mediation in Poland.

THE ENGLISH COURTS OR OTHER NON-POLISH COURTS

If you are in dispute with a Polish organisation which has a base and assets in England, then this first option might be best, if the contract allows it. English law should be specified as well as English court jurisdiction. However difficult issues of conflict of law arise here and care should be taken. For example the Code of Polish Private International Law specifies for contracts that, though the parties are free to choose which law shall apply, the chosen law must be connected with the contract.

The use of English courts is not to be recommended if the Polish defendant has no assets in England but only in Poland. A successful plaintiff in England would then be faced with the task of enforcing an English court judgment in Poland, which is fraught with difficulties. The main difficulty is that Polish law requires there to be an international agreement in place between Poland and another country before it will allow the enforcement in Poland of a judgment obtained in that other country. There is no such agreement in force between England and Poland, and the same problem arises with many other countries.

THE POLISH COURTS

The Polish courts may be a better forum if the Polish defendant has substantial assets in Poland but none outside. Polish courts will usually have jurisdiction if the defendant resides in Poland and if the dispute concerns an obligation which arose in Poland, or is to be performed in Poland.

Courts are divided into district courts (for smaller claims) and provincial courts (for larger ones). Each deal only with disputes relating to their own region and there is no central court as there is in England. Appeals go direct to the Supreme Court. There are plans for an intermediate Court of Appeal to be formed.

In 1989 commercial courts were set up. These commercial courts operate as chambers within provincial or voivodeship courts. Provided the subject matter is of a commercial nature, these courts will have jurisdiction over disputes involving a foreign plaintiff or defendant. Patent disputes and disputes over unfair competition can be heard by these courts.

The commercial system is in its infancy but it is hoped that the judges and advocates of these courts will develop a reasonable degree of expertise in handling commercial disputes, in particular those involving foreign trade and investment.

Proçedure in the commercial courts is similar to the English system with written statements of claim followed by an oral hearing at trial.

Poland has experienced legal advocates who deal with court cases regarding property, criminal, family and other matters. However, there are few practising advocates who have experience of commercial cases. Until recently commercial disputes were dealt with only in arbitration, where academic experts in the relevant legal subject are often used. Lawyers for commercial claims in Poland must therefore be selected with great care.

Polish awards

It is possible to obtain awards of damages and/or specific performance but commercial-style injunctions, such as those freezing a defendant's assets prior to judgment, are not obtainable. Money awards will be granted in zloty, the Polish currency. If an award is obtained, it can then be converted into foreign currency in Poland and taken out of Poland.

Suing a state organisation

In the past, suing a state organisation was regarded as potentially more hazardous than suing a private company because of the possible defence of state immunity. However, state involvement in Polish companies has changed recently. Rather than being direct organs of the state, the relationship of the state to a Polish company is now one of a shareholder to a limited company. These limited companies are private and there arc, in theory at least, no particular difficulties in suing them.

Limitation of actions

As in other countries, it is necessary to bring a court action in Poland within a finite period after the cause of action arose. Care must be taken not to delay as there are different limitation periods depending on the nature of the claim. Time periods can be quite short, so if a dispute arises the legal position should be considered as soon as possible.

Costs

In Poland, court costs must be advanced by the party starting the proceedings. If requested by a defendant, a foreign plaintiff is under a duty to provide a deposit as security for the defendant's costs unless the foreign plaintiff has sufficient assets in Poland to cover potential costs.

The general position on costs is as in England. The loser has to pay the winner's costs. Legal costs in Poland can now be very high, particularly in international commercial matters.

ARBITRATION IN POLAND

An alternative to the courts is to use arbitration as a means of resolving disputes. Arbitration is a well-developed method of dispute resolution in Poland. In the past, foreign traders have been encouraged to submit disputes to arbitration, either by signing contractual provisions in advance or by agreement when the dispute starts. There are four courts of arbitration in Poland, the main one being situated in Warsaw and attached to the Polish Chamber of Commerce. The Polish Chamber of Commerce is a new body and replaces the now extinct Polish Chamber of Foreign Trade. This court delivered 235 awards in 1990 and is both active and experienced in foreign trade disputes.

The dispute is normally heard before three arbitrators though it can be heard before just one. The arbitrators will apply the law which has the closest connection to the dispute, although consideration will be given to the intention of the parties before the dispute arose. Indeed, a particular law can be specified in the initial contract. The decision of the arbitrators is final and there is no right of appeal to the Polish courts. However, a party may request an award of an arbitration court to be set aside on certain grounds including procedural irregularity.

The arbitration procedure is normally an oral hearing in open court. A copy of the court's rules is available in English. The Polish language is used unless both parties request a hearing in a different language. An interpreter will be provided by the court if needed. Awards are in zloty but convertible to non-Polish currency and transferable out of Poland if required.

In addition to formal court arbitrations, the court has a set of rules applicable to *ad hoc* arbitrations. *Ad hoc* arbitrations give the parties complete choice over the rules for the conduct of the arbitration.

The losing party to an arbitration may comply voluntarily. If this is not the case then it is possible to obtain a stamp of enforceability from the Polish courts. The award can then be enforced in Poland as if it were a court judgment.

ARBITRATION IN ENGLAND OR OTHER NON-POLISH TERRITORY

As the Polish system is unfamiliar, arbitration in England or any other country, for example an ICC arbitration in Paris, may be preferred. If so, the contract should deal with the point and should state the law that is to apply.

If England is the chosen place for arbitration then there are the advantages of the familiarity of English law. There is, however, the issue of how an award of an English arbitral tribunal should be enforced. It may be necessary to enforce in Poland if that is where the defendant organisation has its assets.

Enforcing arbitral awards of one country in another country

The 1958 New York convention on arbitration deals with the enforcement of foreign arbitral awards. Both England and Poland are signatories. This means that English arbitral awards can be enforced in Poland and Polish arbitral awards can be enforced in England provided the dispute is of a commercial nature. Enforcement is in accordance with local procedural rules.

The merits of arbitration v. court litigation

For international trade disputes, arbitration, in Poland or elsewhere may well be preferred to court proceedings in Poland. Arbitrators will generally have greater experience in dealing with complex commercial matters and in dealing with any particular linguistic difficulties. Arbitration can also provide a quicker solution than court proceedings in Poland. Costs can be high in both cases, depending on the type of dispute.

If England is to be chosen as the forum for settling a claim against a Polish defendant, then arbitration should be adopted if it may be necessary to enforce the award or judgment in Poland. This is because there is no treaty in place to enforce English court judgments in Poland, or Polish ones in England.

It is possible that with the development of the new Polish commercial courts litigation will become more attractive as a means of resolving disputes, but this development may well be accompanied by a growth in the activities of the Polish Court of Arbitration together with increasing expertise developed by the arbitrators. Certainly, for the time being, arbitration is likely to remain the preferred method of settling foreign trade disputes in Poland.

Part IV

Case Studies

Case Study 1

Trusthouse Forte

Report of an interview with Christopher Melchers, director of corporate development, Trusthouse Forte.

Trusthouse Forte has established a joint venture with Orbis, the Polish state-run tourist agency, in order to refurbish and run the five-star Bristol Hotel in central Warsaw. This ambitious project will have been over four-and-a-half years in the making when the hotel finally opens its doors to the public in October 1992. For a number of reasons this project generated a range of problems not experienced by other Western companies. Firstly, Trusthouse Forte's relationship with Orbis predates the upheavals in 1989 by nearly two years and thus they had to keep a grip on the project against a background of exceptionally rapid and unexpected change. Secondly, the operation of a quality hotel leans heavily on personal service which is seen as one of the most backward aspects of Eastern European economies. Moreover, since it is not possible to bring such an operation slowly on stream, it has to be up and running 100 per cent from day one.

The Bristol Hotel building, constructed at the beginning of the 20th century and designed in the Art Nouveau style by Otto Wagner, occupies a special place in Polish national history. It became the seat of government in the inter-war period, and was one of the few buildings in central Warsaw to survive World War II intact. Subsequently, it was used as a hotel by Orbis who operated it until the late-1970s when it was closed. An Austrian construction company (Hofman & Maculan) was negotiating the contract for its refurbishment, but the financiers (principally Creditanstalt backed by Austrian export credit guarantees) were reluctant to provide the £20 million in foreign currency loans needed to complete the project unless a Western company with a proven record played a part in the finished hotel's operation. Following a series of informal contacts with the Austrians, Trusthouse Forte became involved as part of its strategy to obtain a presence in any major European city where a sufficient volume of businessmen are likely to be looking for high quality accommodation.

Trusthouse Forte's business is centred around hotels, restaurants, and contract catering, generating sales in 1989–90 in excess of £2.4 billion. The hotel division has interests in the UK (where it is the nation's largest hotelier), Europe, the USA, and North Africa. At the time of writing its substantive involvement with ongoing projects in Eastern Europe is limited to joint ventures in Warsaw, Prague and Moscow.

The two-and-a-half years of negotiations that ensued proved complex and difficult. This was partly because of Orbis's initial lack of enthusiasm for the whole deal. Accustomed as it was to control of the whole Polish industry, the arrival of a foreign independent centre of control was not easy to assimilate. This was compounded by the insistence of both Trustehouse Forte and the financiers of the project that Trusthouse Forte be granted full management control. Another group with misgivings about such an organisational structure were the trade unions; large and influential organisations in Poland. Not surprisingly they were reluctant to concede to an employer the right to hire and fire and set wages as they chose. The negotiation process was also complicated by the fact that although Trusthouse Forte was ostensibly dealing with just Orbis, representatives from workers' councils and the local communist hierarchy would often be present at meetings as observers.

During this extended period of negotiations Trusthouse Forte suddenly found itself in the middle of what amounted to a political and economic revolution. Trusthouse Forte's initial purpose had been to set up and run a viable operation behind the iron curtain within the context of an old style communist regime. However, it soon found itself operating in a much more dynamic political environment that provided as many potential pitfalls as opportunities.

The viability of the project was threatened by complications arising from these events. First, the additional uncertainty multiplied the riskiness of the enterprise. Secondly, the cost of the upper layers of management will be quite high because Trusthouse Forte is having to import them and maintain them over a considerable period. The expectation was that this would be counterbalanced by the comparatively low wage levels of indigenous labour. However, economic liberalisation has seen real wage levels catching up with those in Western Europe at a much higher rate than expected. Lastly, the new government has repealed the law which waived the liability of hard currency profits to Polish corporation tax which currently stands at 40 per cent.

On the other hand, the new environment should make doing business more straightforward and profitable as the layers of bureaucracy diminish, the quality and reliability of support services and products rises, and real incomes in Poland increase as the economy revives. Moreover, it is clear that Trusthouse Forte's targeted market niche at the exclusive, quality-end of the market stands to secure particular benefit from the changes.

Eventually, at the end of 1990, the negotiations were concluded and a Polish limited company called Trusthouse Forte Hotel Orbis Bristol Ltd was established under the joint venture laws and a management agreement between this company and Trusthouse Forte was signed. In addition to full management control, Trusthouse Forte has the majority of the equity and directors on the board. Under the joint venture agreement Trusthose Forte has the right to bring in whatever materials it thinks necessary. However, a large proportion of the supplies will be obtained within Poland and a key job is setting up supply lines.

Trusthouse Forte had to deal with the familiar problem for Western investors in Eastern Europe of unclear property rights. Warsaw District City Council, owners of the property in the name of the Polish people, had given the building to Orbis with a perpetual right to use. Trusthouse Forte in turn was now leasing the building from Orbis on a long-term basis. As a result of advice from counsel, informal understandings, and the expectation that in the interests of inward investment the Polish government would never allow the usurpation of a Western company's stake, Trusthouse Forte judged it unlikely to prove a problem. It managed to obtain some additional security for its stake in the form of Polish bank guarantees of Trusthouse Forte's loans for their duration should Trusthouse Forte lose the right to use the Bristol Hotel.

However, the negotiations had been so protracted that the projected cost of the scheme had escalated by 20 per cent. Additional finance was not forthcoming from the existing investors and so the joint venture company had to look elsewhere. Fortunately, at this point the Polish arm of International Finance Corporation (a subsidiary of the World Bank) was looking for projects to fund. The IFC proved to be very helpful to Trusthouse Forte for various reasons. First, it had excellent contacts with local banks and the Polish government at high levels. This proved invaluable for operating efficiently in the Polish bureacratic system, talking to the right people, and getting things done. Second, as well as being able to provide some finance itself, it brought forward other sources. The IFC study of the viability of the project was in broad agreement with Trusthouse Forte's original study and this supplied much credibility with lenders. In particular, the IFC helped secure a large local currency loan from PKO (the largest Polish bank) with an option to convert to Deutschmarks. (Approximately 20 per cent of costs of the joint venture were expected to be denominated in local currency.)

In January 1991 the reconstruction and refurbishment got underway and at the time of writing (March 1991) progress by the Austrian construction company (on a fixed price contract) has been 'good'. Nevertheless the containment of costs remains a continuing concern. This had been a particular issue when it came to agreeing a design for the refurbishment. The Warsaw City Architect's Department, mindful of the building's important historical connections, wanted it renovated to the original specifications. Trusthouse Forte recognised that such an ambitious plan would threaten the viability of the whole project. A compromise was eventually reached whereby all public areas in the hotel would be restored to their former appearance, and all the rest to Trusthouse Forte's exclusive hotel standards.

Initially, Trusthouse Forte is bringing the top management in from outside Poland. The intention is to recruit people who will be most receptive to the new service-based ideas of working for a hotel company. Training will take place both on site and in other THF hotels. It is hoped to grow a nucleus of skilled indigenous staff as rapidly as possible. However, it will be a major task to bring all the local staff up to Trusthouse Forte's Western European standards before the opening.

Because the genesis of the project predates the unforeseen arrival of a market-oriented economy, Trusthouse Forte has had a number of additional problems to surmount. The parameters within which the joint venture has to work have changed beyond recognition and profitabilty has often been threatened. Bringing it this far has required dogged determination and an element of luck – principally the close association with the IFC. In fact the successful assocation with the IFC generated a view within Trusthouse Forte that the underwriting by Western governments or investors of independent financial advice to the other side of a joint venture could be one of the most practical ways to further the move to a profit-based economy. However, there is a sense that most of the major problems are behind Trusthouse Forte which now has the opportunity to capitalise on its first-hand knowledge and experience of operating in Poland.

Case Study 2

Courtaulds Central Trading

Report of an interview with Geoffrey Blackburn, chief executive, Courtaulds Central Trading.

Courtaulds Central Trading (CCT) was established in the early-1960s as a general selling organisation for the Courtaulds Group. The company has been exporting to Poland ever since. Until the late-1970s, the bulk of CCT's business was in textiles and textile fibres. Recently, however, the strategy of the group as a whole has been to move out of basic commodity trading into specialist, value-added products.

The change of corporate profile is reflected in the evolving pattern of CCT's trade with Poland. Exported products now include chemicals, packaging materials and paints, as well as textile fibres. Indeed the economic restructuring which is occurring in Poland may come to complement the changes taking place within Courtaulds itself. Just as the company is moving into more specialised areas, Geoff Blackburn, CCT's Chief Executive, expects the Poles to acquire more sophisticated trading needs.

When Courtaulds first entered the Polish market 30 years ago, foreign trade was wholly state controlled. This held at least some attraction for CCT: centralised decision making, large secure contracts and ease of distribution. The liberalisation of foreign trade which in theory should give the British exporter free access to the end-user, is in reality changing gradually the way CCT does business in Poland.

The sole point of contact for the British exporter would be the FTE responsible for trade in a given field. The FTE system was well suited to a large company like Courtaulds; contracts covering a wide range of goods could be negotiated with a very limited number of contacts in Poland. Geoff Blackburn believes that CCT was set up with this in mind, providing 'centralised selling to fit the centralised buying of the communist system'. CCT generalists would deal with the FTE generalists, and the fact that most FTEs were situated in the capital made for streamlined business trips. 'In general, we could cover all our business in Poland by spending just one week in Warsaw.' Polish comprehensive five-year plans were a big plus for a company used to the mercurial business environment of the West. A single contract with an FTE might cover the entire Polish demand for a given product, well into the future. This gave the company a chance to realise significant and long-term economies of scale. More than this, the contract carried little or no risk for CCT, since all FTE deals were supported by state guarantees.

FTEs made for straightforward distribution arrangements; all contracts were FOB, with the firm taking responsibility only for getting the goods to port. This is becoming rarer in other Eastern bloc countries. Soviet shippers, for example, increasingly demand payment (in hard currency) from the exporters themselves. To date, CCT has not had to offer CIF in any of its Polish contracts. Nor has the company ever had to offer any countertrade in return, although this too is expected to change, especially for firms new to the Polish market.

Polish central planning, for all its advantages, also meant 'bureaucratic and slow decision taking, as well as little or no access to the end-users of our goods'. These problems rebounded particularly on firms trying to enter the Polish market, or trying to export something new. 'You can bet that it would take at least two years to develop any new product.' A firm new to Poland had first to contact an FTE, which might not respond at all, however attractive the product. After a number of visits and considerable perseverance, the newcomer might persuade the FTE to give the product a small trial and carry out lab tests. Only then, probably a good 6–12 months after negotiations began, could the firm actually make an offer to the FTE. The latter was then required to compare this with at least two other offers from competing firms. Eventually a valuable deal might be struck, but clearly the whole process was not for the faint-hearted.

Above all, CCT found trust to be the key factor in their longstanding relationship with Poland. The number of FTE contacts was limited over time, as turnover of personnel was very low. It was important that the same people from the firm went to Poland, and went often. 'The Poles like to see the same faces at least once a month even if, two times out of three, there is no business to discuss. Your physical presence is taken to indicate seriousness.' This kind of steady relationship, once established, was a great asset to CCT when it came to new contracts. 'FTEs would often give us the business over unknowns, even if they were offering a cheaper deal.' It could also shorten the lengthy process of introducing a new product; officials were apparently less wary of innovation if it came from a trusted source.

In the past then, conditions favoured large companies at almost every level. Yet CCT is now having to adapt to developments in Poland which may make it easier for smaller companies to enter the market. The most important of these are the granting of foreign trade rights to individual enterprises, and the internal convertibility of the zloty. Exporters now have access to end-users, who can choose the suppliers with whom they wish to trade. Nevertheless, most enterprises continue to use some kind of intermediary in foreign trade deals. CCT still works with FTEs for two-thirds of its Polish business, while the remainder is with new independent trading agencies, often set up by ex-FTE officials. In the longer run, however, Geoff Blackburn feels that FTEs will all but disappear, with total access to end-users at every stage. Even while FTEs continue to be involved in trade deals, their presence no longer implies the solid financial support of the state banks. Enterprises must now find funding for themselves; a problem which they have (so far) been disconcertingly 'naive' about solving.

Greater dispersion of economic decision making in Poland should benefit small companies producing a narrow range of quality goods. Potential exporters can now approach end-users directly, and tailor contracts to their specific needs. Geoff Blackburn advises caution however; in many respects the old rules about building up a good relationship still apply, while the sheer pace of change has brought its own problems for foreign companies wishing to do business in Poland.

CCT's recent experience in Poland illustrates the pros and cons of the greater economic freedom. The company is glad to gain more access to end-users. Yet, in adapting to this, CCT has had to revert to a more fragmented trading structure. Individual contracts with Polish enterprises have made the generalist approach inappropriate. Each division of the firm now takes on responsibility for contracts in their area, and must provide more elaborate support to accompany any negotiations on the ground. 'Before, we could go and do the deal without even a specialist salesman on our team. Now, a new venture would need linguists, product specialists and creative entrepreneurial personnel to deal with hard currency problems and possible countertrade deals. As well as people with experience of Polish documentation, and a lot of patience.'

Polish managers have no experience of foreign trading; their new tasks, sourcing their own raw material and financing deals themselves, have made them feel extremely vulnerable. Geoff Blackburn advises exporters to respect this, and to anticipate having to provide them with a lot of help on the technical side of completing the deal – for example in arranging lines of credit and transportation. 'Many Polish managers still have to learn, say, what a packing list is.'

CCT had a difficult year in Poland in 1990: the textile fibre side in particular suffered, as economic austerity slashed demand for clothing and related goods. Business has now begun to improve; CCT packaging has 'taken off' over the last few months, with textile fibres also picking up. In the longer term, the company sees a good future trading to Poland, as the country begins to demand the kind of speciality goods which would have been (quite literally) unheard of before. 'We may soon be approaching the Poles with some of the products of the Group's new acquisitions; aerospace sealants, for example. Now who would have wasted their time doing that a few years ago?'

On balance, Geoff Blackburn thinks small companies should go into Poland now, although they should not expect quick returns. Firms who become known now will reap benefits later (maybe much later) when Polish enterprises are in a position to launch themselves on the Western marketplace. In an alien environment, Polish managers may then look kindly, and lucratively, on a familiar face.

Case Study 3

Radio Solidarity

Report of an interview with Alastair Shaw, chairman, Radiotrust plc.

Radio Solidarity was born when Poland was under martial law, and operated clandestinely for seven years before emerging into the open. During those dark years, the presenters and technicians kept Poland's hopes alive with uncensored news broadcasts and free speech. On air for minutes at a time before having to pack up and move their transmitter, the presenters would ask their audience to switch their apartment lights on and off so that other listeners could see that they were not alone. Staff used smuggled-in equipment and lived in constant fear of arrest.

The coming to power of Tadeusz Mazowiecki's Solidarity government in August 1989 meant that the radio station was soon given a frequency for legal operations in the Warsaw area.

Station officials visited the UK in the hope of finding funding and know-how. The Independent Broadcasting Authority put them in touch with Radiotrust plc, a quoted investment trust which invests in the equity of commercial radio stations. Radiotrust, which was floated on the London Stock Exchange in July 1989, has built up stakes in 20 radio stations in the UK, and was looking to expand abroad.

Chairman Alastair Shaw did not see immediate opportunities in Western European markets. Either commercial radio was not permitted - as in Holland - or the market was considered to be too mature. He said, 'We chose Poland as the first overseas investment site for Radiotrust because of its population - much larger than that of Hungary or Czechoslovakia - and because the Mazowiecki government had taken some painful decisions, tackling the problems of transition to a market economy in a very brave way.

Radio Solidarity carries commercial advertising. The Polish state radio and television enterprise also now carry adverts but these are aired in a haphazard manner. There is only one other commercial station setting up in Poland, with emphasis on international rather than local news. Despite the weak economy, advertising in Poland is a business with great growth potential - albeit from an almost non-existent base. Plenty of enterprises, state, private and foreign, want to get their brand name across among consumers hitherto starved of choice.

After the initial contacts had been made, a business plan was drawn up and a financial package was structured in February 1990. A total investment equivalent to £240,000 was provided by Radiotrust and Abtrust New European Investment Trust plc.

Although all the money has come from these two British trusts, their combined equity holding amounts to just 43 per cent, split between 17.5 per cent for Radiotrust and 25.5 per cent for Aberdeen Trust. Radio Solidarity Foundation (a charitable institution supporting worthwhile projects) will retain 51 per cent of the equity. Ludomir Lasocki, the UK-born Pole who was instrumental in making the whole deal happen has five per cent, and the remaining one per cent is held by Polish state radio.

While the British investors could have taken a 100 per cent stake in the equity, they chose to leave the majority in Polish hands. 'We wanted the operation to be run by Poles for Poles', explained Alastair Shaw. He says that Radiotrust, not being an income fund, is not looking for annual dividends from this investment: 'We seek capital growth rather than dividend income'. 'We want to make this investment grow - we're looking to set up wholly-owned subsidiaries of Radio Solidarity in Poznań, then eventually in Łódź, Kraków and Gdańsk'. While accepting that this Polish venture is high-risk - the highest risk in Radiotrust's portfolio - the investment is relatively small. The trust considers the sum invested to be a low price to pay for a strategic stake in a growing market.

Radiotrust has identified several exit routes for its investment. Either Radio Solidarity will eventually be sold to a larger Western media or publishing group, or its shares will be floated on Poland's fledgling stock exchange in three to five years time. Mr Shaw is not worried about repatriation of profits, saying that there are few restrictions.

The £240,000 investment was meant to cover the first two years of Radio Solidarity's operations, on the assumption of no advertising revenue whatsoever. The money was meant to have been enough to pay for the salaries of the 28 staff as well as paying for transmitting equipment and computers. 'We didn't want them coming back every few months telling us they'd run out of operating capital', explained Mr Shaw. As it is, the station, which came on air in its present format in June 1990, is now cash-positive. Reaching up to 1.5 million listeners in and around Warsaw, it has succeeded in attracting over 40 advertisers - a mixture of insurers, airlines, travel agencies, shops, hotels and manufacturers, from Western European, US and Polish firms. Three of the staff are employed to sell air-time.

Although no independent audience research agency operates yet in Warsaw, Radio Solidarity claims great loyalty from the people who listened to it during the years of martial law. 'All the indications are that the station is very popular. There are phone-ins with government ministers, which vent public anger - a good thing in a new democracy. It is creating a community radio spirit,' says Mr Shaw.

The programming is a mixture of 25 per cent talk and 75 per cent music, with the musical emphasis being on contemporary and classic (1960s) pop. 'It's like a cross between London's Capital and LBC radios'. The staff are all local, most of whom worked on the radio clandestinely. Salaries are extremely low by Western standards, though competitive for Warsaw. 'The cost of talented people here is low. We didn't need to do any technical or professional training' explains Mr Shaw, 'we did, however, have to stress certain financial disciplines such as having monthly accounts.'

Radio Solidarity's managing director was brought over to the UK to see how British commercial stations operated; Mr Shaw or Mr Lasocki visit Poland for two to four days each month to monitor progress. Auditors have been appointed to help prepare accounts. This hands-off approach reveals a faith in the Polish management. 'If things weren't going so well, we'd have to spend a lot more time in Warsaw', says Mr Shaw.

What are the problems faced in the creation of this enterprise? 'The only real problem is macroeconomic' says Mr Shaw. 'With the twin shocks of the cessation of the subsidised Soviet oil supplies and the recession in the West, the Polish economy has been hit hard. Within two or three years, I hope these two waves of imported difficulties will have subsided.'

The negotiating process proved to be long and hard. 'You don't set up these deals in one trip' says Mr Shaw. 'The Polish managing director of Radio Solidarity spent nine months talking to the Polish Investment Agency, the Industry Ministry, the Communications Ministry and other government departments. Agreement was needed from all these bodies before the investment deal could be concluded. Despite the first-rate entrée of a Radio Solidarity business card, long hours of negotiating in government corridors had to be endured before the deal was finalised. This was a job for a Pole – it could not have been done from London.'

Alastair Shaw's experience in dealing with the Polish ministries reveals differences between them in terms of efficiency and attitude. 'The main ministry in the Radio Solidarity project was Communications – they were good. But the Industry Ministry, with whom we didn't have that much contact on the radio side, but with whom I was dealing on other projects, are very bureaucratic and tend to hold things up.'

Another area of difference between business culture in the UK and Poland is the attitudes to financial reporting. 'Western investors live, sleep and breathe profit and loss accounts and balance sheets. The Poles I've been dealing with say they understand the technical jargon associated with accountancy – but do they? I've had to take care to explain and educate the management in Warsaw about the importance of accounting discipline; keeping investors informed of the bad news as well as good'.

Mr Shaw considers that there are many small and medium-sized projects around suitable for British investment. 'The big merchant banks and accountancy firms are only interested in the big projects – they do not want to assess the vast number of smaller projects that are capable of being progressed. There is a major gap to be filled. I have been impressed by the commercial mindedness of the Poles and their innate ability. They seem to be more willing to get involved in a market economy than the Czechs or Slovaks; our investment in a Prague radio station will be despite the Czechs and not because of them.'

Case Study 4

ECH

Report of an interview with John Oswald, managing director, EC Harris Project Management.

Management practices like quality and cost control have been generally quite alien to even the best Polish companies. The potential of combining the technical skills and traditional markets of a relatively successful Polish company with Western management and marketing skills has been seized by ECH, a major international company of surveyors and project managers.

Its Polish partners, Hydrotrest, specialise in the erection of large infrastructure projects such as dams, hydro-electric power stations and water treatment works. Besides the domestic Polish market, the company has worked in other Eastern European states and in the Middle East. Most projects have been commissioned by government agencies. In 42 years of existence, the competition facing Hydrotrest has, to say the least, been limited; in bidding for construction contracts, it has faced one competitive tender in its history. A lack of competition meant there was little incentive to strive for efficiency.

ECH itself specialises in all aspects of the industrial property business, involving financial management, technical design, construction management, and the provision of development funds. Links have been fostered with Hydrotrest through an intermediary. ECH has agreed to provide the Poles with expert guidance in all aspects of the industrial property and construction business.

The advantages which may accrue to Hydrotrest are clear, but why has ECH decided to enter the market? John Oswald, Managing Director of EC Harris Project Management – 'The company had traditionally held markets in the UK and the Far East. In the mid-1980s, the UK markets slowed, and the natural progression was into Western Europe. Recently this market has become sluggish, hence our interest in Eastern Europe.'

Western firms entering the region may expect to find cheap labour and large markets ready for mass consumption. But this does not explain, says Oswald, why most talk of expansion is limited to other Eastern European countries – 'How can people talk about Hungary being the ideal route into Western Europe? For us, in terms of logistics, Poland is far more suitable. It has a population of 38 million, compared to 11 million in Hungary. More people in concentrated areas means a larger demand for our type of business.'

As regards labour, Oswald praises the Poles. 'Polish contractors look skilled and competent in terms of basic civil engineering. Much of their work is exported to the Middle East, and the work-force is always willing to spend a year or two working away from home.' So, after looking at density, population spread and the relative skills and expertise, Poland has become the country targeted by ECH for major growth in the next five to ten years.

The next step for Oswald and his team was to decide the method of entry into Poland. Although the details of the contract are not yet finalised, it seems clear that a joint venture company will be formed. The equity of the company will be held by ECH and a UK investment company (major shareholdings) and Hydrotrest (minor shareholdings). The span of activities performed by these three companies is wide ranging. Such a combination of skills is essential if firms wish to survive these difficult times in Poland, says Oswald. 'For firms considering the Polish market, I think that any company must provide a wide range of integrated services. The market economy is so underdeveloped that there is no question of relying on specialisation of different functions. No one firm would survive if they just offered one element in the property-contruction process.' Vertically integrated firms, or amalgamations of firms will then have the greatest chance of success in Poland at this stage.

There were particular characteristics of Hydrotrest which attracted Oswald: 'Although the Polish workers are technically competent, problems lie in terms of fine finishing. They don't have the quality control – their final product could never be marketed to Western-style specification. In addition, the firm has developed in a very sheltered market. There has been no consideration of efficiency throughout the company's history.'

Such shortcomings provide great opportunities for ECH, or any Western company, to raise performance through greater efficiency. At the heart of ECH's involvement with Hydrotrest is the notion of synergy – the technical, construction skills of the Poles combined with the marketing and management capabilities of ECH has the potential to be a great success. The Middle East connection is another reason underlying ECH's attraction to Hydrotrest. Both companies have worked extensively in the area, and demand for reconstruction in the war-torn cities of Iraq and Kuwait is likely to create lucrative opportunities to expand.

Hydrotrest are undertaking a review of the existing management structure and an analysis of management roles and objectives. On the marketing side, the aim is to review and revitalise the marketing, PR and selling functions. ECH will undertake further work in the more technical areas. It will introduce up to date estimating, buying and tender procedures, introduce resource programme monitoring, and quality control functions will be set up, dealing with both construction and operations. ECH also mentions that operatives and staff will be given 'general training'. The initial period of restructuring the company's procedures and techniques will take from six to nine months. After this, monitoring of changes will be necessary, and ECH expects this process to take anything from 12 to 18 months. After this period of time, ECH expects to maintain a continuing light involvement in Hydrotrest. This provisional scheme of work is indicative of the problems facing all companies in Poland. It involves an overhaul of a complete system of management.

When asked to list a few areas which give him cause for concern, Oswald does not hesitate in selecting at least half a dozen. 'Peculiar to our business is the problem of land acquisition. In Poland, and many other Eastern European countries, the rights over property are disputed fiercely.' No one is sure who is entitled to land in the newly liberalised Eastern economies; is it the state, or the workers of the land, or possibly other nationalities who feel that the land is historically theirs? Whatever the outcome of these disputes, there are sure to be battles. For a company dealing in property, disputes over the legal ownership of land can only cause unnecessary delay and inefficiency.

Another problem which looms large over ECH is that of pollution and the environment. 'The design of many old infrastructure projects has led to immense contamination and environmental pollution. In some ways, the problem of designing new water treatment works is greater in Poland than in the Third World. In order to build infrastructure in Poland, it might be necessary to demolish existing installations and start from scratch. These problems could easily extend the build time of any new project, as much work might be needed on making old installations safe.'

This uncertainty has consequences for the joint venture as ECH and its investment partner will be attempting to raise finance for new projects. How will the consortium attempt to resolve the problem of excessive risk? 'The financial packages are likely to be a cocktail of funds from Polish banks and overseas banks and investors. The riskiness is deterring some of the large pension funds from investing substantially in Poland, but I'm hopeful that many European banks will be interested in providing finance for our deals.' It remains to be seen whether sufficient funds can indeed be raised.

When does John Oswald expect to see a return from this venture? 'Realistically, our thoughts are of a positive return in five to ten years time. In the short term, we hope to see our costs reflected in the increased performance of Hydrotrest. There is so much potential to introduce sophisticated management techniques that we expect to see a pretty rapid improvement in efficiency, but we really accept that a certain amount of investment is needed. Of course, during this time we will learn more about the markets of Eastern Europe, and hope that Hydrotrest will be just one of a whole number of new development activies for us in the region.'

The joint venture is still at an embryonic stage, but there is evidence to suggest that marriages between Polish and Western firms may provide benefits for both sides. Valuable synergies may well exist between the parties, and if the logistical problems can be minimised, entry into Poland may well prove profitable. John Oswald certainly sees much potential: 'It is a question of education; all the resources are there - technical know-how, enthusiasm and expertise; it's just the way that it is managed, co-ordinated and controlled.' The problems of Poland may be substantial, but not everyone thinks that they are insurmountable.

Case Study 5

Maiden Posters

Report of an interview with Julian Macey, director (with responsibility for Eastern and Central Europe), Arthur Maiden Ltd.

Cities in the former Eastern bloc used to be drab, colourless places quite different from Western cities. The reason - there was no advertising. No adverts on the sides of buses or trams, no bright displays in shop windows - but above all no large billboards carrying colourful posters.

But things are changing rapidly. Many Eastern European trams are now gaily decorated, advertising consumer goods, airlines and banking services. Shops are full of Western goods. Eastern European consumers are faced with having to decide between the bewildering plethora of new products suddenly available. 'A consumer market is beginning to develop; competition between brands is emerging. Polish consumers' desire for well-known branded goods is boosted by improved distribution channels', says Julian Macey of Arthur Maiden Ltd, Britain's largest independent poster advertising company.

To help consumers make the choice, providers of goods and services entering the market are looking at ways of spreading their message and Maiden saw this as an excellent opportunity for growth.

Poland was identified as offering potential for development. Personal contacts led Mr Macey to the Polish marketing consultancy firm, Marco, with which a joint venture was set up last year. Employing four Poles in a Warsaw office to develop operations, the joint venture company, Maiden Poland was established with the intention of administering poster sites on which Western firms could buy space in London for hard currency. The joint venture route was chosen to secure and motivate a good local partner. The Polish partner's expertise guided the joint venture through Poland's

Commercial Code; Maiden also sought advice in the UK from a law firm specialising in Eastern Europe.

Sales are split evenly between advertising agencies, who take a commission for placing the advertisement, and directly to manufacturers.

Maiden did not initially envisage a sales role for their Warsaw office. But soon after the first posters went up, Polish firms began expressing an interest in buying advertising. Western firms setting up offices in Warsaw are also going to be more likely to book advertising directly rather than seeking approval from head offices, so a need to train Maiden Poland's staff in advertising sales was quickly identified.

The sites themselves are stainless steel structures, either 48 or 96-sheet sized, and illuminated. They are free-standing or attached to buildings. Costing around £4,000 each, they are manufactured in the UK, and transported by road to Poland, where they are erected on location. Maiden Poland hope to have 50 poster sites up in Poland by the end of 1991, in city centre and airport road locations mostly in Warsaw, but a few in Gdańsk and Poznań. These are chosen on the basis of excellent visibility and backed up with government traffic flow statistics. No independent audience research organisation currently exists in Poland to monitor audience reaction to posters as in the UK, so official statistics are the best guide to placing sites.

The locations chosen, Maiden Poland will seek agreement with the property owners, offering to pay them rent, then seek permission from local authorities and the police – the poster site is then erected. 'There are many bodies whom we may have to approach – Warsaw's Grass and Tree Authority is one' says Mr Macey. Electricity for illumination is drawn from sub-street mains, or from traffic lights, or from the buildings on which the poster sites are located.

'We're selling sites for around $2,000 a month. Rental, rates or taxes, and electricity account for 30 per cent of the selling prices; then there is maintenance, the overheads of the Warsaw office and transport costs', says Mr Macey. Assuming all 50 posters are sold at full rate with half sold to agencies for a commission, Maiden Poland could see an income of over £250,000 during the course of 1992.

Overheads are low; staff costs for the four Poles employed by the joint venture start at £2,500 a year for the bilingual secretary. Though low by UK standards, this represents a monthly salary two to three times higher than what a Pole would earn working in a state enterprise.

Maiden Poland currently has little western competition, and existing Polish posters tend to be 'hand painted, crude and badly positioned' according to Mr Macey.

Given the complete lack of precedent, there was much uncertainty on the Polish side about the operational questions of erecting poster sites. 'There are no Polish planning regulations pertaining to this form of advertising; the UK has strict planning laws. We've transplanted our responsible attitudes to Poland. We've taken a lot of time and effort to tell the authorities what poster advertising is about, and overcoming their initial concerns. Adherence to UK-style best practice will give Maiden the edge over competitors entering the market later, and operating to slacker standards.

All poster sites are prominently branded with the words 'Maiden Poland'. 'The Japanese entering these markets like to be assured that everything is done legally. Some of the old posters that have been up for years are technically illegal. By placing our name on our posters, it guarantees that everything is above board', says Mr Macey.

Maiden has brought over joint venture staff to the UK for ten days of training, visiting the poster structure manufacturers as well as regional sales offices. Mr Macey describes the cultural differences between East and West. 'They are very enthusiastic, but have a certain naïvety about business. At first it was difficult to instil confidence in our staff; initially they thought it was a bit of a pipe dream and they needed continual reassurance.'

Maiden Poland did not use large Western consultants in Warsaw - all the fact-finding and spade work was done by the joint venture staff. 'Time-consuming errors were made, and on some occasions the wrong channels were pursued. Matters were not helped by the archaic commercial laws. However, the law is changing for the better all the time', says Mr Macey. He sees a continually improving business scene too. 'First, our clients came on to the market. Then the media owners such as ourselves came along. Finally, the advertising agencies arrive. The agencies' initial response to our sales pitches has been superb, but their commitment has been slow. However, we see a great potential for Japanese clients - there is a tremendous demand in Poland for consumer electronics'. Maiden's investment in the Polish market is small, but the company does not consider the investment to be risky. 'We've already identified further sites; our investment follows demand.'

Income is through the London office which sells sites to Western companies wishing to buy posters in Poland. Of the first five sites sold, one was bought by J Walter Thomson in London on behalf of a client, the remaining four were sold directly to a Dutch-based jeans manufacturer. Although London effectively handles the selling, Maiden's sales staff visit regional and Western European advertisers, proposing the concept of advertising in Poland. Maiden's Polish subsidiary is paid in the UK in hard currency, and from that expenses and overheads are paid. Nearly all outgoings are paid in zlotys - ie rents, rates, taxes and salaries. Mr Macey considers it will be at least three years before the repatriation of profits made in Poland will be a problem, and by then he expects the zloty should have become fully convertible.

Poland has also the potential to become a manufacturing centre for poster structures, then transporting them to locations throughout Central and Eastern Europe. This would bring substantial savings in labour and transportation, although some more specialist parts of the frame assemblies would have to come from the UK. Problems had been encountered during the transportation of poster sites to Poland from the UK, such as customs delays and a road accident. 'Early frustrations have largely been overcome as Maiden Poland staff fathomed their way through the paperwork, and through the use of an experienced road distribution company', says Mr Macey.

Apart from these early teething troubles, Mr Macey sees no more hurdles ahead, only upside. He is happy with the control over the Warsaw operation; Maiden Poland's general manager provides him with monthly management accounts. Mr Macey visits the Warsaw office every six weeks, and feel that this represents a balance between hands-on and hands-off management with which the Poles are happy.

Appendices

Appendix 1

Opportunities by Sector

AGRICULTURE

The agricultural sector has an importance to Poland's economy which is out of proportion to its output. It contributes around 15 per cent of the country's GDP, but it employs some 40 per cent of the working population. These figures hint at the inefficiency of the state-run farms and the institutions which allocate resources to the sector.

The communists' attempts to socialise Polish farming over the last 40 years were less than wholehearted: 80 per cent of the sector's total output comes from private farms. Polish farms are relatively small concerns, with an average size of 7 hectares. This is too small to benefit from economies of scale, which start to apply when a farm's land area gets to around 15 hectares. Buying and selling land in Poland is still an exceedingly difficult process, and farms are unable to evolve into efficient units in response to market pressures.

Poland is a country of great agricultural potential, with plenty of good soil and a favourable climate. Its farms are well-known in the region for the quality of their meat and vegetables, and fruit such as apples, raspberries, strawberries and currants. This potential has not been fully realised because of shortages of inputs and mis-allocation of resources. Fertilizers, machinery and spare parts are in short supply everywhere, and supplies of seeds, plant protection chemicals and animal feed are unreliable. When resources (particularly credit) have been available, greater priority has been given to the country's less productive socialised farms.

The absence of market pricing has impeded the rational development of Polish farms. In August 1990 price controls were removed, and farmers had more incentive to raise production. However, the effects of free market pricing were muted by the continued dominance of government bodies in the processing and marketing of farm produce. Private farmers can bypass these organisations to a certain extent, but they remain partially tied, because the government bodies control the allocation of inputs like fertilizers and machinery, and they control the farmers' social security scheme.

Agricultural research services are traditionally of a high standard in Poland. However, they are poorly administered: many agencies overlap unhelpfully, while other areas have important gaps. More fundamentally, too little of the research carried out is directed towards the small farms which make the greatest contribution to overall output.

The problems raised by a transition to a market economy are not as great for farmers as for industrial enterprises: successful competition in the international market for agricultural produce tends to demand less investment in machinery and training. But liberalisation measures seem to command less support in the agricultural sector, and are proceeding more slowly there. Poland's farmers are calling on the government to protect them from foreign imports, and are pressing their demands with strikes and road blockades.

In the medium term, agriculture is one of the sectors where Poland, along with other countries in the region, has comparative trade advantages. But in the short term the picture is still highly confused.

The outlook for agriculture is characterised by the World Bank as follows:

- *Grains:* There is considerable potential to expand substantially grain output through increases of yield rather than in area.
- *Sugar:* The country is now self-sufficient and in some years has an exportable surplus.
- *Potatoes:* significant gains in yield would allow production requirements to be met on a considerably smaller area;
- *Dairy:* Poland now meets most of its own needs for dairy products. With improvements in both milk production and processing it should be able to supply the domestic market fully, and export some speciality products;
- *Meat:* Poland has always been a livestock and meat exporter, primarily to European and US markets.

- *Fruit and vegetables:* Except for citrus fruit Poland now meets most of its fruit and vegetable needs and has some surplus for export. It has a particularly well-developed fruit industry.
- *Rape seeds:* Poland is unable to produce commercially either soyabeans or sunflowers but it has had recent success with rape seed as a source of high protein livestock feed and edible oils.

FOOD PROCESSING

Food processing in Poland is considerably less developed than in the West, but it is an important sector of the economy nonetheless: 10 per cent of the workforce and 9 per cent of the country's fixed assets are employed in the sector. Food processing produces 20 per cent of the country's industrial output, and 10 per cent of its exports.

Food processing - and particularly meat processing - was accorded investment priority in the early-1970s, but then fell out of favour: construction of uncompleted projects was halted and established plants were allowed to deteriorate. It has been estimated that over 60 per cent of Poland's food processing machinery has exceeded its useful working life. In some product areas the figure is higher: around 70 per cent in meat processing, alcohol production and edible oil processing.

In any case, the effectiveness of the investment boom was reduced by its concentration in a relatively small number of large scale food processing plants. This entails long distance transportation of produce from the country's numerous small farms. Many agricultural areas are seriously short of processing facilities. For instance, only 50 per cent of the produce of the Zamość district is processed within the district.

Packaging is another problem. Even paper packaging is unavailable in many areas, which means that produce is often spoilt or in poor condition by the time it reaches its market.

The move to value-added products such as convenience foods is some way off for most Polish producers. Western firms may be expected to establish such operations in the nearer future, but progress in this direction has been slow to date. However, there are significant investment opportunities for Western firms in providing basic processing facilities such as storage and packaging.

ENGINEERING

Polish engineering enterprises employ some 1.5 million people, and account for around a quarter of GDP. Under investment has been particularly acute in this sector, and large parts of the industry operate with obsolete equipment. The significance of this was disguised in the days of Comecon, when customers had little or no access to the more modern technology of Western firms. This insularity has now been breached.

Even more important, with the move to hard currency trading in what was Comecon, many customers of Polish engineering enterprises have either disappeared, or cannot obtain the currency to pay for their goods.

The prospect is brighter for the longer term, however. Many Polish engineering enterprises employ highly educated engineers and well trained workers. With investment in new plant, revamped production procedures, and new management controls, these plants could become very competitive on world markets due to Poland's low labour costs.

The industry ministry's Industrial Development Agency (IDA) has significant funds to facilitate this sort of restructuring. One example of its activities is the transformation of the Waryński Excavator Works, planned and implemented with the help of the Boston Consulting Group.

Polish engineering firms which enjoy a reputation for good product quality include the following: Stalowa Wola, earth moving equipment; Łucznik, sewing machines; Romert, bicycles; Star, Trucks; FSM, Fiat 126 cars; Świdnik, aviation equipment; Cegielski, ship engines; and Ursus, farming equipment.

SHIPBUILDING AND SHIP REPAIR

Shipbuilding began in Poland in the 1950s, and today Poland is the world's fourth largest shipbuilder. Merchant ships make up most of the industry's work, and Poland has a reputation for producing relatively unsophisticated ships of good quality at low prices.

The shipyards of Gdańsk were the birthplace of Solidarity, and shipbuilding has a special place in the hearts of many of today's Polish leaders. Foreign investors in this industry may find an especially warm welcome, therefore.

The industry has inevitably spawned a large number of component suppliers, including manufacturers of engines, electrical and electronic equipment, navigation equipment and so on. The main shipyards are listed in Table A1.1.

Table A1.1 *Poland's principal shipyards*

Name (Location)	*Widest berth catered for*
Gdańsk	36m
Northern (Gdańsk)	16m
Wisla (Gdańsk)	10m
Gdynia	70m
Ustka	10m
Szczecin	25m

These yards are not highly specialised, but some do enjoy particular reputations for certain types of vessels. For instance, the Gdańsk yard is well known for fishing vessels, while Gdynia is best known for producing tankers and large bulk carriers.

Poland also boasts a number of ship repair yards which undertake overhauls, reconstruction and repair (see Table A1.2).

Table A1.2 *Poland's principal ship repair yards*

Name	*Location*	*Tonnage catered for*
Gdańsk	Gdańsk	32,000
Nauta	Gdynia	5,000
Rounia	Gdańsk	No docking facilities
Naval yard	Gdynia	5,000
Gryfia	Szczecin	10,000
Parnica	Szczecin	No docking facilities
Świnoujście	Świnoujście	5,000

CHEMICALS

The chemical industry (including oil refining) accounts for around 12 per cent of Poland's GDP, which is a small proportion considering the country's wealth of relevant natural resources. Poland has significant reserves of coal, silver, sulphur, copper and zinc. It also has rich deposits of limestone, gypsum, ceramic clay and barite, silicon earth and fluorspar.

The industry was seen as a priority sector in the 1960s, when it received 19 per cent of all industrial investment, but in the late-1980s the figure fell below 10 per cent. The number of production lines in large factories has remained practically unchanged since 1980, and only around 15 per cent of the industry's production processes are automated.

There are around 400 large chemical plants in Poland, including 10 very large complexes. More than half the industry's work-force is employed by plants with 2000 or more workers. Although some plants, such as the fertilizer plant at Puławy, are modern and well equipped, the majority are very inefficient in their consumption of energy. Energy prices were kept well below world levels under the communists, and plants had little incentive to improve their efficiency.

Poland's chemical industry installations do not lend themselves to upgrading, and much of the inward investment in this sector is expected to be on a greenfield basis. Production of inorganic materials such as sulphur and sodium chloride are likely to present attractive investment opportunities, as are more extensive processing of fluorspar, anhydrite and barite. Polish farms will represent a growing market for nitrogenous and phosphatic fertilizers and pesticides.

ELECTRONICS

Electronics was a vogue industry in Poland during the 1970s. New plant was constructed, and new technology was introduced. Polish universities began to turn out engineers and technicians equipped to develop and run the growing industry. But in the 1980s resources became more scarce, and today the industry seems very dated from a Western viewpoint. Virtually no facilities for microelectronics have been established.

The largest electronics enterprises are located in and around Warsaw, producing transmission equipment, radios, television sets and telephones. Among the best known names are:

- Electric Lamps Production Works;
- Radio Works;
- State Transmission Works;
- 'Tewa' Semiconductors Plant;
- Warsaw Television Works;
- Telephone Appliances Works; and
- The Piaseczno Works.

The Piaseczno Works is one of Poland's very few 1980s electronics plants, making cathode ray oscilloscopes, transmitting tubes and picture tubes.

Further north, the shipyards spawned their own electronics industry, including internationally known firms such as Elmar, Telkom-Telmar, Unimor and Radmor.

To date, most Western investments in Poland's electronics industry are concerned with unsophisticated assembling operations. The acquisition by Philips of Polam-Pila, a manufacturer of fluorescent lights, may be a precursor of more significant capital investments in the future.

TEXTILES AND CLOTHING

Textiles and clothing represent two contrasting models of industrial development in communist Poland. Textile firms were established on a grand scale, but central planning rendered them inefficient and unprofitable. Clothing firms, on the other hand, tended to remain small and relatively entrepreneurial.

Textile production has a long history in Poland, with some of the firms trading today having been established in the 18th century. The main textile centre is Łódź, with lesser concentrations around Częstochowa and Warsaw.

The industry received substantial levels of investment under communism, but the allocation of resources, as usual, was inconsistent, and modern equipment is often found alongside very old plant. The majority of the spinning and weaving machines are of East European origin. With several honourable exceptions, such as the corduroy from Harnam and the linen from Żyrardów, the produce of Polish textile manufacturers is therefore of indifferent quality.

The textile industry suffered a serious blow in 1990 when cheap supplies of cotton from the Soviet Union suddenly stopped. This severely curtailed its competitiveness – both within Poland and abroad. Many firms are on the verge of bankruptcy, and some of them are strong candidates for investment by Western firms. •

Poland's clothing enterprises, by contrast, continue to thrive. Many of the most expensive garments sold in Paris and London are actually produced by Polish workers as sub-contract tailors.

These firms tend to be small workshops, with no more than 50 employees. They can be found wherever factories and industrial centres attract large numbers of women looking for work, but the largest centre is Łódź, with its textile traditions.

RETAILING

Many shops and restaurants have already become private operations, and the improvements - particularly in the shops - have been dramatic.

Little attempt has yet been made by Polish retailers to establish brand names, and most of those which exist have poor reputations. A partial exception is the Pewex chain which retails foreign imported goods. Establishing nationwide brands is clearly an area of opportunity for Western firms. One firm already doing this is Kodak, which is establishing a chain of photo processing outlets.

TOURISM

Tourism stands out as an under-developed opportunity in Poland. The country boasts many attractions, such as Warsaw old town, Kraków's Wawel castle, the lake district and the Tatra mountains, yet its income from tourism is only a quarter of Hungary's.

The main tourist organisation is Orbis, which includes a chain of hotels, travel agencies and a car rental network. Orbis is due for privatisation shortly, and is certain to attract favourable attention. A number of private tourist companies have also been established, but none are significant as yet.

Western investment in the sector to date focuses on the provision of hotel accommodation, particularly high class hotels, which are in short supply at present. A Marriott was completed in Warsaw in 1989, and has been very successful. Ten more four and five-star hotels are planned or under construction in central Warsaw at the time of writing.

Another opportunity area is holiday camps. Many large Polish companies had their own holiday camps and motels for employees. The financial difficulties these companies have found themselves in mean these facilities are often neglected or up for sale.

PROPERTY

Economic reform has created great interest among foreigners in the possibility of direct property investment in Poland. Current law on the acquisition of long-term interests in land and property for foreigners requires a special consent issued by the Minister of Internal Affairs. These problems can be simply overcome by the foreign partner initially taking a 49 per cent interest in a company with Polish partners.

Land can still be purchased quite cheaply with, for example Warsaw, prices ranging from US$8 per square metre on the city boundary to US$200 per square metre plus in the centre although the average price is between US$30–50 per square metre.

Building costs range from US$200–400 per square metre for residential and office developments based on Polish construction methods to US$1,000–1,500 per square metre for high quality, air-conditioned office accommodation.

Selling prices range from US$650-1,000 per square metre for residential accommodation whilst rental income for offices is valued between US$27–55 per square foot in central Warsaw.

About 70 per cent of all land and buildings within city and township boundaries is owned by the state although the right of use is generally enjoyed by state institutions. Outside city boundaries the land is mainly private.

The Polish government is now in the process of transferring property ownership, subject to claim, to the original families who owned it prior to World War II or selling it on the open market, although the latter process is limited with most successful deals being joint venture agreements.

This applies less to industry and business of which more than 80 per cent was destroyed during the war. It is, therefore, generally considered that in this area, most of the value has been generated since 1945.

COAL

Poland has one of the world's largest coal industries. In 1987 it was the world's fourth largest producer and third largest exporter. The powerful coal lobby has managed to ensure that government investments have focused on maintaining and expanding supply rather than cutting demand. However, much of Poland's coal is of poor quality, and it is expensive to recover.

Industry minister Andrzej Zawiślak has been described as an economic wet in Polish terms, but he has produced a strategic plan to rationalise the country's mines. Restructuring will undoubtedly aggravate the labour unrest already apparent in the mines.

OIL

Indigenous reserves of oil are negligible, and the vast majority of Poland's oil has traditionally been imported from the USSR via the Friendship pipeline. In the late-1980s these supplies were made at prices well below world levels, but the days of cheap oil came to an abrupt halt in 1990, when trade with the USSR shifted to a hard currency basis.

Even at world prices, Soviet supplies are far from certain due to the political and economic confusion there. Imports from the USSR were around 13 million tonnes per year in the late-1980s, but are unlikely to exceed 5 million tonnes in the 1990s. Much of the shortfall will be made up from the Middle East, particularly Iran.

One of Poland's most urgent problems is its logistical difficulty in dealing with this switch of oil sourcing. Its oil industry infrastructure is geared up to receive the bulk of its supplies from the east. To allow oil imports from other sources, the unloading and storage facilities at Gdańsk port's oil terminal will have to be expanded and modernised. The country's refineries also require modernisation, to allow them to switch between the very different types of crude which come from the Soviet Union and the Middle East.

LIST OF PRIORITY SECTORS FOR INVESTMENT BY FOREIGN INVESTMENT COMPANIES (Council of Ministers Decree No 17, 6 February, 1989)

1. Agro-processing industry

- Production of machinery for food-processing industry and catering (including freezing and cooling equipment).
- Production of baby foods and special dietary products.
- Production of protein concentrates, animal feed additives and mineral pre-mixes.
- Potato processing.
- Fruit and vegetable processing.
- Herb production and processing.

2. Production of pharmaceuticals and medical equipment

- Manufacture of medical and laboratory products.

- Manufacture of rehabilitation equipment.
- Manufacture of wheelchairs (with electric or combustion engines).
- Manufacture of pharmaceutical and herbal products.
- Manufacture of laboratory re-agents, tests, isotopes and radioactive products etc.

3. ***Chemical and paper industry***

- Manufacture of highly concentrated fertilisers.
- Manufacture of crop protection products.
- Manufacture of polyester, styrene, epoxy and polyurethane.
- Manufacture of paper and boards.

4. ***Construction materials***

- Manufacture of finishing equipment for civil buildings.
- Manufacture of crop protection products.
- Manufacture of metal plumbing.
- Manufacture of plastic products for construction/building industry.
- Manufacture of finishing, and insulating products, high quality and sanitary ceramics.
- Manufacture of energy, water and gas measuring equipment.

5. ***Environment protection***

- Manufacture of equipment for the protection of the environment.
- Construction of waste treatment plants (biological and mechanical).

6. ***Modern technologies***

- Introduction of energy-, fuel-, raw-material-saving technologies, based on original scientific research, including patents, know-how and licences and their application to the manufacture of products.

- Manufacture of energy-, fuel-, raw-material-saving machinery and equipment.

7. Telecommunication, electronics and electronic products

- Manufacture of modern telecommunication equipment.
- Manufacture of telecommunication cables.
- Manufacture of computer systems, electronic data processing equipment and computer software.
- Manufacture of optical fibres and optical cables and equipment for their production.
- Manufacture of industrial robots.
- Technologies and measurement equipment for VLSI and LSI.
- Manufacture of equipment for surface assembly.
- Manufacture of modern electronic components (passive and active).
- Manufacture of materials for the electronics industry (including low tonnage chemistry).
- Manufacture of quartz pipes and derivatives for electronics industry.
- Manufacture of laminates for integrated circuits.

8. Manufacture of scientific, control and measuring equipment

9. Printing and office automation equipment

- Manufacture of printing equipment (including small scale).
- Manufacture of modern office automation equipment.

10. Products of power metallurgy

11. Finished products

- Manufacture of new generation household equipment, of higher standards and exploitation parameters.
- Manufacture of new generation appliances, on the basis of technologies that were not applied in Poland.
- Manufacture of metal cutting tools.

12. *Packaging*

- Manufacturing of packaging and package-producing equipment.
- Manufacture of packages and packaging material.

13. *Transport*

- Manufacture of servicing equipment for rail, road, air and water transport.
- manufacture of equipment for the mechanization of freight loading.

14. *Tourism*

- Construction and exploitation of hotels, recreational and tourist facilities.

Appendix 2

Foreign Investment Act Permit

APPLICATION FORM

1. Names, data and addresses of the future partners:

....

....

2. Addresses for delivery of mail in connection with establishment of the Company:

....

....

3. The name and seat of the future Company:

....

....

4. Purpose of establishment of the Company (to be provided item by item):

....

5. Subject and scope of economic activity of the Company (forecast for 5 years)

1) subject of activity (item by item),
2) planned production capacity[1],
3) estimated sales (domestic and export),
4) estimated imports.

[1] Production means manufacturing and services

6. Estimated number of employees of the Company, including number of expatriots:

....

7. Resources needed to start the activity:
   1) Total investment outlays,
   2) Value of the equity,
   3) External sources of finance (credits, loans, etc).

9. Shares in equity capital by partners:

.... %

.... %

10. Forms on contribution to equity capital by individual partners (in zlotys and in foreign exchange):

....

partner

— Total ....

— in cash ....

— in Kind ....

....

partner

— Total ....

— in cash ....

— in Kind ....

11. Other informations, which according to applicants are relevant to the issuance of the permit:

....

<u>Enclosures to application:</u>

1. The draft of the foundation act of the Company initiated by all partners.

2. Economic and financial feasibility study of the Company inclusive of market analysis, techno-organisational analysis and financial analysis.

Such analysis may be based upon UNIDO methodology described in published in Poland 'Guidelines for preparation of an industrial feasibility study' by Instytut Wydawniczy Związków Zawodowych, Warszawa 1986[2].

3. Documents describing legal status of the future partners.

4. Documents describing financial standing of the future partners (ie bank statements, commercial investigators reports, annual financial statements etc).

In case of contribution of all or part of the foreign enterprise established under the Law of 6th July 1982, to the equity capital of the future Company, the following should in addition be attached:

1) Declaration of the applicant describing the ways to meet creditors obligations arising out of activities of the foreign enterprise.

2) The proof, verified by licenced accountants, of purchase against convertible foreign exchange of resources included in the value of convertible foreign exchange of resources included in the value of contributed foreign enterprise (or its part), or statement from Treasury Chamber, that foreign enterprise has effected foreign exchange input of the minimum value of US$50,000.

[1] Production means manufacturing and services

[2] Except in cases included in Article 42 Paragraph 3 of the Law of 23 Dec, 1988 on Economic Activity with the Participation of Foreign Partners (Dz- Ustaw No 41/88)

[2] Except in cases included in Article 42 Paragraph 3 of the Law of 23 Dec, 1988 on Economic Activity with the Participation of Foreign Partners (Dz- Ustaw No 41/88)

Appendix 3

Sources of Finance

THE KNOW-HOW FUND

In the summer of 1989 the UK government put together a package of financial aid for Poland known as the Know-How Fund. The objective of the fund (total value £50 million) is to provide advice and expertise to assist Poland in establishing democratic institutions and a free market economy. The fund is administered by the Joint Assistance Unit whose tasks are: to identify potential areas of need; to confirm with the relevant Polish authorities that assistance in the area concerned would be beneficial and welcomed; and to find UK companies to provide the assistance required.

Areas of need so far identified have been banking, financial services, energy, accountancy, management and development, English language training and broadcasting. The fund also finances feasibility studies by UK businesses for proposed projects and management training for employees of a Polish joint venture partner, in each case up to a maximum of £50,000. A separate fund of £15 million to provide advice and assistance for agricultural development is also planned.

OPERATION PHARE

The EC has a variety of aid programmes targeted at Poland and Eastern Europe generally. At the Paris summit of OECD countries on 14 and 15 July 1989 it was agreed that the commitments would co-ordinate Western aid to Poland and Hungary in the PHARE programme. The programme includes the following measures:

1. lifting of all quantitative restrictions in 1990;
2. an ECU300 million budget (to be spent by the end of 1991) for private sector cooperative projects;

3. the European Investment Bank to make loans of between ECU800–1000 million to Poland and Hungary over three years starting from 1989;
4. establishment of the European Training Foundation; and
5. establishment of Tempus Exchange Programme to develop cooperation in higher education.

THE WORLD BANK PROGRAMME FOR POLAND

One of the most important elements of the international financial support for the Polish economic reforms as well as an important source for financing investment projects in Poland is the World Bank's loan programme. Below is a short description of the ongoing and future programmes financed by the World Bank in Poland.

1. *Industrial Export Development Project* Development of industrial exports, improvements in production facilities, assistance in purchasing licences and in technology transfer, improvement of the banking system, restructuring of industry, development of the private sector. Credit line managed by the National Bank of Poland and available through a number of commercial banks. Loan - US$260 million.
2. *Agroindustries Export Development Project* Development of private food-processing sector, assistance in increasing export of processed agricultural products. Credit line managed by the Bank for Food Economy and available through a number of commercial banks. Loan - US$100 million.
3. *Environment Management Project* Development of policy, regulatory, institutional and investment action to improve the environment. Project run by the Ministry of Environmental Protection. Loan - US$18 million.
4. *Transport I (General)* Assistance in restructuring the transport system, introduction of modern organisation, management and maintenance procedures. Loan of US$4.8 million managed by the Ministry of Transportation.
5. *Transport I* Assistance in modernising the railway network; rolling-stock and track maintenance, signalling and telecommunication systems. Loan of US$145 million extended to PKP (Polish Railway Company).
6. *Energy Resources Development Project* Assistance in develop-

ment and rehabilitation of gas fields, expansion of storage and transmission facilities, adoption of new gas processing and desulphurisation technologies. Project run by the Polish Oil and Gas Mining Company. Loan - US$250 million.

7. *SAL I* Direct support for the Polish government's economic transformation programme which has three objectives: stabilisation, structural reforms and restoration of growth. Loan of US$300 million extended to the Ministry of Finance.

In the next six months another seven programmes will be submitted for the approval to the Board of the Bank. These include the following:

- Industrial restructuring and privatisation.
- Financial institutions development.
- Heat supply restructuring.
- Housing finance.
- Telecommunications.
- Employment services.
- Agricultural adjustment and development.

Several of the loans will be in the form of credit lines available to the domestic and foreign investors in Poland.

OTHER PROGRAMMES

- *The Agreement for the Promotion and Reciprocal Protection of Investments* was signed by Poland and the UK on 8 December 1987 and came into force on 14 April 1988. The Agreement set out to 'create favourable conditions for greater investment by investors' of both countries and to this end makes provision for compensation in the event of financial loss or in the event of nationalisation or other expropriation of a foreign investor's property.
- *The European Bank for Reconstruction and Development* provides a full range of financial services and instruments to finance private sector projects necessary for the transition to a market-oriented economy. The bank's headquarters are in London, and it is owned as to 51 per cent by the EC and member states.

Appendix 4

Bibliography and Sources of Further Information

BIBLIOGRAPHY

An Agricultural Strategy for Poland, EEC/WB Polish Task Force, Warsaw, July 1990.

Business in the New Free Poland, Foreign Investment Agency, Warsaw, 1990.

Directory of Polish Export Production, AGPOL, Warsaw, 1990.

Eastern Europe Business Opportunities, Bulgaria, Czechoslovakia, Hungary, Poland, Romania, Unipost SA, Belgium, January 1991 (unpublished).

'Economic Review', *Polish News Bulletin of the British and American Embassies*, Warsaw, 29 January 1991.

Foreign Investor's Guide to Poland, Foreign Investment Agency, Warsaw, 1990.

Funkcjonowanie inweatycij zagranicznych w Polsce, [The Operation of Foreign Trade in Poland], Instytut Koniunktur i Cen Handlu Zagranicznego, Warsaw, 1990.

Hints to Exporters to Poland, DTI, HMSO, Edinburgh Press, 1990/91.

List of Prohibited Articles, International Bureau of the Universal Postal Union, UPU, Berne, 1987.

Poland's Economic and Trade Policy in 1990, Instytut Koniunktur i Cen Handlu Zagranicznego, Warsaw, 1990.

Poland - statistical data 1990, Central Statistical Office, Warsaw, 1990.

Poland - statistical data 1991, Central Statistical Office, Warsaw, 1991.

Polityka Ekonomiczna i Handlowa Polski w 1991 r., [Poland's Economic and Trade Policy in 1991], Instytut Koniunktur i Cen Handlu Zagranicznego, Warsaw, 1991.

Polityka Rozwoju Handlu Zagranicznego w Polsce, [Foreign Trade Development Policy in Poland], Instytut Koniunktur i Cen Handlu Zagranicznego, UNDP World Bank, Warsaw, 1990.

Pologne (Rep. Pop), Stratégies de Développement des Services Postaux d'Europe, Charles Leroy, UPU, Berne, 1988 (unpublished).

Polski Handel Zagraniczny w 1989 r., [Polish Foreign Trade in 1989], Instytut Koniunktur i Cen Handlu Zagranicznego, Warsaw, 1990.

Statistical Information, Central Statistical Office, Warsaw, Jan. 1991.

SOURCES OF FURTHER INFORMATION

Colin Rose
British Postal Consultancy Service
Royal Mail International Headquarters
Alder House
1 Aldersgate Street
London EC1A 1AL
Tel: 44 (71) 601 1407

Eric Yull
Manager - Poland
British Telecom
Business Communications Division
Aeradio House
Hayes Road
Southall
Middlesex UB2 5NJ
Tel: 44 (81) 843 3516
Fax: 44 (81) 843 3270
Telex: 24114 BTIAL G

Maurice Childs
Head of East European Department
CBI
Centre Point
103 New Oxford Street
London WC1A 1DU
Tel: 44 (71) 379 7400
Fax: 44 (71) 240 1578

Craig Eadie
Frere Cholmeley
28 Lincoln's Inn Fields
London WC2A 3HH
Tel: 44 (71) 405 7878
Fax: 44 (71) 405 9056

Jerzy Mula
The Polish Investment Company plc
Buchanan House
3 St James's Square
London SW1Y 4JU
Tel: 44 (71) 333 8844
Fax: 44 (71) 333 0072

Peter Jasilkowski
The Polish Investment Company
ul Smolna 8
00-375 Warsaw
Tel: 48 (22) 26 82 10/07

Simon Goode
Saatchi & Saatchi Advertising Worldwide
80 Charlotte Street
London W1A 1AQ
Tel: 44 (71) 636 5060
Fax: 44 (71) 436 8905

Archibald Campbell
DRT Eastern Europe Liaison
Touche Ross & Co
Hill House
1 Little New Street
London EC4A 3TR
Tel: 44 (71) 936 3000
Fax: 44 (71) 583 8517
Telex: 884739 TRLNDN G

Jan Maciejewicz/George Szyman
DRT Poland
Aleje Ujazdowskie 6A
00-461 Warsaw
Tel: 48 (22) 29 32 85
48 (2) 625 5545
Fax: 48 (22) 29 01 07
Satellite: 48 (39) 12 06 43

George Sloczynski
BSB Saatchi & Saatchi Marco
ul Moliera 6
00-950 Warsaw
Tel: 48 (22) 26 40 04
Fax: 48 (22) 26 65 37

Department of Trade and Industry
Polish Desk
1 Victoria Street
London SW1H 0ET
Tel: 44 (71) 215 4735

East European Trade Council
Suite 10
Westminster Palace Gardens
Artillery Row
London SW1P 1RL
Tel: 44 (71) 222 7622

Polish Commercial Counsellor's Office
15 Devonshire Street
London W1N 2AR
Tel: 44 (71) 580 5481

Polish Embassy
47 Portland Place
London W1N 3AG
Tel: 44 (71) 580 4324

American Embassy
Wiljska 20
Warsaw
Tel: 48 (22) 28 30 41

British Embassy
Aleja Roz
Warsaw
Tel: 48 (22) 28 10 01/5
Telex: 815694 prod pl

Ministry of Agriculture and Food Economy
ul Wspólna 30
00-930 Warsaw
Tel: 48 (22) 21 03 11
Telex: 814597/8

Ministry of Culture and Arts
ul Krakowskie Przedmiescie 15/17
00-950 Warsaw
Tel: 48 (22) 26 62 51
Telex: 813762 bwkz pl

Ministry of Defence
ul Klonowa 1
02-653 Warsaw
Tel: 48 (22) 21 02 61

Ministry of Environmental Protection and Natural Resources
ul Wawelska 52/54
02-067 Warsaw
Tel: 48 (22) 25 00 01
Telex: 812816
817157 wodro pl

Ministry of Finance
ul Swietokrzyska 12
00-916 Warsaw
Tel: 48 (22) 20 03 11
Telex: 815592 minfin pl

Ministry of Foreign Affairs
Al 1 Armii Wojska Polskiego 23
00-918 Warsaw
Tel: 48 (22) 28 84 51
Telex: 814301 msz

Ministry of Foreign Economic Relations
Pl Trzech Krzyzy 5
00-507 Warsaw,
Tel: 48 (2) 693 5500
Fax: 48 (22) 28 68 08
Telex: 814501 mhz pl

Ministry of Health and Social Assistance
ul Miodowa 15
00-246 Warsaw
Tel: 48 (22) 31 34 41
Telex: 813864

Ministry of Industry
ul Wspólna 4
00-926 Warsaw,
Tel: 48 (22) 21 03 51
Telex: 814267
814261

Ministry of the Interior
ul Rakowiecka 2
00-904 Warsaw
Tel: 48 (22) 21 02 51

Ministry of Justice
Al Ujazdowskie 11
00-950 Warsaw
Tel: 48 (22) 28 44 31
Telex: 813891

The Ministry of Labour and Social Policy
Socjalnych
ul Nowogrodzka 1/5
00-513 Warsaw
Tel: 48 (22) 28 90 41
Telex: 814710 minprs pl

Ministry of National Education
Al 1 Armii Wojska Polskiego
00-918 Warsaw
Tel: 48 (22) 28 04 01
Telex: 813523 men

Ministry of Ownership Changes (Property Transformation)
Tel: 48 (22) 28 32 61

Ministry of Physical Planning and Construction
Department of International Relations
ul Wsponla 2
00-926 Warsaw
Tel: 48 (22) 21 27 25

Ministry of Post and Telecommunications
Pl Malachowskiego 2
00-940 Warsaw
Tel: 48 (22) 26 10 71
Telex: 813001

Ministry of Territorial Planning and Construction
Przestrzennej i Budownictwa
ul. Wspólna 2
00-926 Warsaw
Tel: 48 (22) 21 03 51
Telex: 814411
814416

Ministry of Transport
Pl Malachowskiego 2
00-940 Warsaw
Tel: 48 (22) 26 10 71
Telex: 813001

Ministry of Transportation and Shipping
ul Chalubinskiego 4/6
00-928 Warsaw
Tel: 48 (22) 24 40 00
Telex: 816651

Bank for Food Economy
Bank Gospodarki Zywnosciowej
ul Swietokrzyska 12
00-916 Warsaw
Tel: 48 (22) 20 03 11
Telex: 813869

Bank PEKAO SA
Bank Polska Kasa Opieki SA
ul R Traugutta 7/9
00-950 Warsaw
Tel: 48 (22) 26 92 11
Telex: 816442

Foreign Trade Bank
Bank Handlowy w Warszawie SA
ul T Chalubinskiego 8
00-950 Warsaw
Tel: 48 (22) 30 03 00
Telex: 814811

National Bank of Poland
Narodowy Bank Polski
ul Swietokrzyska 11/21
00-950 Warsaw
Tel: 48 (22) 20 46 21
Telex: 814681

State Savings Bank
Bank Panstwowy - Powszechna Kasa Oszczednosci
ul Swietokrzyska 11/21
00-950 Warsaw
Tel: 48 (22) 20 03 21
Telex: 814625

Anti Monopoly Office
Plac Powstancow
Warsawy 1
00-950 Warsaw
Tel: 48 (22) 26 90 41
48 (22) 26 34 14
Telex: 8142915
Fax: 48 (22) 26 50 76

Central Customs Office
ul Swietokrzyska 12
00-916 Warsaw
Tel: 48 (22) 20 03 11

Central Statistical Office
Al Niepodleglosci 208
00-925 Warsaw
Tel: 48 (22) 25 32 41

EEC (Warsaw)
Aleje Ujazdowskilie 14
Warsaw
Tel: 48 (22) 21 64 01/2

Foreign Investment Agency
Agencja d/s Inwestycji Zagranicznych
Aleje Roz 2
00-556 Warsaw
Tel: 48 (22) 29 57 17
48 (22) 21 62 61
Fax: 48 (22) 21 84 27
Telex: 817225

Foreign Investors' Chamber of Industry and Commerce
ul Krakowskie Przedmiescie 64
00-325 Warsaw
Tel: 48 (22) 26 32 01
Telex: 817105

Industrial Development Fund
5th Floor
ul Wspolna 4
Warsaw
Tel: 48 (22) 28 09 34

Institute of Finance
Swietokrzyska 12
Warsaw
Tel: 48 (22) 26 97 14

Institute of Market Economy Research
Gdynskich Kosynierow 11
Gdansk
Tel: 48 (58) 31 18 16
Fax: 48 (58) 31 01 33

Institute of the World Economy
Al Niepodleglosci 12/14
Warsaw
Tel: 48 (22) 49 12 51

International Finance Corporation (World Bank)
ul Stawki 2
Warsaw
Tel: 48 (2) 635 0553

Patent Office
Al Niepodleglosci 188/192
00-950 Warsaw
Tel: 48 (22) 25 59 10
Telex: 813716 clnt pl

Polish Chamber of Foreign Trade
ul Trebacka 4
00-074 Warsaw
Tel: 48 (22) 29 52 41
Telex: 814361

Vice President's Secretariat
Tel: 48 (22) 26 00 17

Export Dept
Tel: 48 (22) 27 47 49

Legal Advice and Information Centre
Tel: 48 (22) 26 18 62

Polish Committee of Normalisation, Measures and Quality
ul Elektorliana 2
00-950 Warsaw
Tel: 48 (22) 20 02 41
Telex: 813642

Polish Press Agency
Tel: 48 (22) 28 00 01
48 (22) 21 85 18

Polservice
(FTO) Head Office
18 Chalunbinskiego St
00-612 Warsaw
Tel: 48 (22) 30 05 21
48 (22) 30 24 58
Fax: 48 (22) 30 00 76

Senate of Polish Republic
6 Wiejska Street
Warsaw
Tel: 48 (2) 614 2284

United Nations Industrial Development Organisation (UNIDO)
Stawki 2
00-950 Warsaw
Tel: 48 (2) 635 6086/7112/8552

Warsaw Voice
ul Bagatela 12
00-585 Warsaw
Tel: 48 (22) 21 13 28

Central Post Office
Swietokrzyska 31/33
Warsaw
Fax: 48 (22) 30 00 21

International Road Freight Office
Westgate House
Westgate Road
Newcastle NE1 1TW
Tel: 44 (91) 261 0031

KOMERTEL
Centrum Radiokomunikacji i Telekomunikacji
ul Nowogrodzka 45
Warsaw
Tel: 48 (22) 29 35 66

LOT
ul Warynskiego 9
Warsaw
Tel: 48 (22) 21 70 21
Telex: 814327/8

MarCo Ltd
4/6 Warsaw
Tel: 48 (22) 25 23 54
48 (22) 25 22 26
Fax: 48 (22) 25 05 91

Parcelforce National Enquiry Centre
(International Datapost and parcel services)
Tel: 0800 22 44 66 (toll free)

Polska Poczta Telegraf Telefon
General Headquarters
Plac Malachowskiego 2
00-940 Warsaw
Tel: 48 (22) 26 10 71
48 (22) 26 14 11
Telex: 813001

Royal Mail International
(International business letter mail)
Tel: 0800 58 19 60 (toll free)

Index